# CYBORG

VOLUME 1
UNPLUGGED

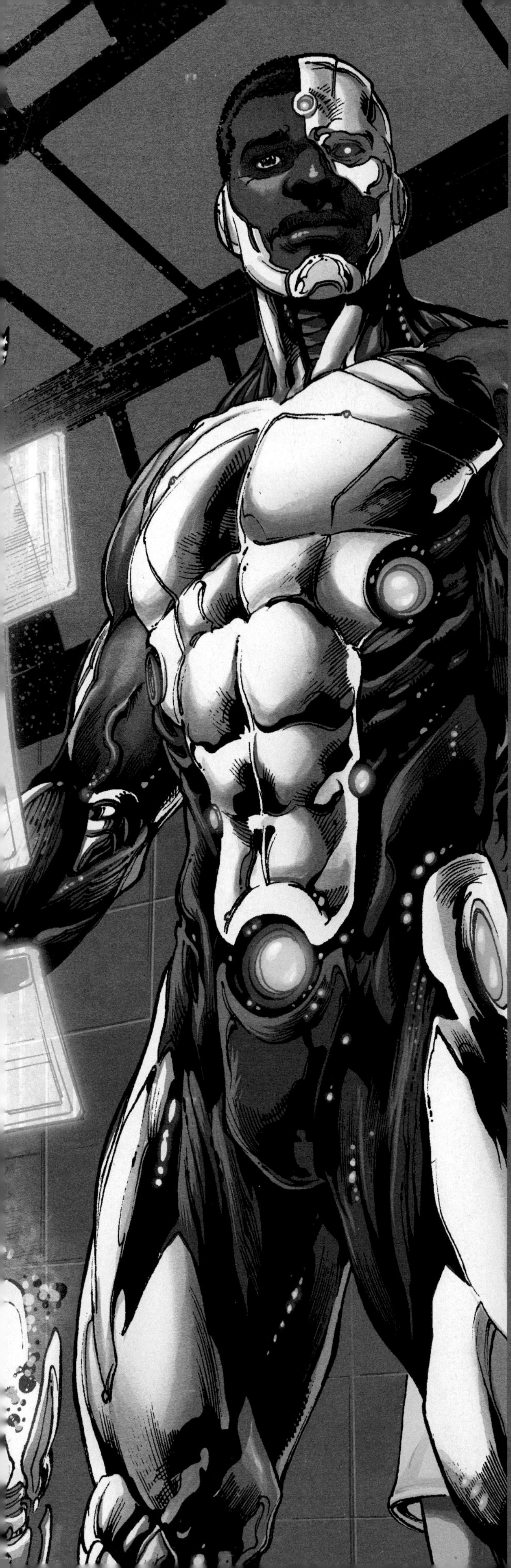

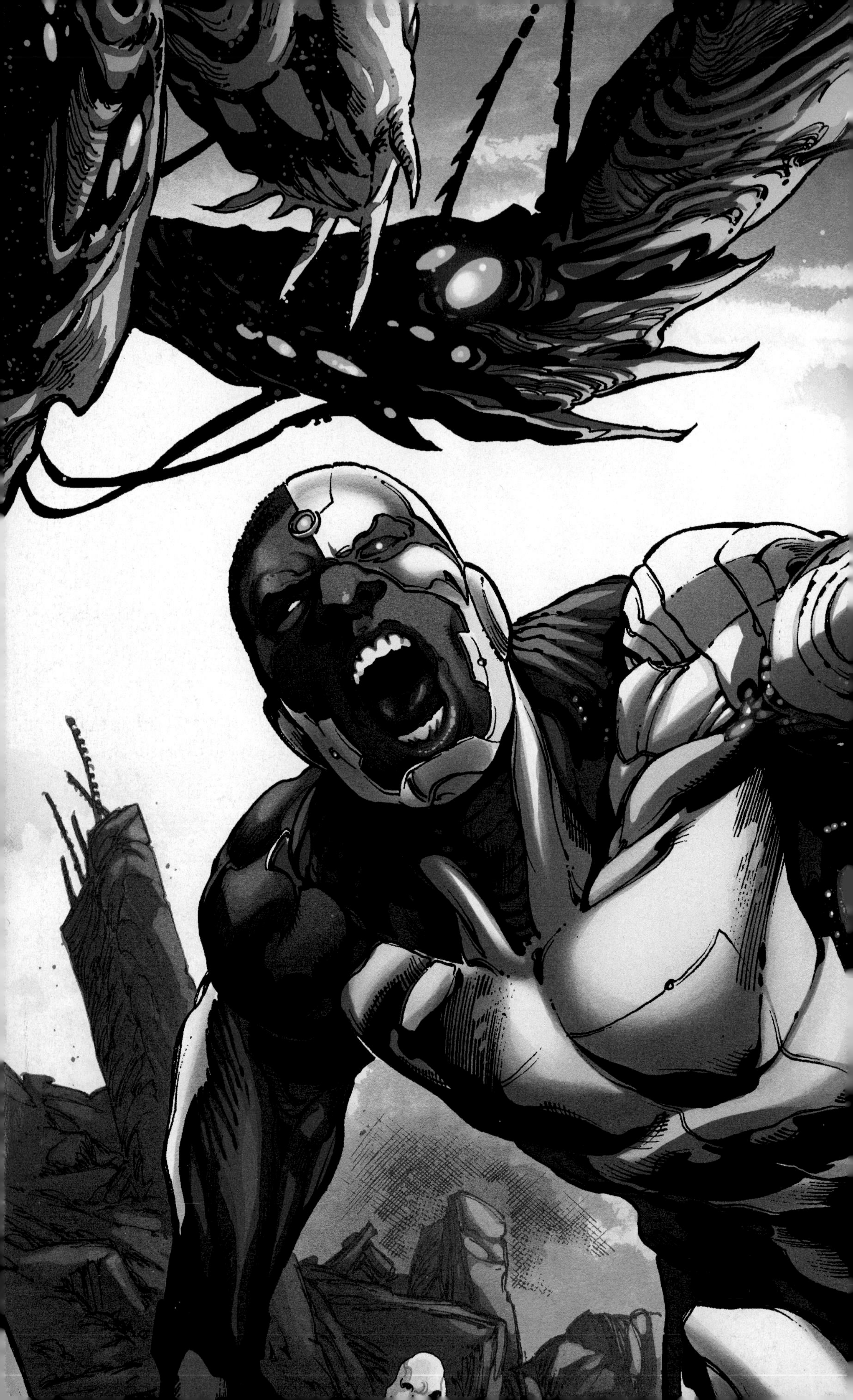

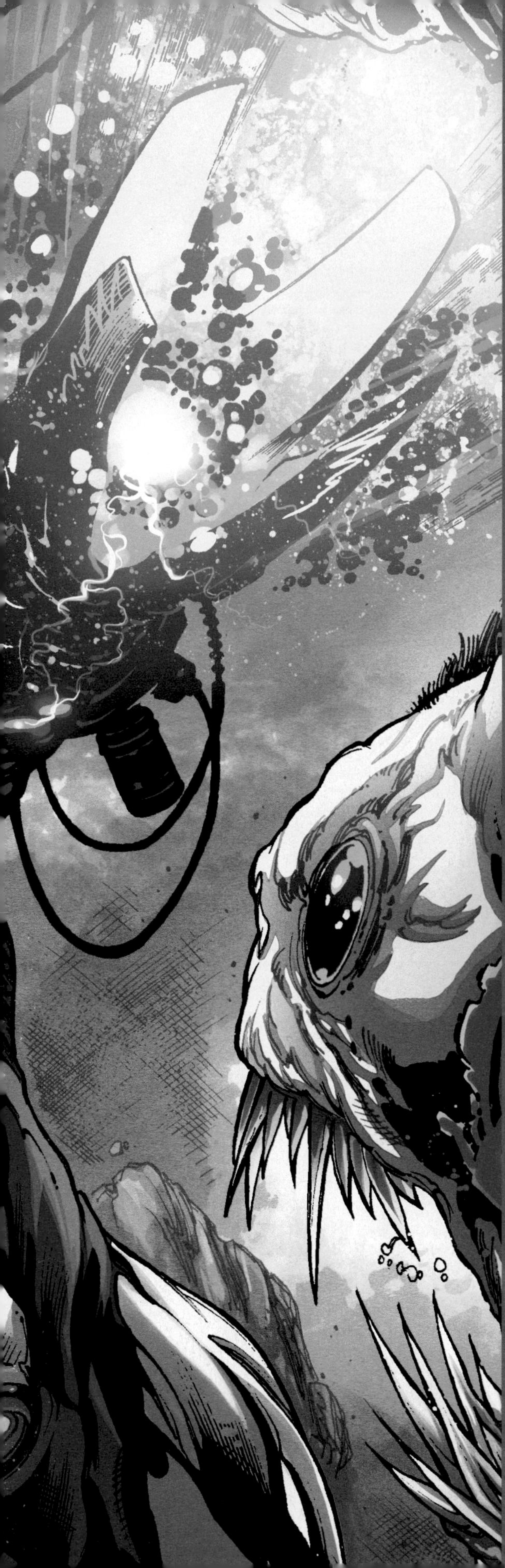

# CYBORG

VOLUME 1

## UNPLUGGED

WRITTEN BY
**DAVID F. WALKER**

PENCILS BY
**IVAN REIS**
**EDUARDO PANSICA**
**FELIPE WATANABE**
**DANIEL HDR**
**CLIFF RICHARDS**

INKS BY
**JOE PRADO**
**RAY McCARTHY**
**SCOTT HANNA**
**OCLAIR ALBERT**
**WAYNE FAUCHER**
**JULIO FERREIRA**
**ANDY OWENS**
**JUAN CASTRO**
**CLIFF RICHARDS**
**IVAN REIS**

COLOR BY
**ADRIANO LUCAS**
**PETE PANTAZIS**

LETTERS BY
**ROB LEIGH**
**COREY BREEN**
**TRAVIS LANHAM**

CYBORG CREATED BY
**MARV WOLFMAN and**
**GEORGE PÉREZ**

HARVEY RICHARDS Editor - Original Series
AMEDEO TURTURRO Assistant Editor - Original Series
JEB WOODARD Group Editor - Collected Editions
PAUL SANTOS Editor - Collected Edition
STEVE COOK Design Director - Books

BOB HARRAS Senior VP - Editor-in-Chief, DC Comics

DIANE NELSON President
DAN DIDIO and JIM LEE Co-Publishers
GEOFF JOHNS Chief Creative Officer
AMIT DESAI Senior VP - Marketing & Global Franchise Management
NAIRI GARDINER Senior VP - Finance
SAM ADES VP - Digital Marketing
BOBBIE CHASE VP - Talent Development
MARK CHIARELLO Senior VP - Art, Design & Collected Editions
JOHN CUNNINGHAM VP - Content Strategy
ANNE DEPIES VP - Strategy Planning & Reporting
DON FALLETTI VP - Manufacturing Operations
LAWRENCE GANEM VP - Editorial Administration & Talent Relations
ALISON GILL Senior VP - Manufacturing & Operations
HANK KANALZ Senior VP - Editorial Strategy & Administration
JAY KOGAN VP - Legal Affairs
DEREK MADDALENA Senior VP - Sales & Business Development
JACK MAHAN VP - Business Affairs
DAN MIRON VP - Sales Planning & Trade Development
NICK NAPOLITANO VP - Manufacturing Administration
CAROL ROEDER VP - Marketing
EDDIE SCANNELL VP - Mass Account & Digital Sales
COURTNEY SIMMONS Senior VP - Publicity & Communications
JIM (SKI) SOKOLOWSKI VP - Comic Book Specialty & Newsstand Sales
SANDY YI Senior VP - Global Franchise Management

CYBORG VOLUME 1: UNPLUGGED



DC Comics, 2900 West Alameda Avenue, Burbank, CA 91505
Printed by RR Donnelley, Salem, VA, USA. 02/19/16 First Printing.

Library of Congress Cataloging-in-Publication Data is available.

ISBN: 978-1-4012-6119-1

PEFC Certified
Printed on paper from sustainably managed forests and controlled sources
PEFC
PEFC/29-31-75
www.pefc.org

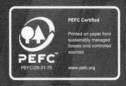

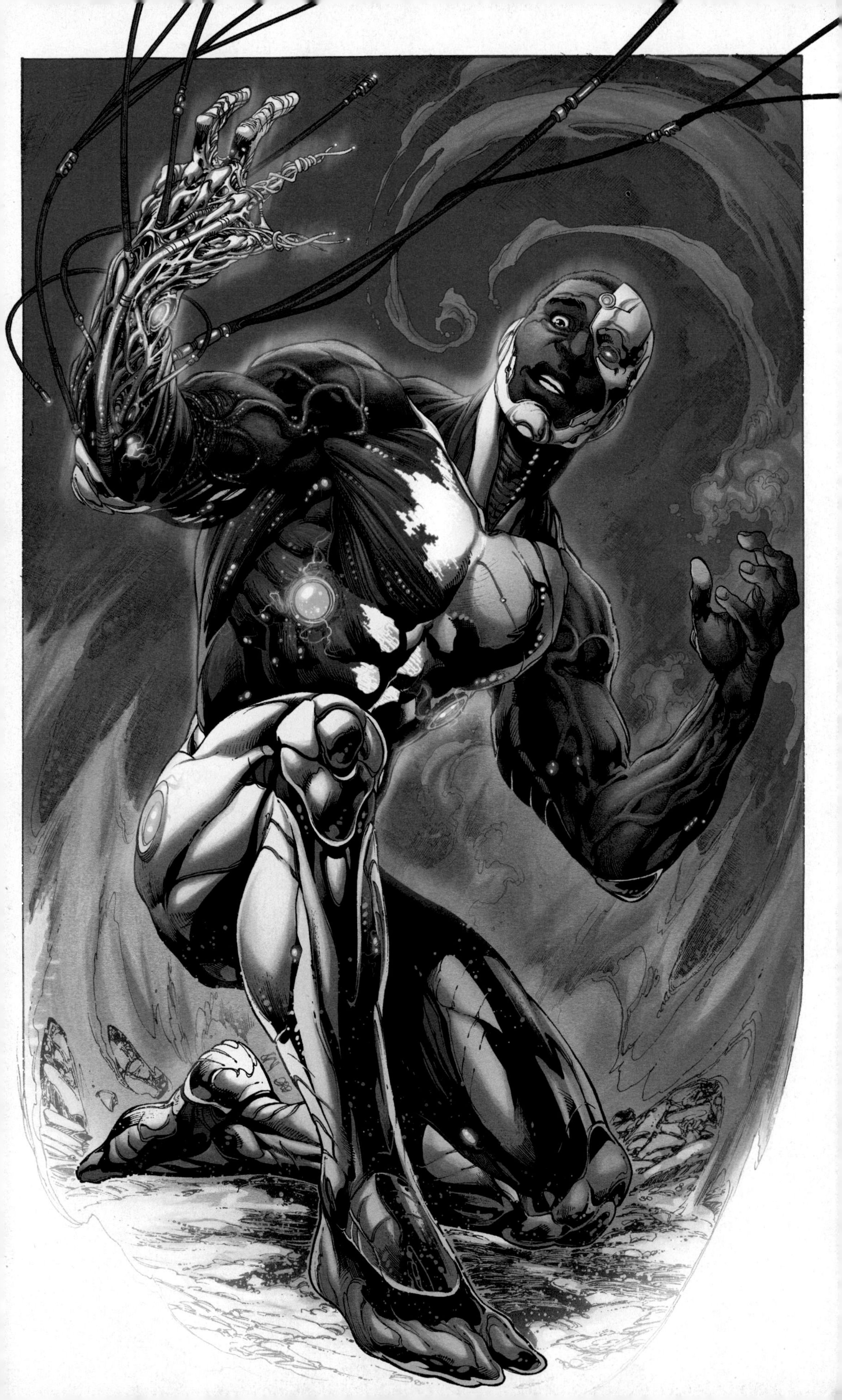

**DAVID F. WALKER** writer   **IVAN REIS** penciller   **JOE PRADO** artist   **ADRIANO LUCAS** colorist   **ROB LEIGH** letterer

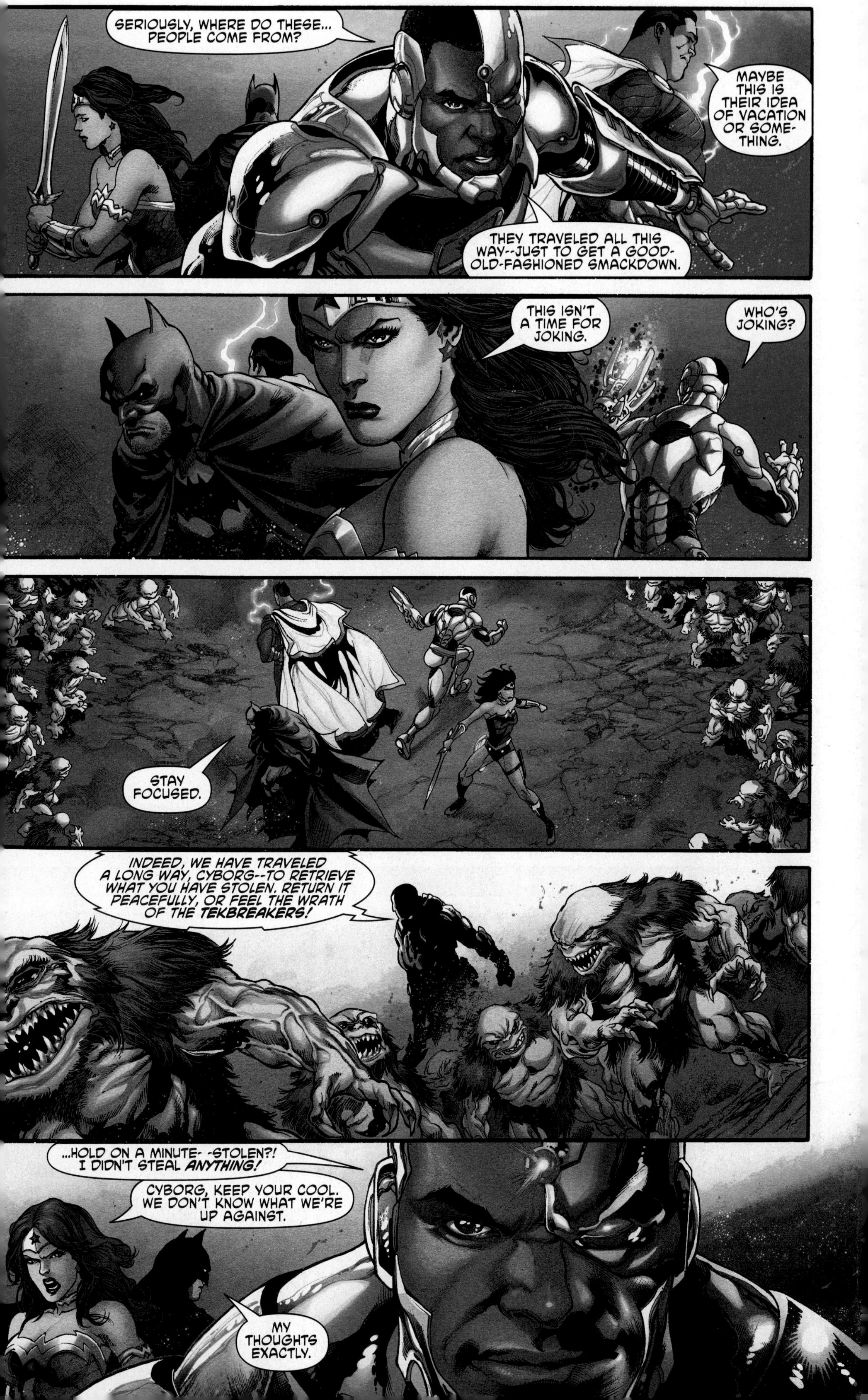
SERIOUSLY, WHERE DO THESE... PEOPLE COME FROM?
MAYBE THIS IS THEIR IDEA OF VACATION OR SOME-THING.
THEY TRAVELED ALL THIS WAY--JUST TO GET A GOOD-OLD-FASHIONED SMACKDOWN.
THIS ISN'T A TIME FOR JOKING.
WHO'S JOKING?
STAY FOCUSED.
INDEED, WE HAVE TRAVELED A LONG WAY, CYBORG--TO RETRIEVE WHAT YOU HAVE STOLEN. RETURN IT PEACEFULLY, OR FEEL THE WRATH OF THE TEKBREAKERS!
...HOLD ON A MINUTE- -STOLEN?! I DIDN'T STEAL ANYTHING!
CYBORG, KEEP YOUR COOL. WE DON'T KNOW WHAT WE'RE UP AGAINST.
MY THOUGHTS EXACTLY.

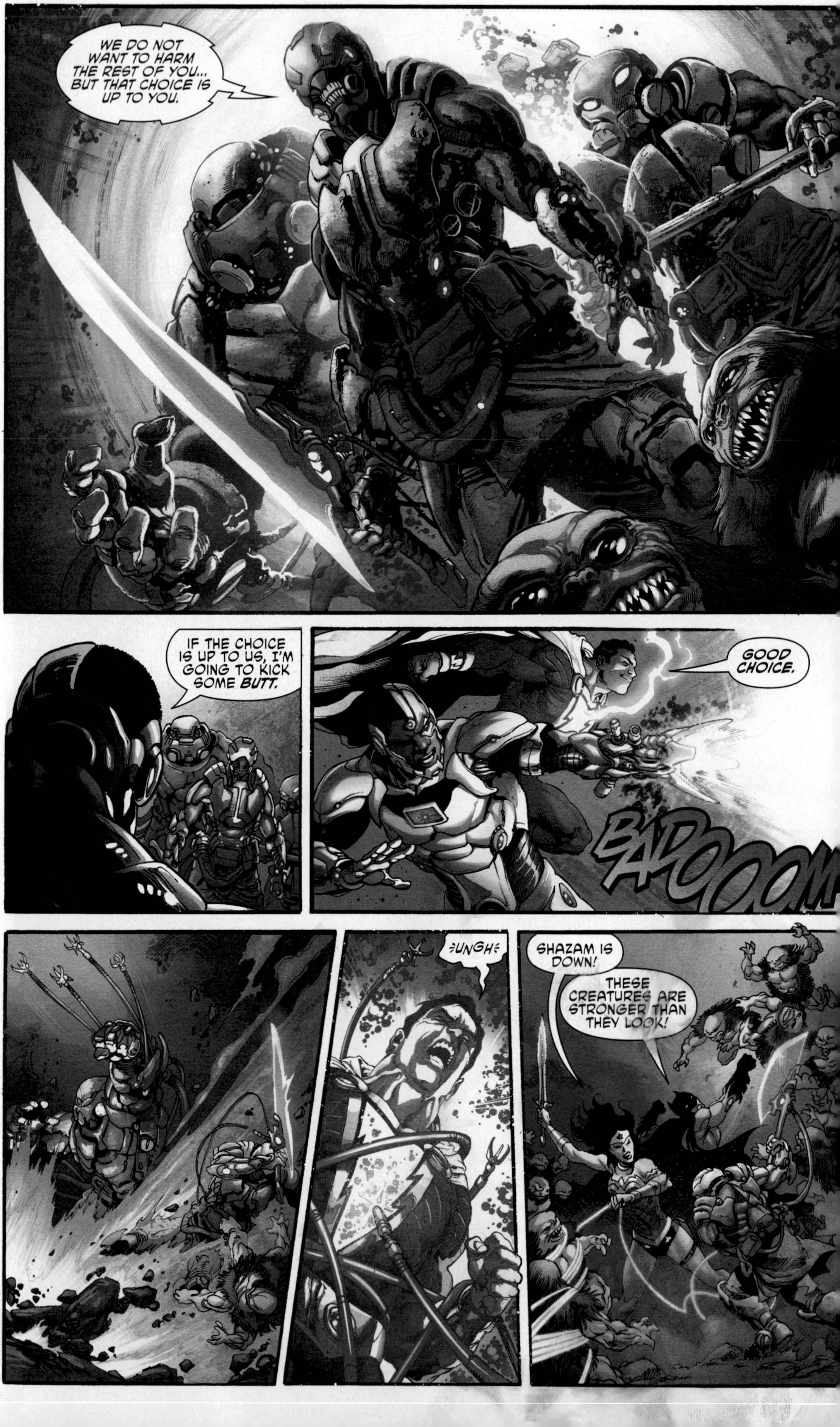
WE DO NOT WANT TO HARM THE REST OF YOU... BUT THAT CHOICE IS UP TO YOU.
IF THE CHOICE IS UP TO US, I'M GOING TO KICK SOME BUTT.
GOOD CHOICE.
BADOOOOM
UNGH
SHAZAM IS DOWN!
THESE CREATURES ARE STRONGER THAN THEY LOOK!

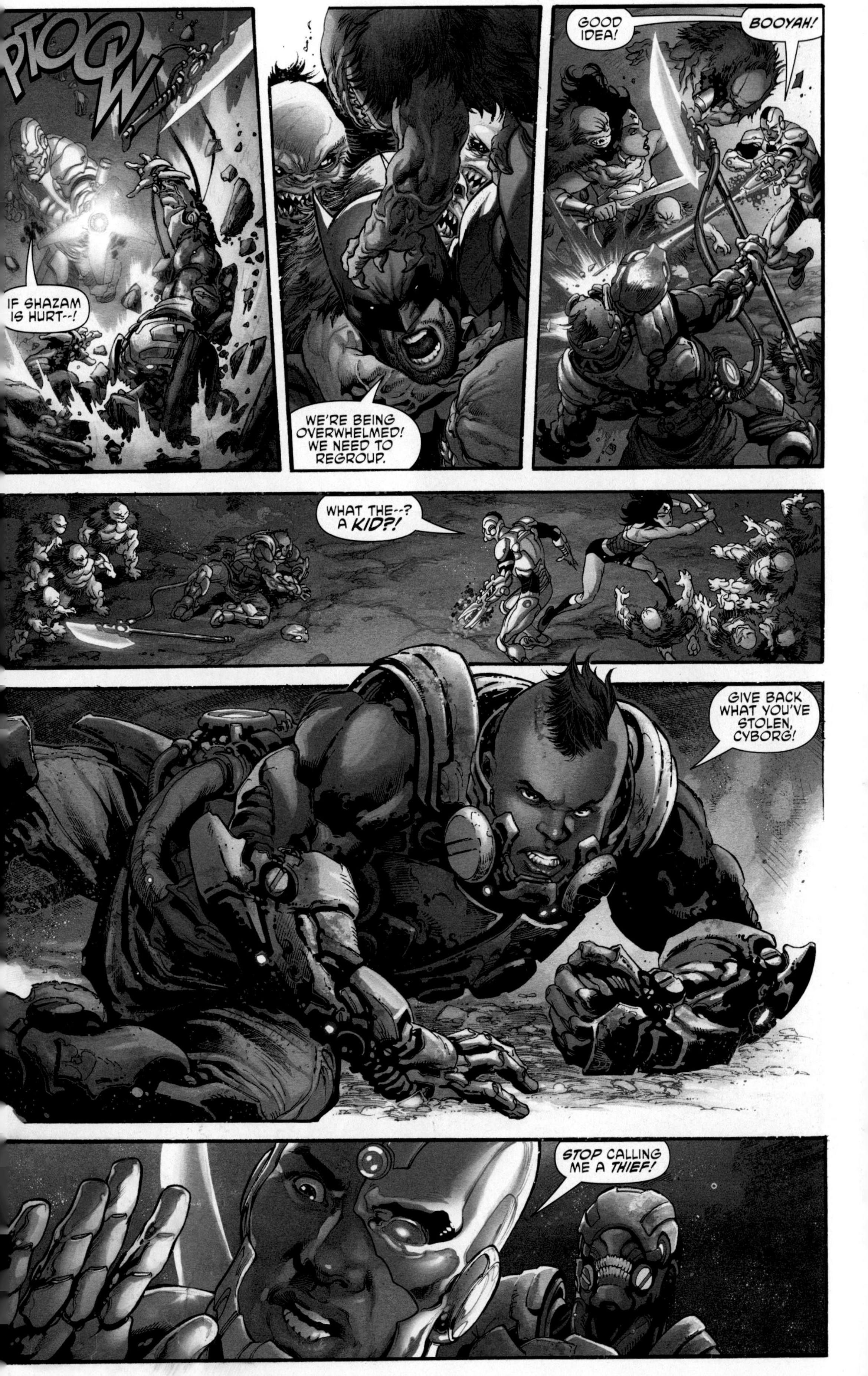
PTOOW
IF SHAZAM IS HURT--!
WE'RE BEING OVERWHELMED! WE NEED TO REGROUP.
GOOD IDEA!
BOOYAH!
WHAT THE--? A KID?!
GIVE BACK WHAT YOU'VE STOLEN, CYBORG!
STOP CALLING ME A THIEF!

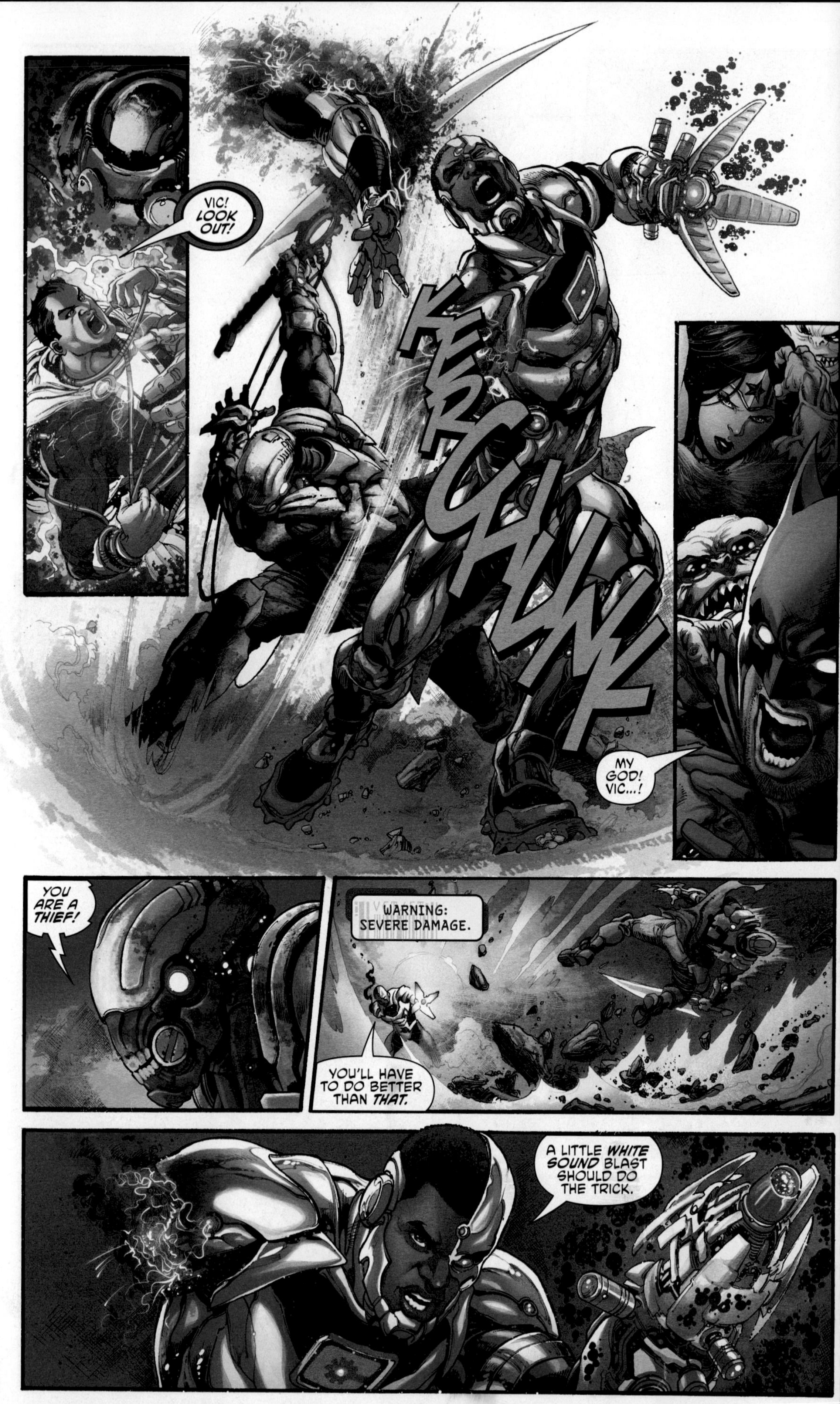
VIC! LOOK OUT!
KERCHUNK
MY GOD! VIC...!
YOU ARE A THIEF!
WARNING: SEVERE DAMAGE.
YOU'LL HAVE TO DO BETTER THAN THAT.
A LITTLE WHITE SOUND BLAST SHOULD DO THE TRICK.

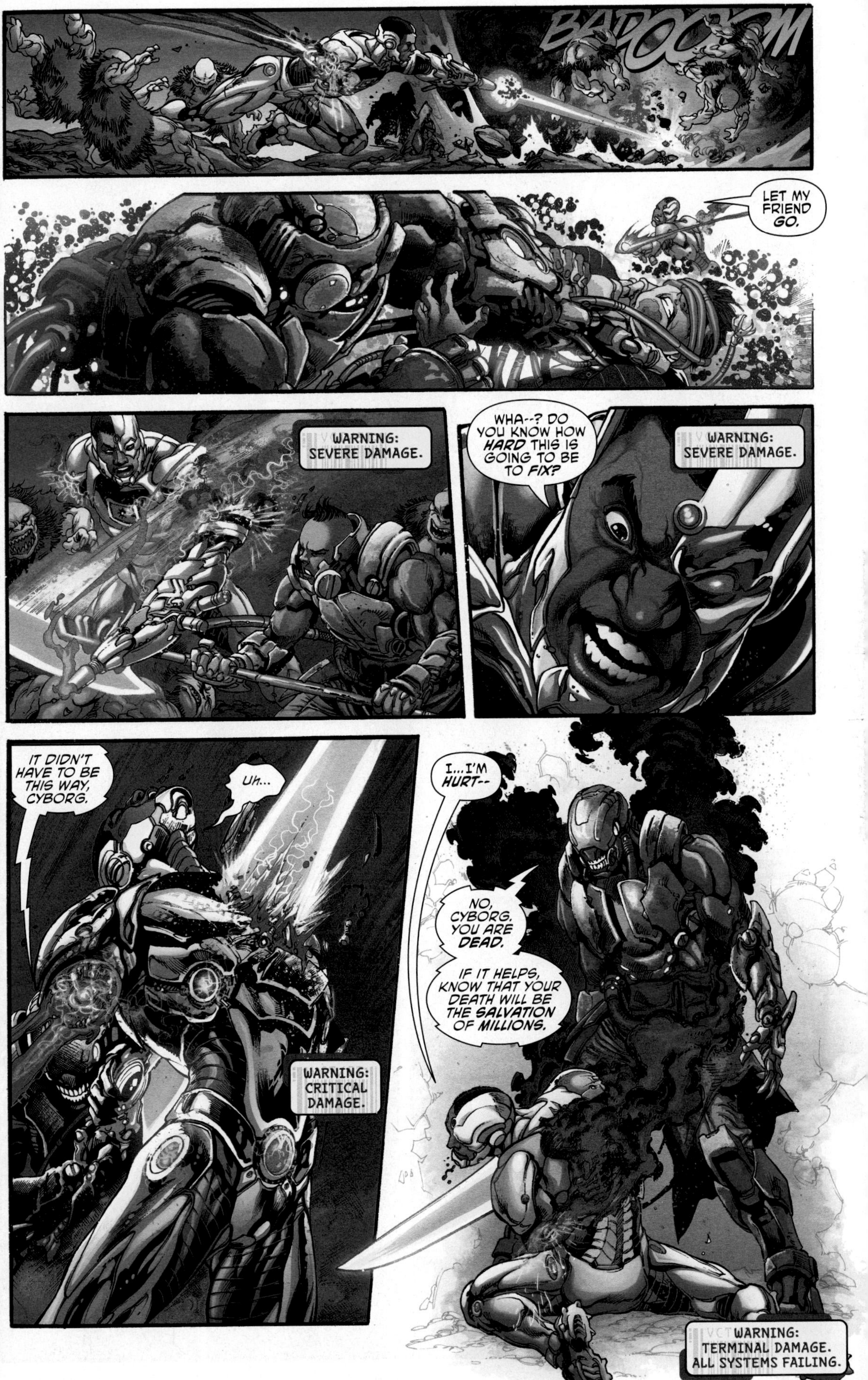
BADOOOM
LET MY FRIEND GO.
WARNING: SEVERE DAMAGE.
WHA--? DO YOU KNOW HOW HARD THIS IS GOING TO BE TO FIX?
WARNING: SEVERE DAMAGE.
IT DIDN'T HAVE TO BE THIS WAY, CYBORG.
Uh...
WARNING: CRITICAL DAMAGE.
I...I'M HURT--
NO, CYBORG. YOU ARE DEAD.
IF IT HELPS, KNOW THAT YOUR DEATH WILL BE THE SALVATION OF MILLIONS.
WARNING: TERMINAL DAMAGE. ALL SYSTEMS FAILING.

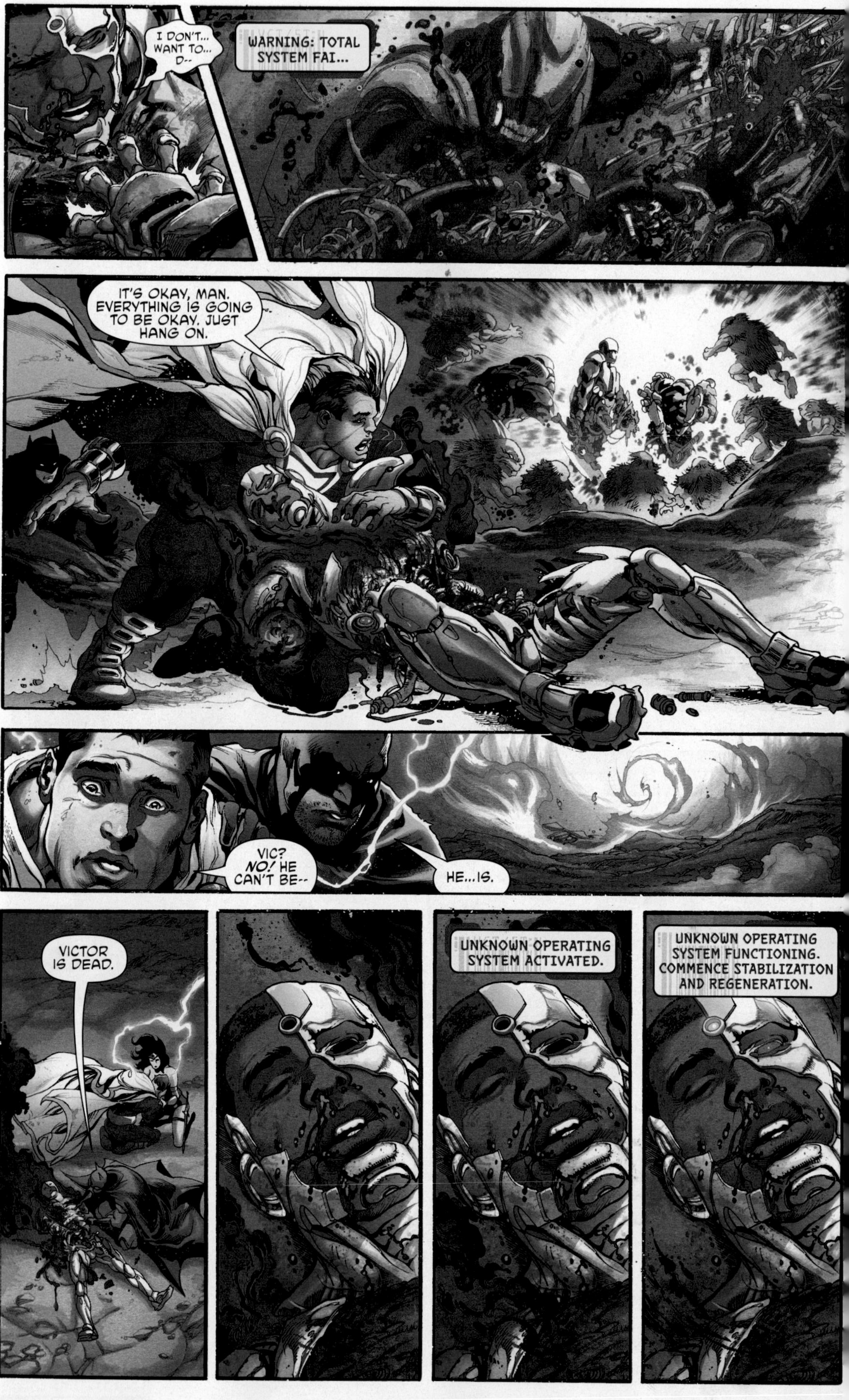

I DON'T... WANT TO... D--
WARNING: TOTAL SYSTEM FAI...
IT'S OKAY, MAN. EVERYTHING IS GOING TO BE OKAY. JUST HANG ON.
VIC? NO! HE CAN'T BE--
HE...IS.
VICTOR IS DEAD.
UNKNOWN OPERATING SYSTEM ACTIVATED.
UNKNOWN OPERATING SYSTEM FUNCTIONING. COMMENCE STABILIZATION AND REGENERATION.

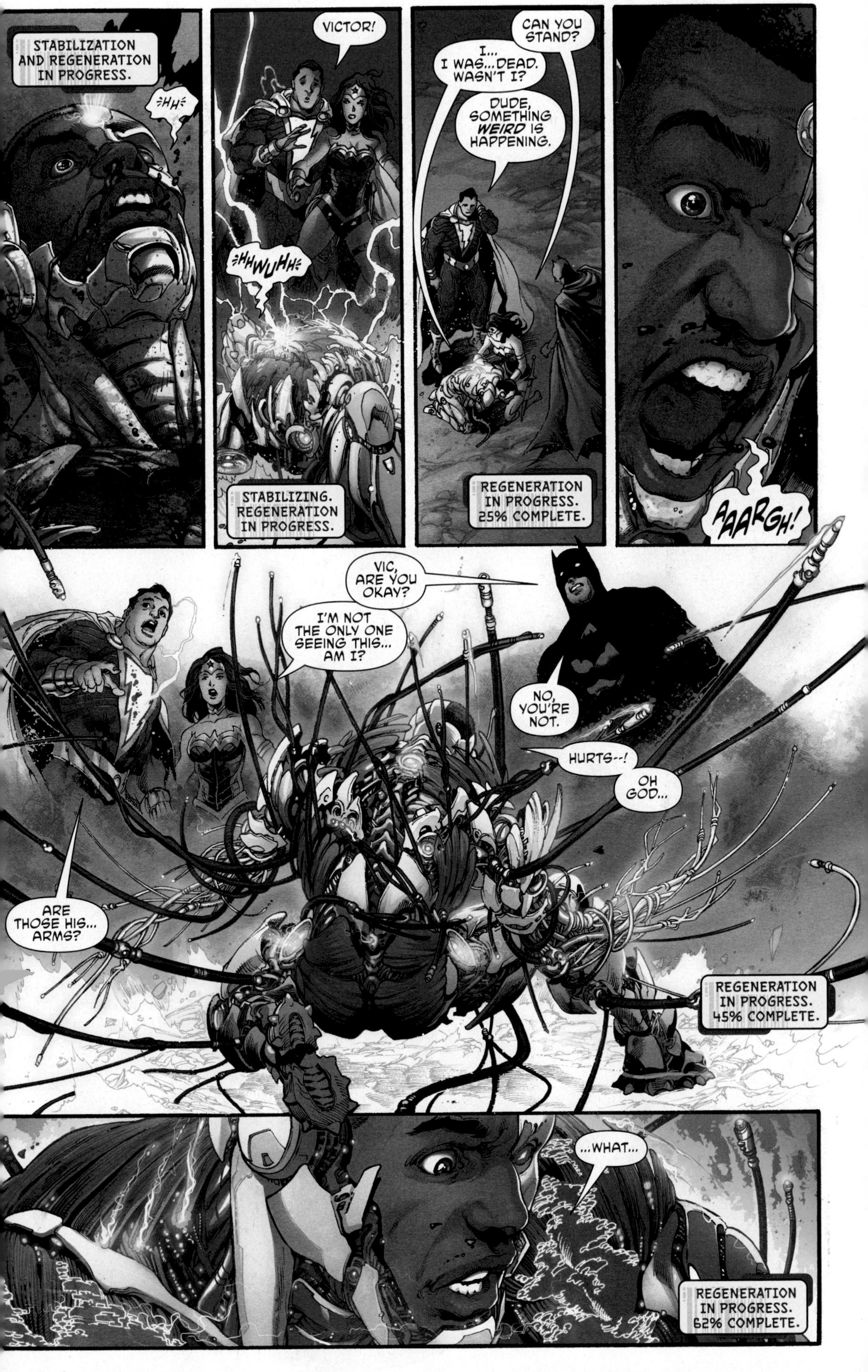
STABILIZATION AND REGENERATION IN PROGRESS.
HH
VICTOR!
HHWUHH
STABILIZING. REGENERATION IN PROGRESS.
CAN YOU STAND?
I... I WAS...DEAD. WASN'T I?
DUDE, SOMETHING WEIRD IS HAPPENING.
REGENERATION IN PROGRESS. 25% COMPLETE.
AAARGH!
VIC, ARE YOU OKAY?
I'M NOT THE ONLY ONE SEEING THIS... AM I?
NO, YOU'RE NOT.
HURTS--!
OH GOD...
ARE THOSE HIS... ARMS?
REGENERATION IN PROGRESS. 45% COMPLETE.
...WHAT...
REGENERATION IN PROGRESS. 62% COMPLETE.

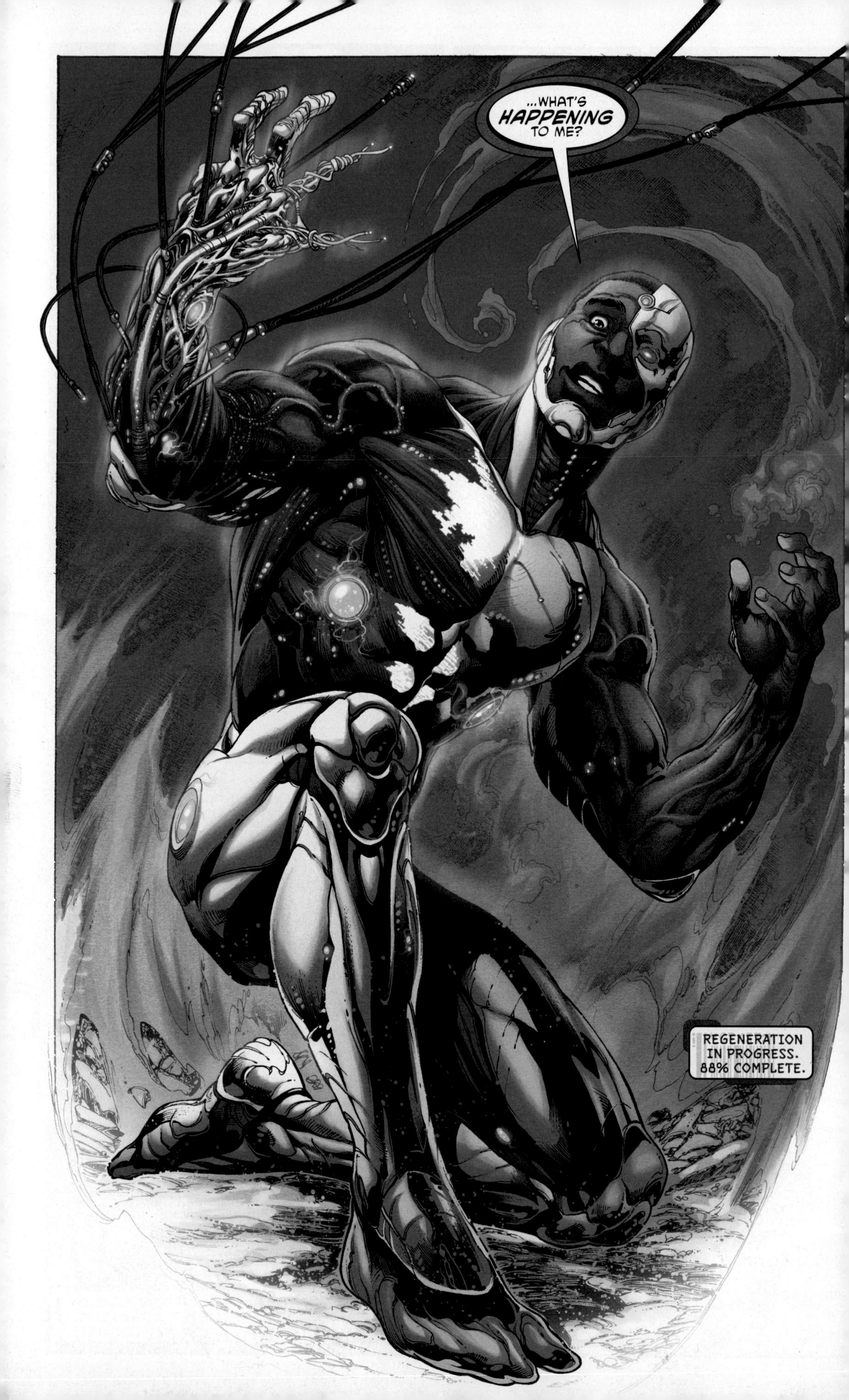
...WHAT'S HAPPENING TO ME?
REGENERATION IN PROGRESS. 88% COMPLETE.

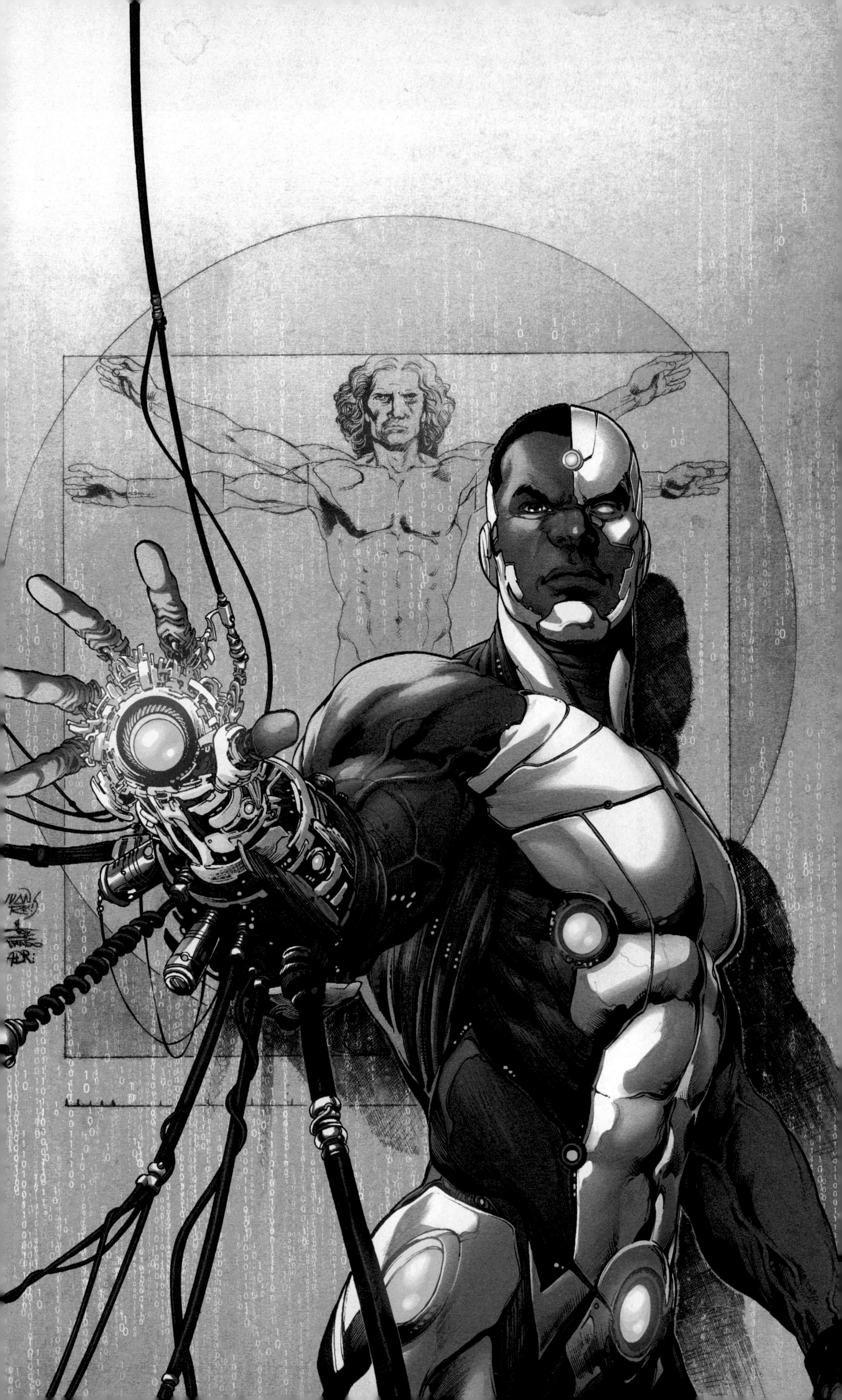

**UNPLUGGED**

**IVAN REIS** penciller **JOE PRADO** inker **ADRIANO LUCAS** colorist **ROB LEIGH** letterer
**IVAN REIS, JOE PRADO** and **ADRIANO LUCAS** cover art

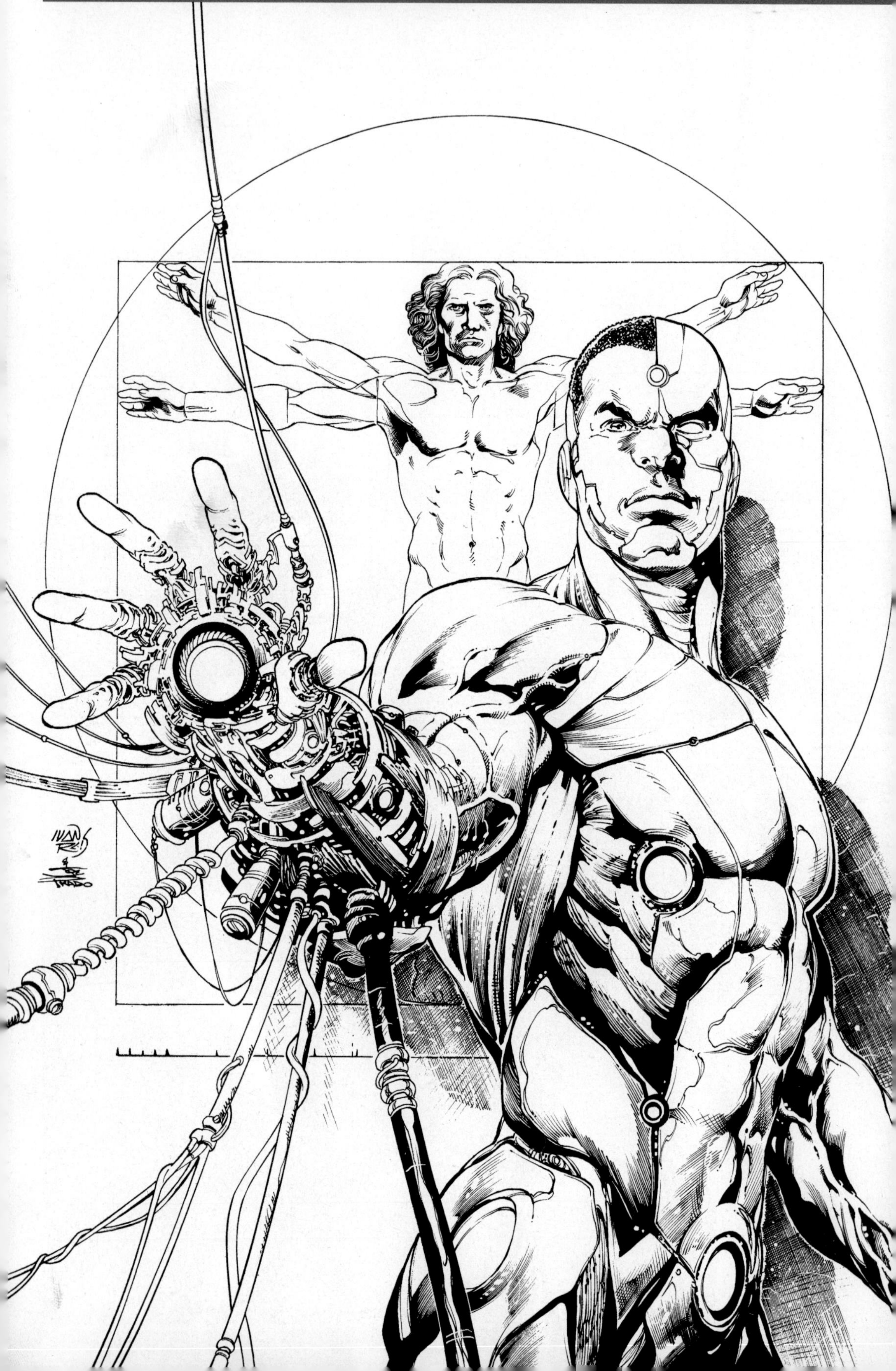

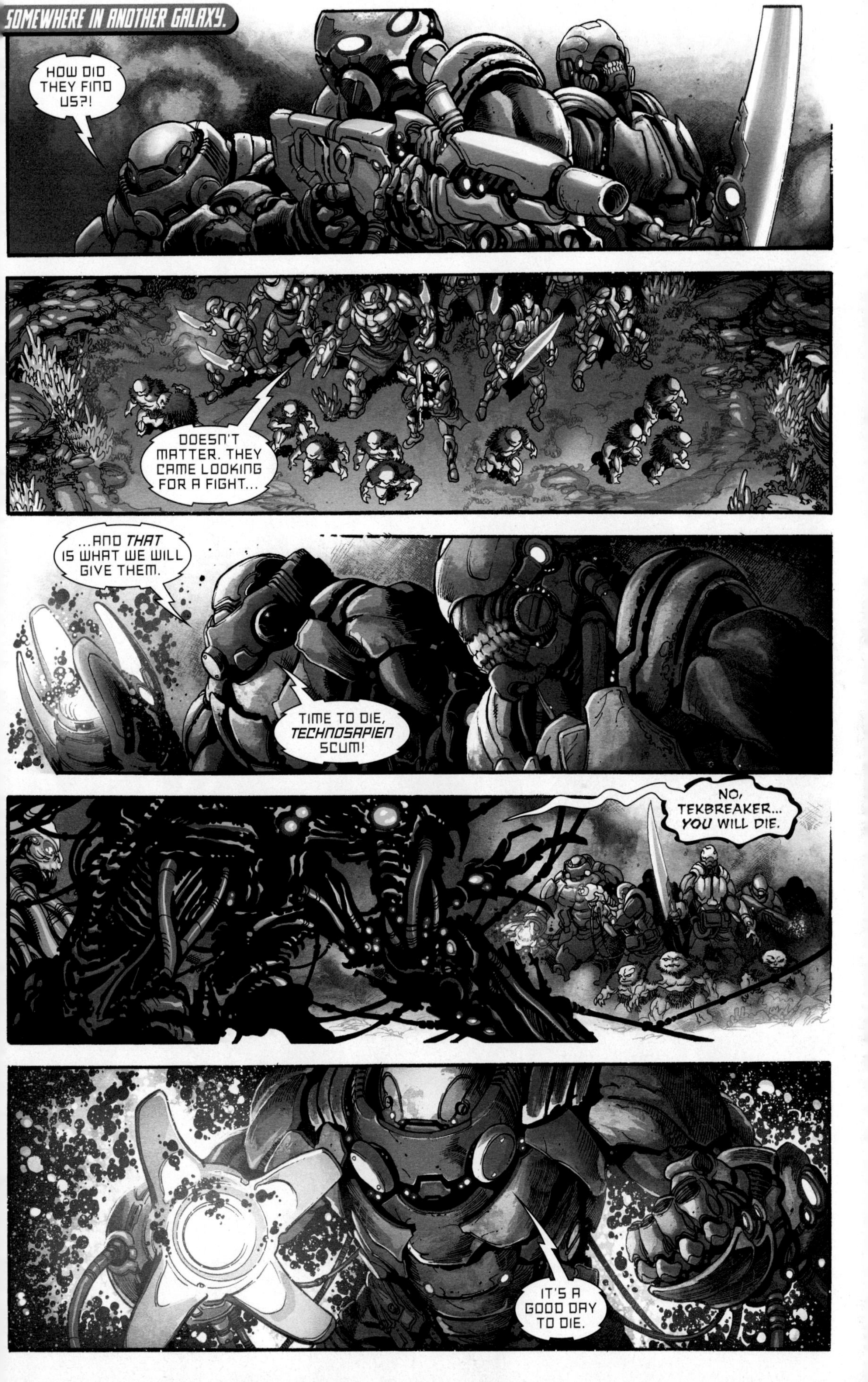
SOMEWHERE IN ANOTHER GALAXY.
HOW DID THEY FIND US?!
DOESN'T MATTER. THEY CAME LOOKING FOR A FIGHT...
...AND THAT IS WHAT WE WILL GIVE THEM.
TIME TO DIE, TECHNOSAPIEN SCUM!
NO, TEKBREAKER... YOU WILL DIE.
IT'S A GOOD DAY TO DIE.

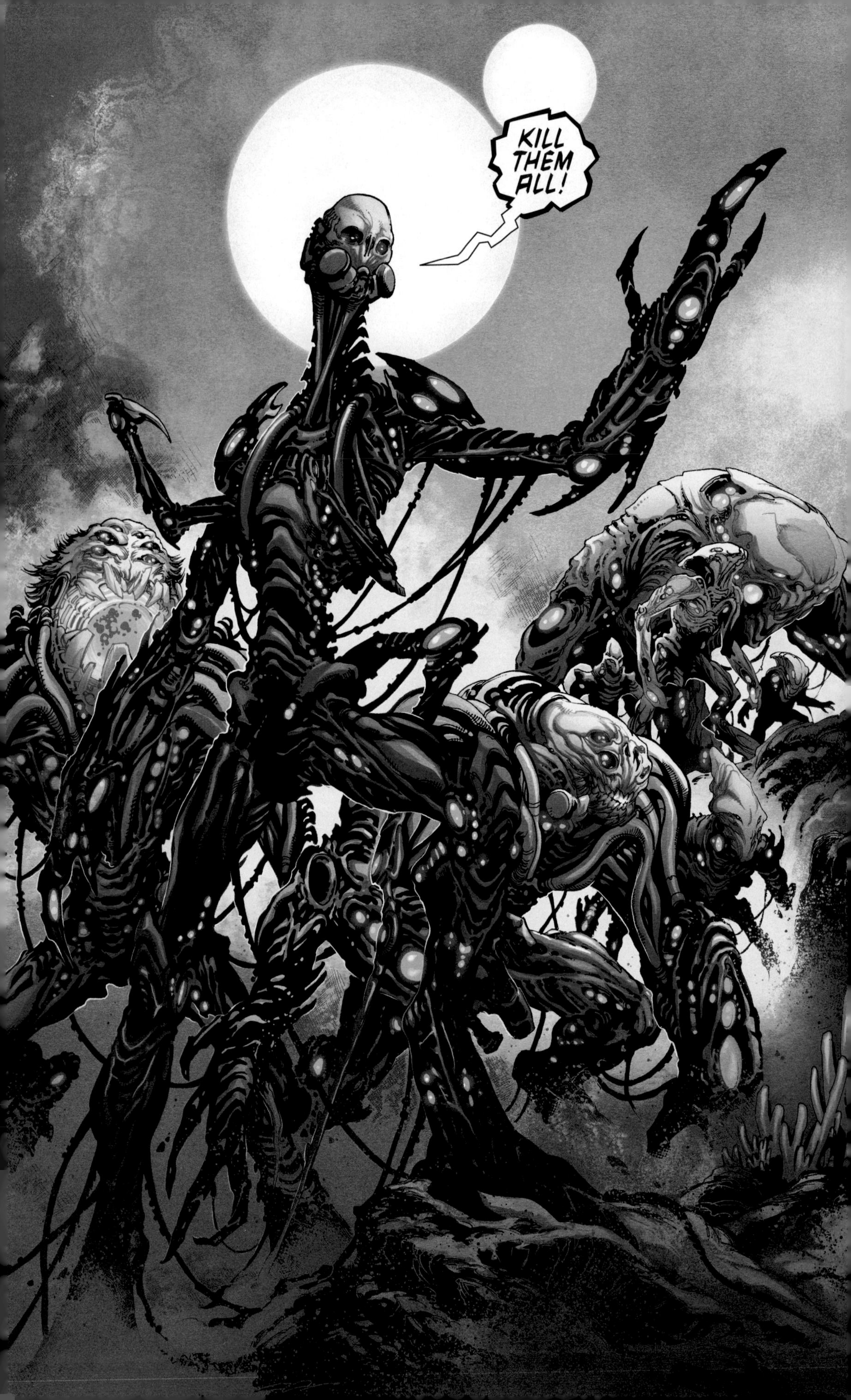
KILL THEM ALL!

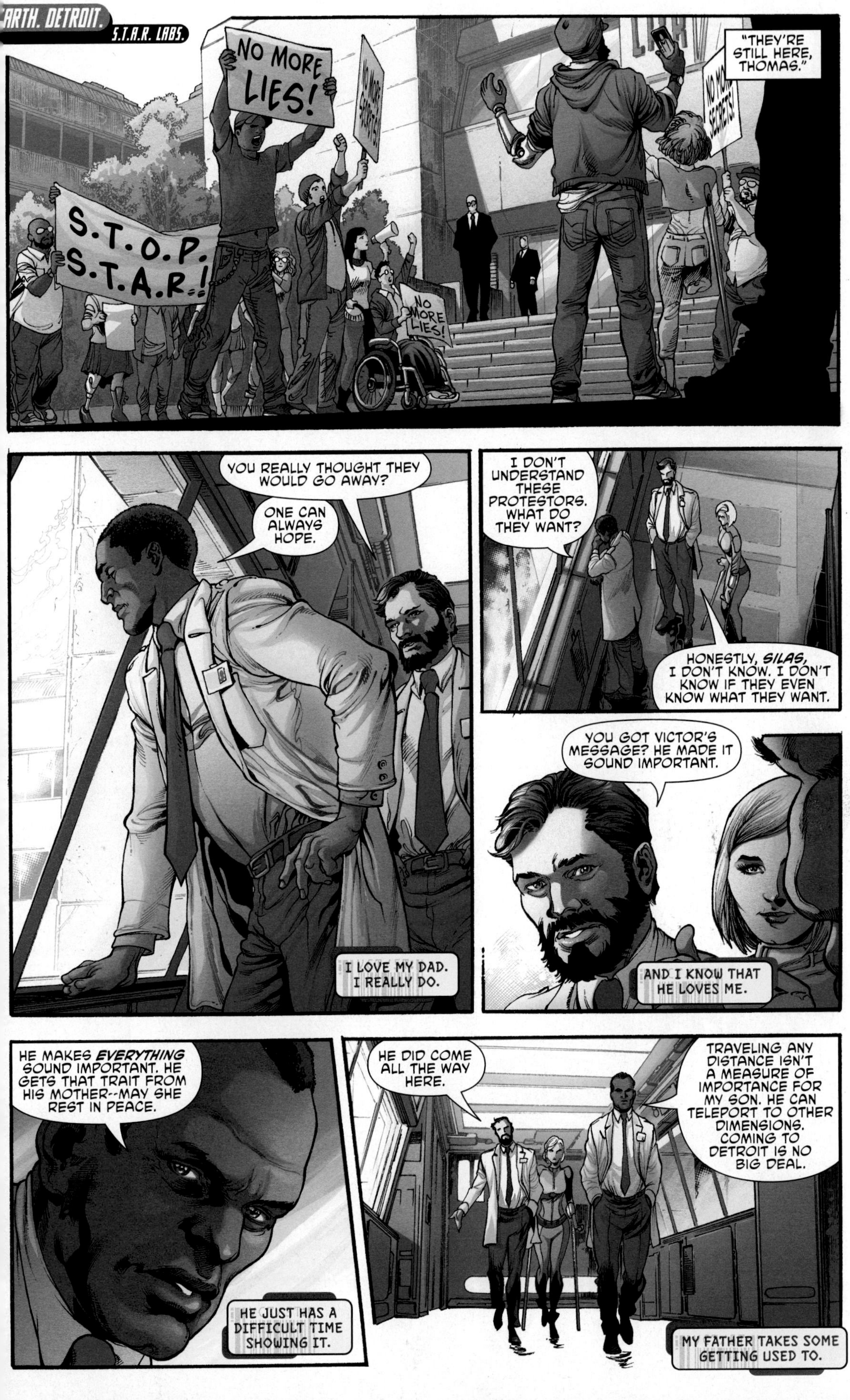
ARTH. DETROIT.
S.T.A.R. LABS.
NO MORE LIES!
NO MORE SECRETS!
S.T.O.P. S.T.A.R.!
NO MORE LIES!
NO MORE SECRETS!
"THEY'RE STILL HERE, THOMAS."
YOU REALLY THOUGHT THEY WOULD GO AWAY?
ONE CAN ALWAYS HOPE.
I LOVE MY DAD. I REALLY DO.
I DON'T UNDERSTAND THESE PROTESTORS. WHAT DO THEY WANT?
HONESTLY, SILAS, I DON'T KNOW. I DON'T KNOW IF THEY EVEN KNOW WHAT THEY WANT.
YOU GOT VICTOR'S MESSAGE? HE MADE IT SOUND IMPORTANT.
AND I KNOW THAT HE LOVES ME.
HE MAKES EVERYTHING SOUND IMPORTANT. HE GETS THAT TRAIT FROM HIS MOTHER--MAY SHE REST IN PEACE.
HE JUST HAS A DIFFICULT TIME SHOWING IT.
HE DID COME ALL THE WAY HERE.
TRAVELING ANY DISTANCE ISN'T A MEASURE OF IMPORTANCE FOR MY SON. HE CAN TELEPORT TO OTHER DIMENSIONS. COMING TO DETROIT IS NO BIG DEAL.
MY FATHER TAKES SOME GETTING USED TO.

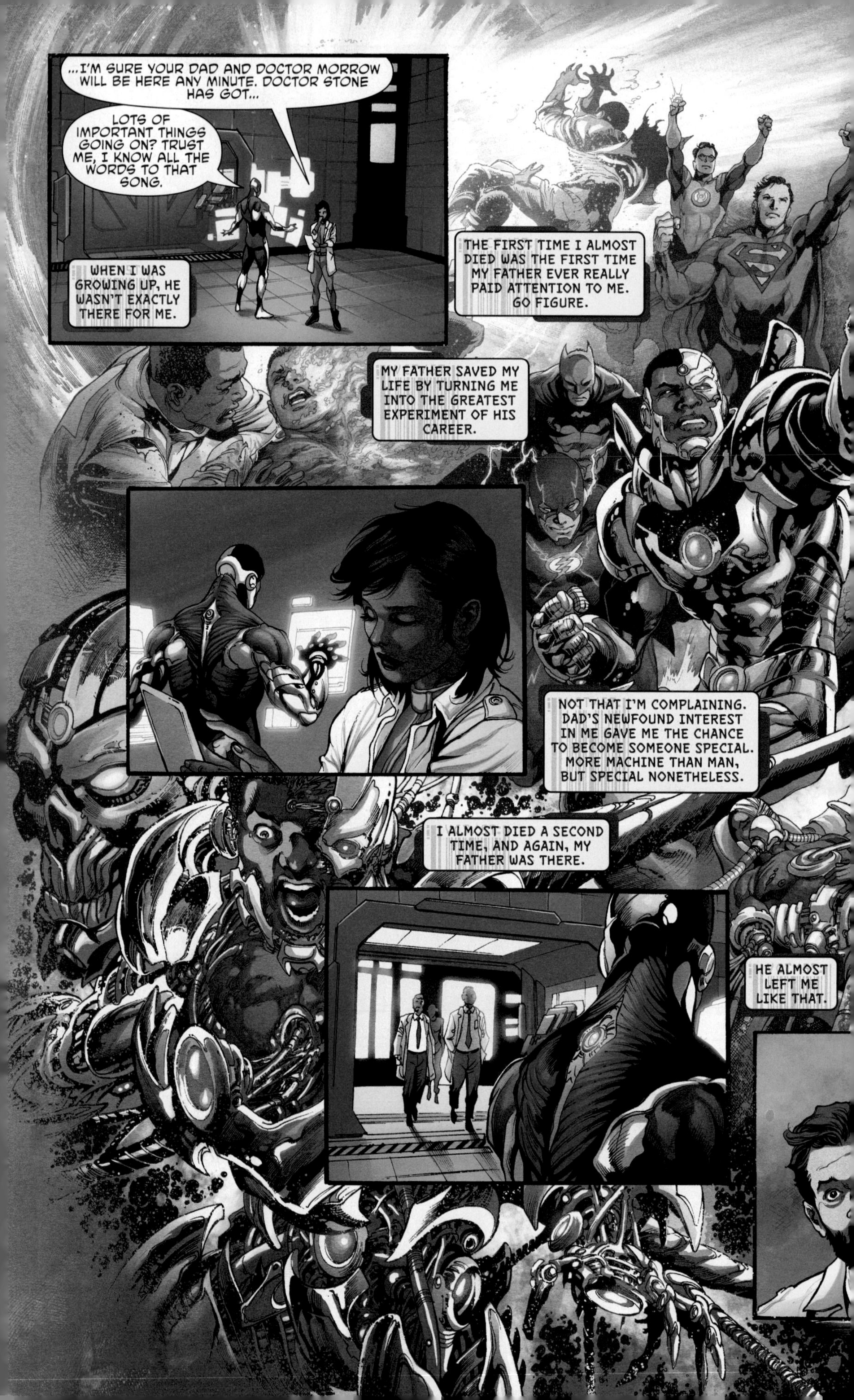
...I'M SURE YOUR DAD AND DOCTOR MORROW WILL BE HERE ANY MINUTE. DOCTOR STONE HAS GOT...
LOTS OF IMPORTANT THINGS GOING ON? TRUST ME, I KNOW ALL THE WORDS TO THAT SONG.
WHEN I WAS GROWING UP, HE WASN'T EXACTLY THERE FOR ME.
THE FIRST TIME I ALMOST DIED WAS THE FIRST TIME MY FATHER EVER REALLY PAID ATTENTION TO ME. GO FIGURE.
MY FATHER SAVED MY LIFE BY TURNING ME INTO THE GREATEST EXPERIMENT OF HIS CAREER.
NOT THAT I'M COMPLAINING. DAD'S NEWFOUND INTEREST IN ME GAVE ME THE CHANCE TO BECOME SOMEONE SPECIAL. MORE MACHINE THAN MAN, BUT SPECIAL NONETHELESS.
I ALMOST DIED A SECOND TIME, AND AGAIN, MY FATHER WAS THERE.
HE ALMOST LEFT ME LIKE THAT.

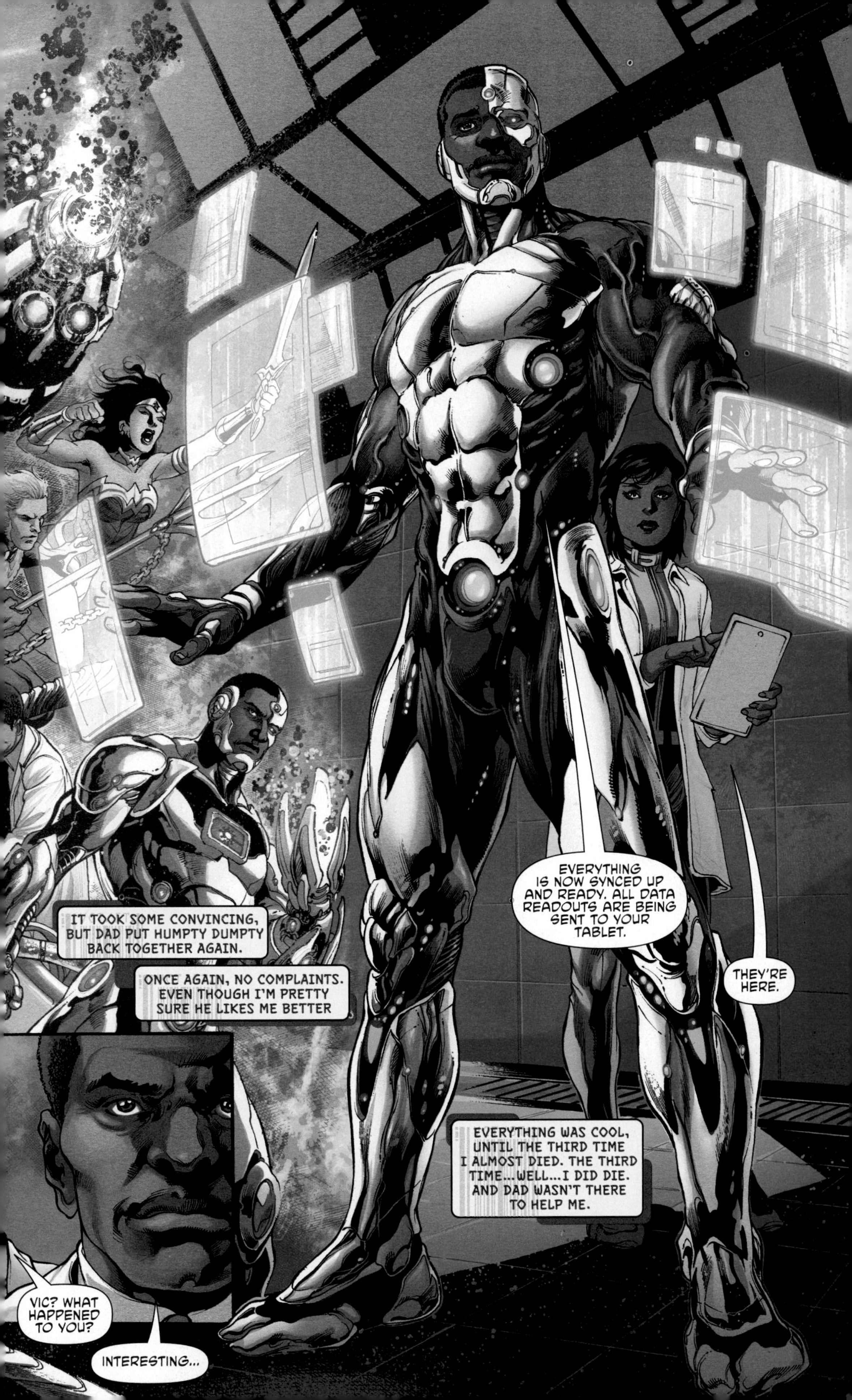
IT TOOK SOME CONVINCING, BUT DAD PUT HUMPTY DUMPTY BACK TOGETHER AGAIN.
ONCE AGAIN, NO COMPLAINTS. EVEN THOUGH I'M PRETTY SURE HE LIKES ME BETTER
EVERYTHING IS NOW SYNCED UP AND READY. ALL DATA READOUTS ARE BEING SENT TO YOUR TABLET.
THEY'RE HERE.
EVERYTHING WAS COOL, UNTIL THE THIRD TIME I ALMOST DIED. THE THIRD TIME...WELL...I DID DIE. AND DAD WASN'T THERE TO HELP ME.
VIC? WHAT HAPPENED TO YOU?
INTERESTING...

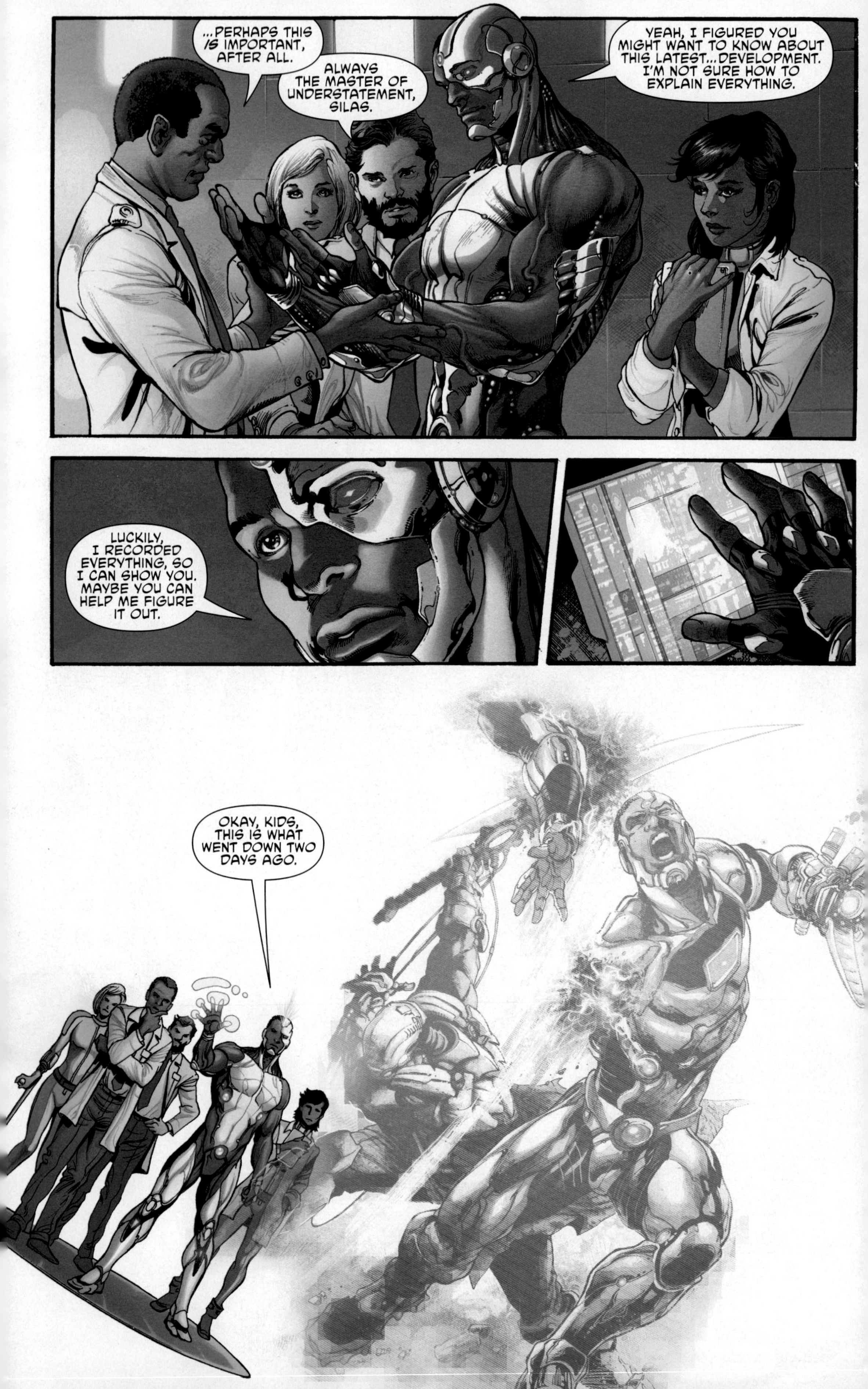
...PERHAPS THIS IS IMPORTANT, AFTER ALL.
ALWAYS THE MASTER OF UNDERSTATEMENT, SILAS.
YEAH, I FIGURED YOU MIGHT WANT TO KNOW ABOUT THIS LATEST...DEVELOPMENT. I'M NOT SURE HOW TO EXPLAIN EVERYTHING.
LUCKILY, I RECORDED EVERYTHING, SO I CAN SHOW YOU. MAYBE YOU CAN HELP ME FIGURE IT OUT.
OKAY, KIDS, THIS IS WHAT WENT DOWN TWO DAYS AGO.

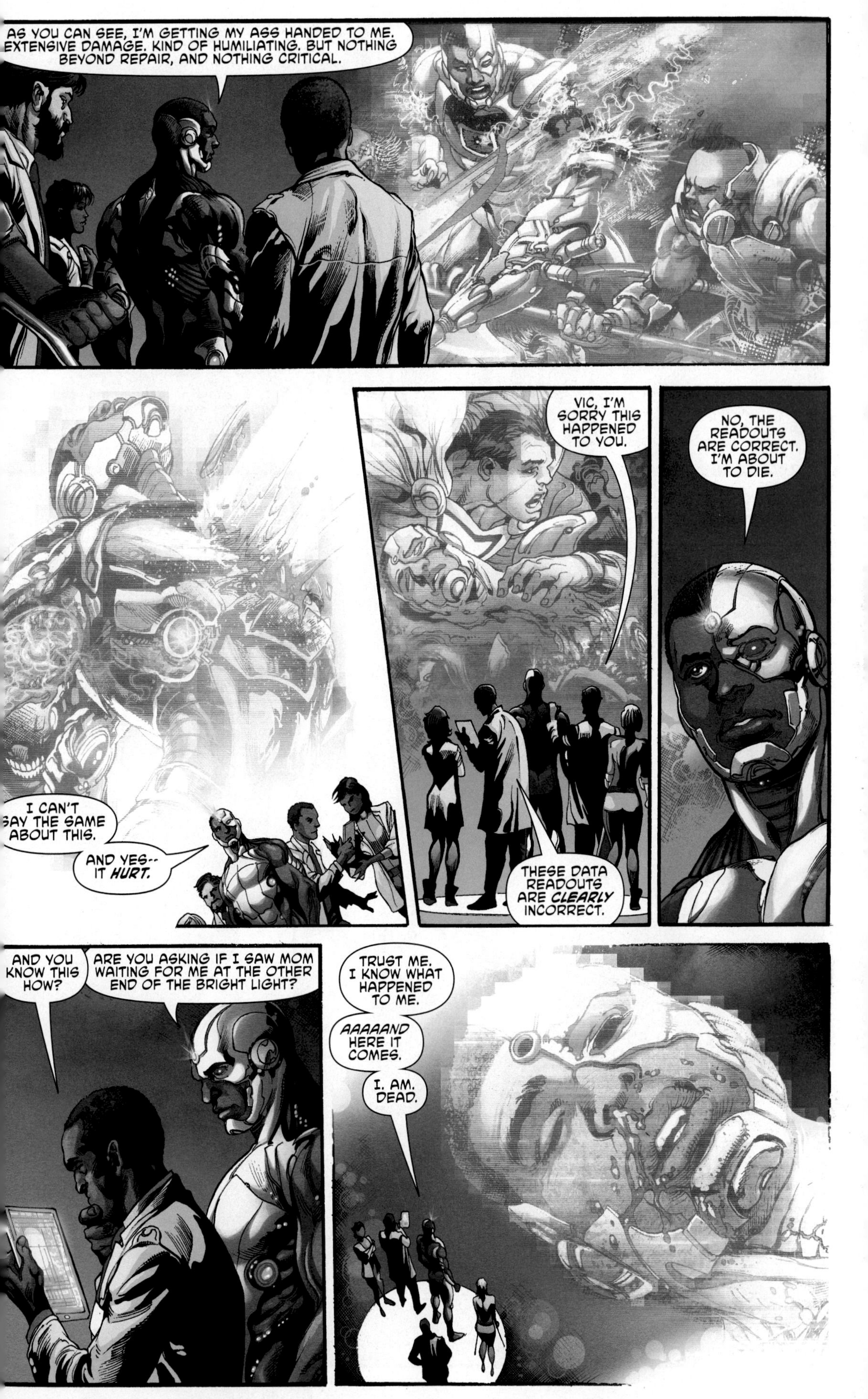

AS YOU CAN SEE, I'M GETTING MY ASS HANDED TO ME. EXTENSIVE DAMAGE. KIND OF HUMILIATING. BUT NOTHING BEYOND REPAIR, AND NOTHING CRITICAL.
I CAN'T SAY THE SAME ABOUT THIS.
AND YES-- IT HURT.
VIC, I'M SORRY THIS HAPPENED TO YOU.
THESE DATA READOUTS ARE CLEARLY INCORRECT.
NO, THE READOUTS ARE CORRECT. I'M ABOUT TO DIE.
AND YOU KNOW THIS HOW?
ARE YOU ASKING IF I SAW MOM WAITING FOR ME AT THE OTHER END OF THE BRIGHT LIGHT?
TRUST ME. I KNOW WHAT HAPPENED TO ME.
AAAAAND HERE IT COMES.
I. AM. DEAD.

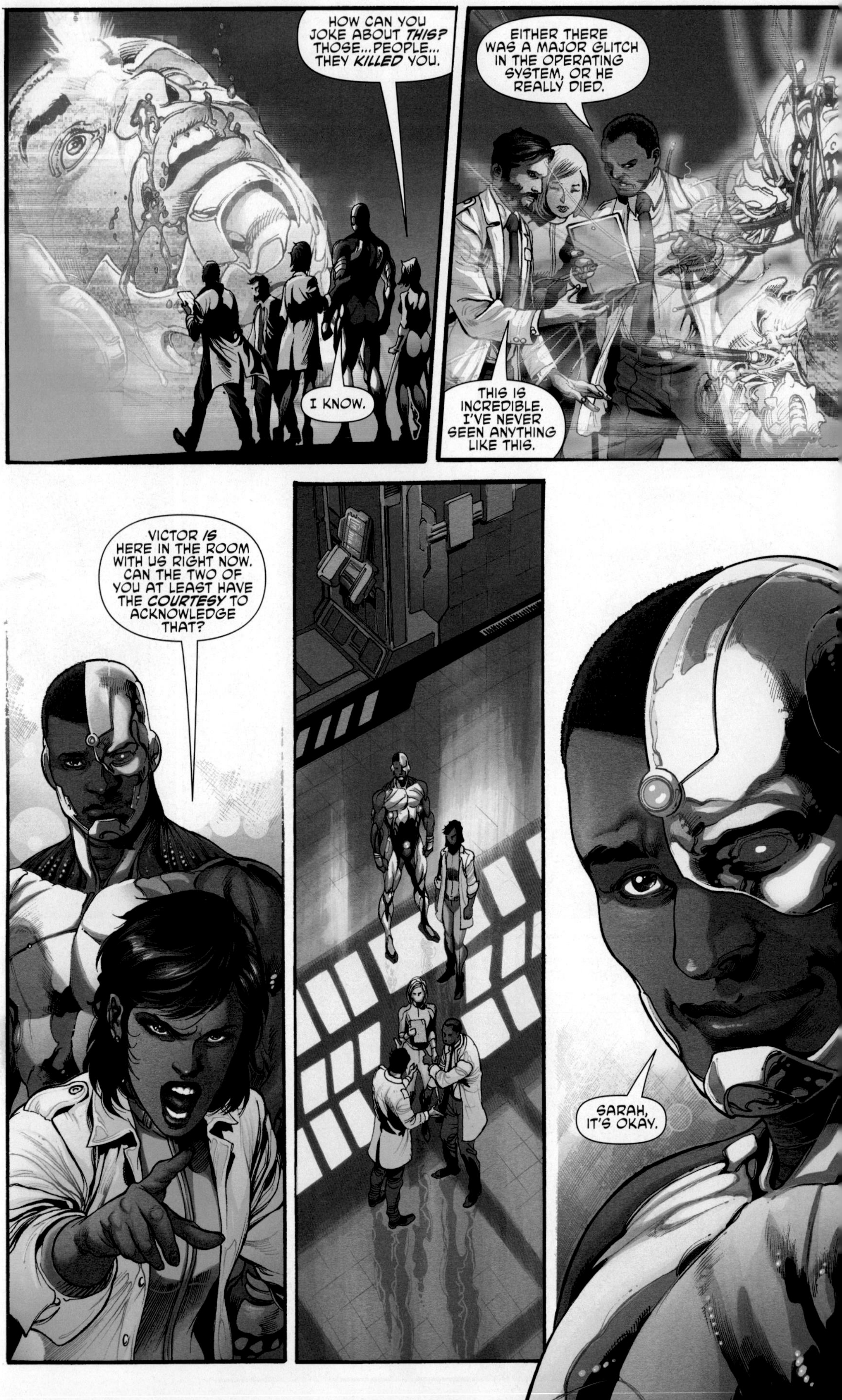
HOW CAN YOU JOKE ABOUT *THIS?* THOSE...PEOPLE... THEY *KILLED* YOU.
I KNOW.
EITHER THERE WAS A MAJOR GLITCH IN THE OPERATING SYSTEM, OR HE REALLY DIED.
THIS IS INCREDIBLE. I'VE NEVER SEEN ANYTHING LIKE THIS.
VICTOR *IS* HERE IN THE ROOM WITH US RIGHT NOW. CAN THE TWO OF YOU AT LEAST HAVE THE *COURTESY* TO ACKNOWLEDGE THAT?
SARAH, IT'S OKAY.

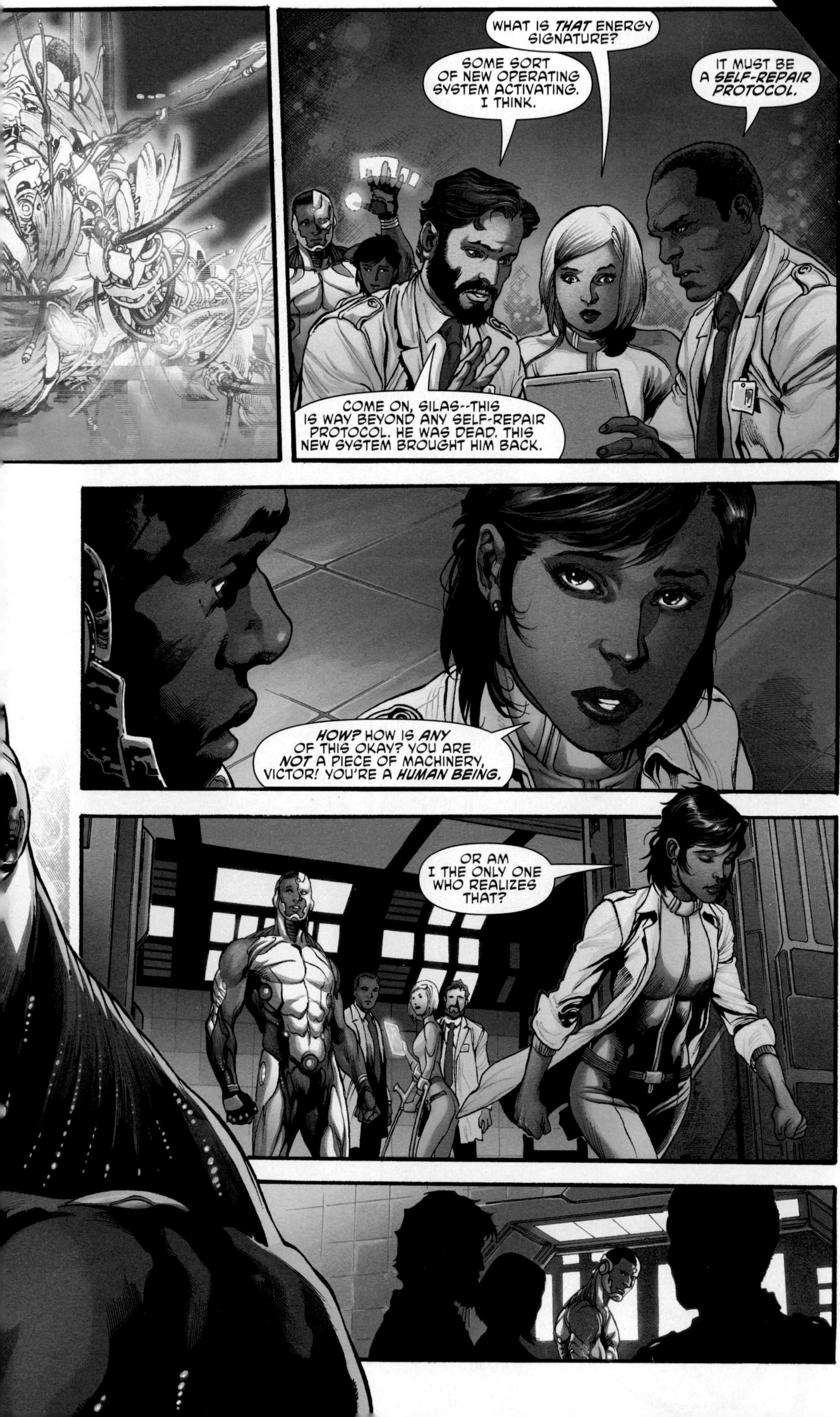
WHAT IS *THAT* ENERGY SIGNATURE?
SOME SORT OF NEW OPERATING SYSTEM ACTIVATING. I THINK.
IT MUST BE A *SELF-REPAIR PROTOCOL.*
COME ON, SILAS--THIS IS WAY BEYOND ANY SELF-REPAIR PROTOCOL. HE WAS DEAD. THIS NEW SYSTEM BROUGHT HIM BACK.
*HOW?* HOW IS *ANY* OF THIS OKAY? YOU ARE *NOT* A PIECE OF MACHINERY, VICTOR! YOU'RE A *HUMAN BEING.*
OR AM I THE ONLY ONE WHO REALIZES THAT?

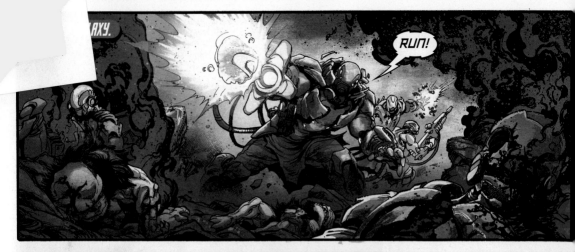

RUN!

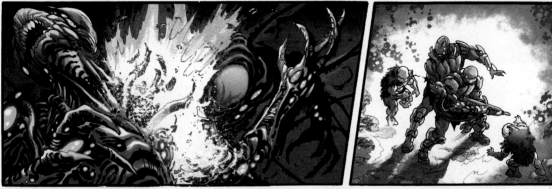

NO! LET ME GO!

THERE'S NO HELPING HIM!

SOMEONE HAS TO LIVE TO FIGHT ANOTHER DAY. THAT IS THE ONLY WAY WE WILL WIN THIS WAR.

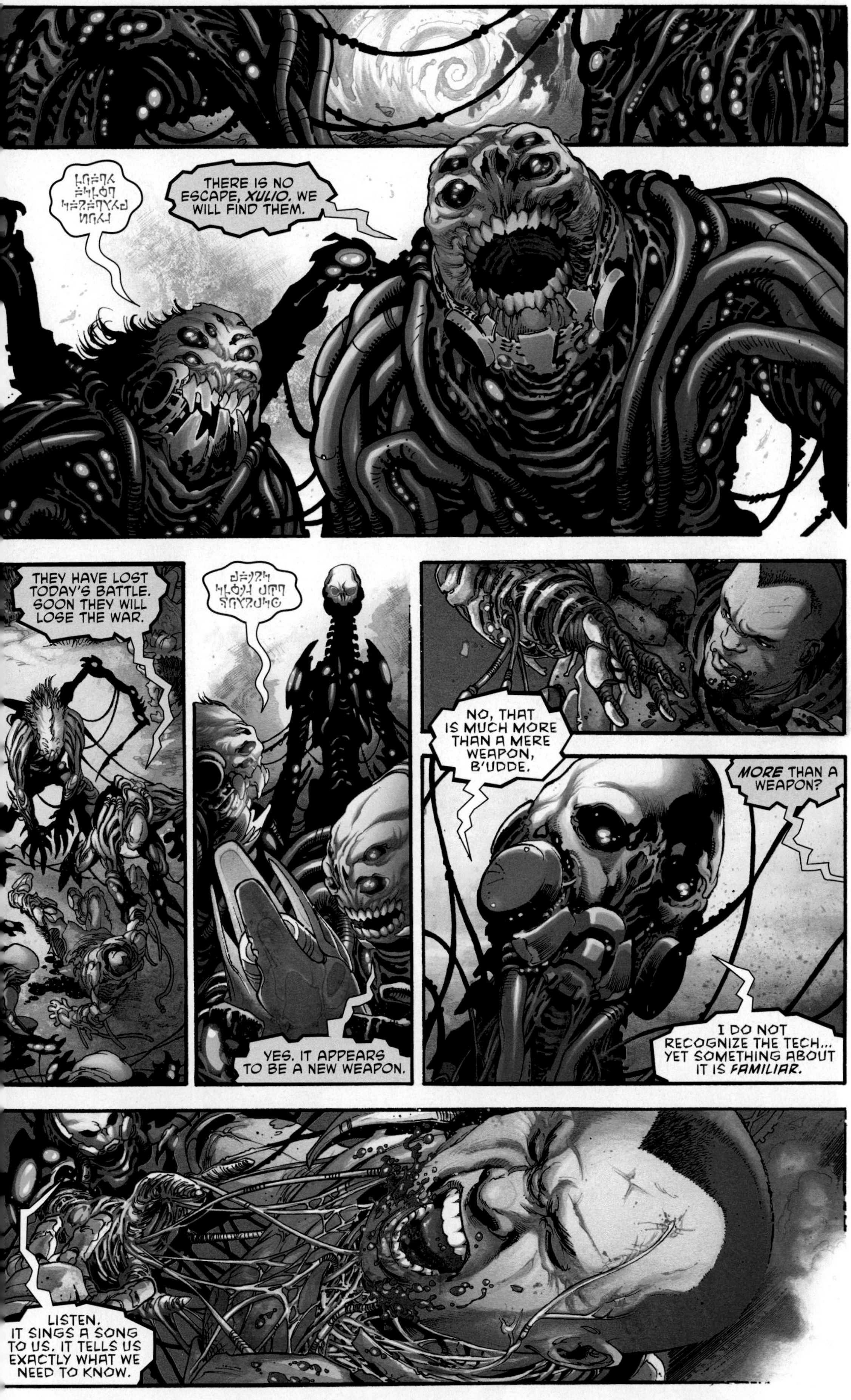
THERE IS NO ESCAPE, XULIO. WE WILL FIND THEM.
THEY HAVE LOST TODAY'S BATTLE. SOON THEY WILL LOSE THE WAR.
YES. IT APPEARS TO BE A NEW WEAPON.
NO, THAT IS MUCH MORE THAN A MERE WEAPON, B'UDDE.
MORE THAN A WEAPON?
I DO NOT RECOGNIZE THE TECH... YET SOMETHING ABOUT IT IS FAMILIAR.
LISTEN. IT SINGS A SONG TO US. IT TELLS US EXACTLY WHAT WE NEED TO KNOW.

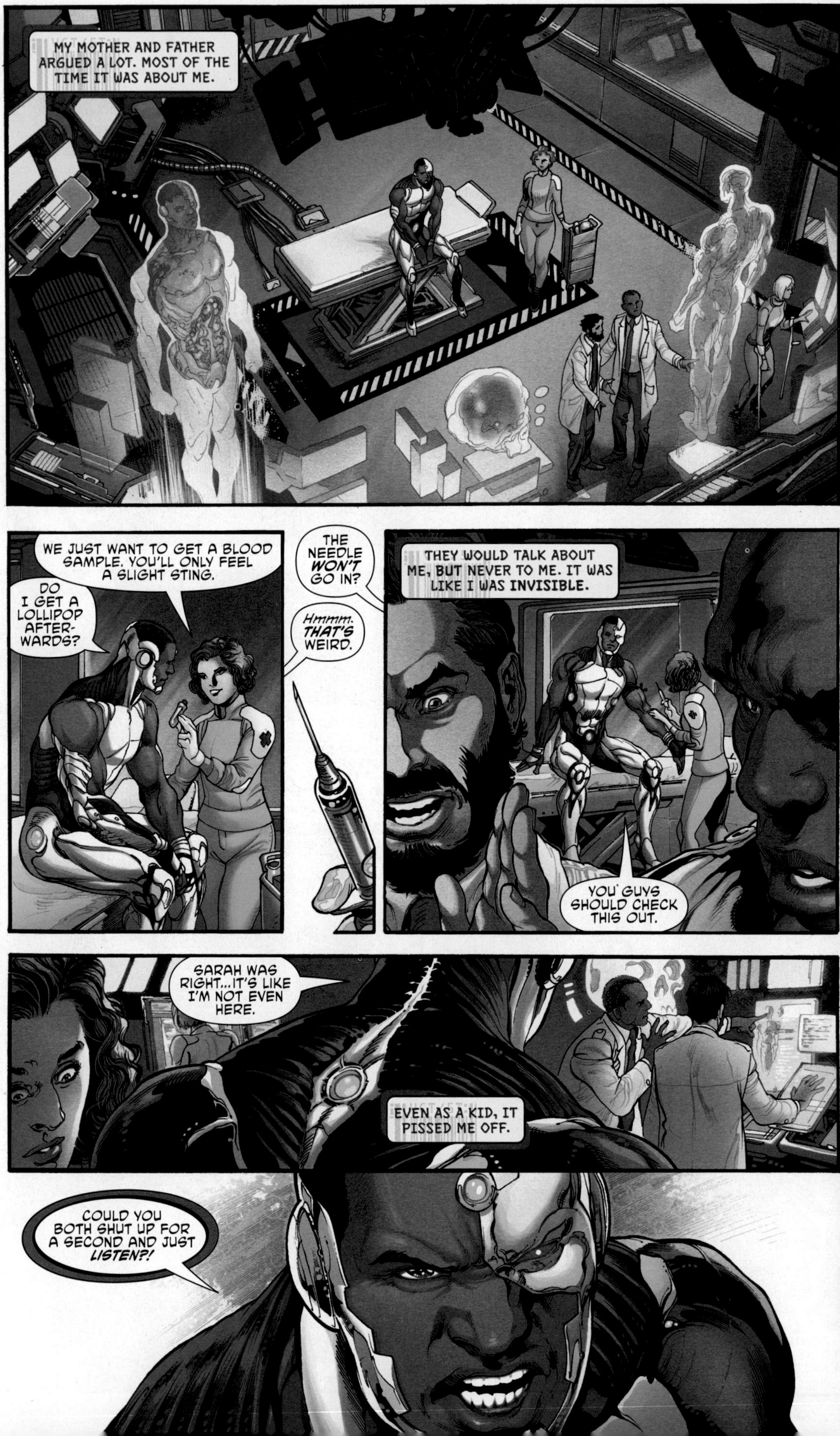
MY MOTHER AND FATHER ARGUED A LOT. MOST OF THE TIME IT WAS ABOUT ME.
WE JUST WANT TO GET A BLOOD SAMPLE. YOU'LL ONLY FEEL A SLIGHT STING.
DO I GET A LOLLIPOP AFTER-WARDS?
THE NEEDLE *WON'T* GO IN?
*Hmmm. THAT'S* WEIRD.
THEY WOULD TALK ABOUT ME, BUT NEVER TO ME. IT WAS LIKE I WAS INVISIBLE.
YOU GUYS SHOULD CHECK THIS OUT.
SARAH WAS RIGHT...IT'S LIKE I'M NOT EVEN HERE.
EVEN AS A KID, IT PISSED ME OFF.
COULD YOU BOTH SHUT UP FOR A SECOND AND JUST *LISTEN?!*

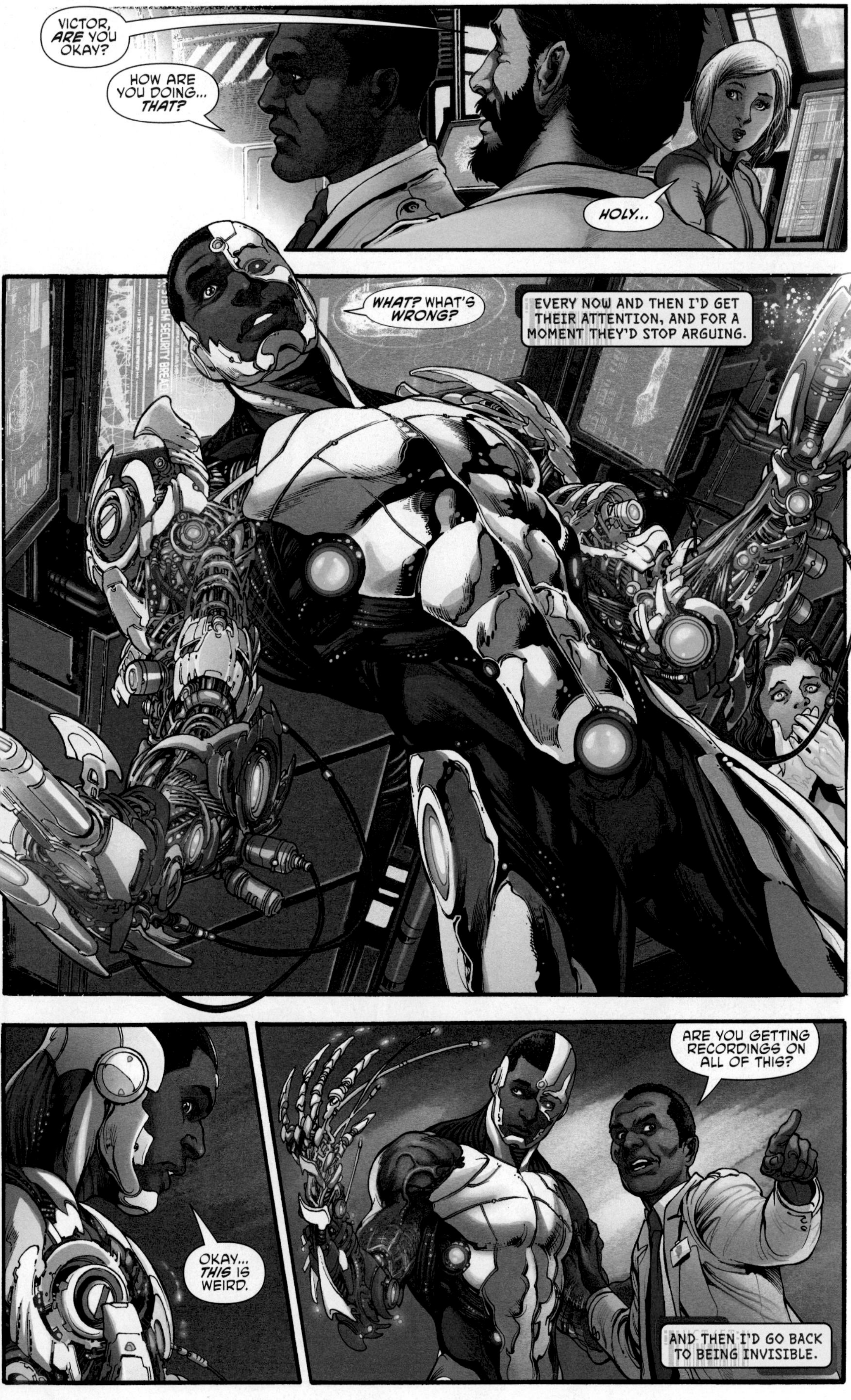
VICTOR, ARE YOU OKAY?
HOW ARE YOU DOING... THAT?
HOLY...
WHAT? WHAT'S WRONG?
EVERY NOW AND THEN I'D GET THEIR ATTENTION, AND FOR A MOMENT THEY'D STOP ARGUING.
OKAY... THIS IS WEIRD.
ARE YOU GETTING RECORDINGS ON ALL OF THIS?
AND THEN I'D GO BACK TO BEING INVISIBLE.

RUN A FULL SYSTEM ANALYSIS. CROSS-REFERENCE IT TO EVERYTHING WE HAVE ON RECORD.

ON IT.

BEING MORE MACHINE THAN MAN BRINGS A LOT OF UNWANTED ATTENTION.

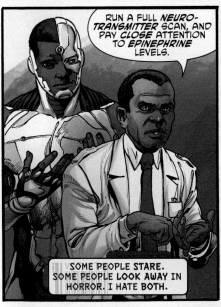

RUN A FULL *NEURO-TRANSMITTER* SCAN, AND PAY *CLOSE* ATTENTION TO *EPINEPHRINE* LEVELS.

SOME PEOPLE STARE. SOME PEOPLE LOOK AWAY IN HORROR. I HATE BOTH.

LOOK AT ALL THIS *ACTIVITY* IN THE LIMBIC SYSTEM OF THE BRAIN--*ESPECIALLY* THE AMYGDALA.

THAT'S *NOTHING.* LOOK AT THE ENERGY READINGS ON THE *NEURO-CYBER* CONDUCTORS.

IT SOUNDS WEIRD, BUT I'D RATHER HAVE THEM STARE, OR EVEN BE REPULSED, THAN TO HAVE THEM ACT LIKE I'M *NOT THERE.*

ARE YOU... OKAY?

*HONESTLY?* I DON'T KNOW.

IT'S BETTER TO BE THE MONSTER IN THE ROOM THAT EVERYONE FEARS OR PITIES THAN TO BE THE THING THEY **DON'T EVEN SEE.**

BUT THANKS FOR ASKING.

I HATE BEING INVISIBLE.

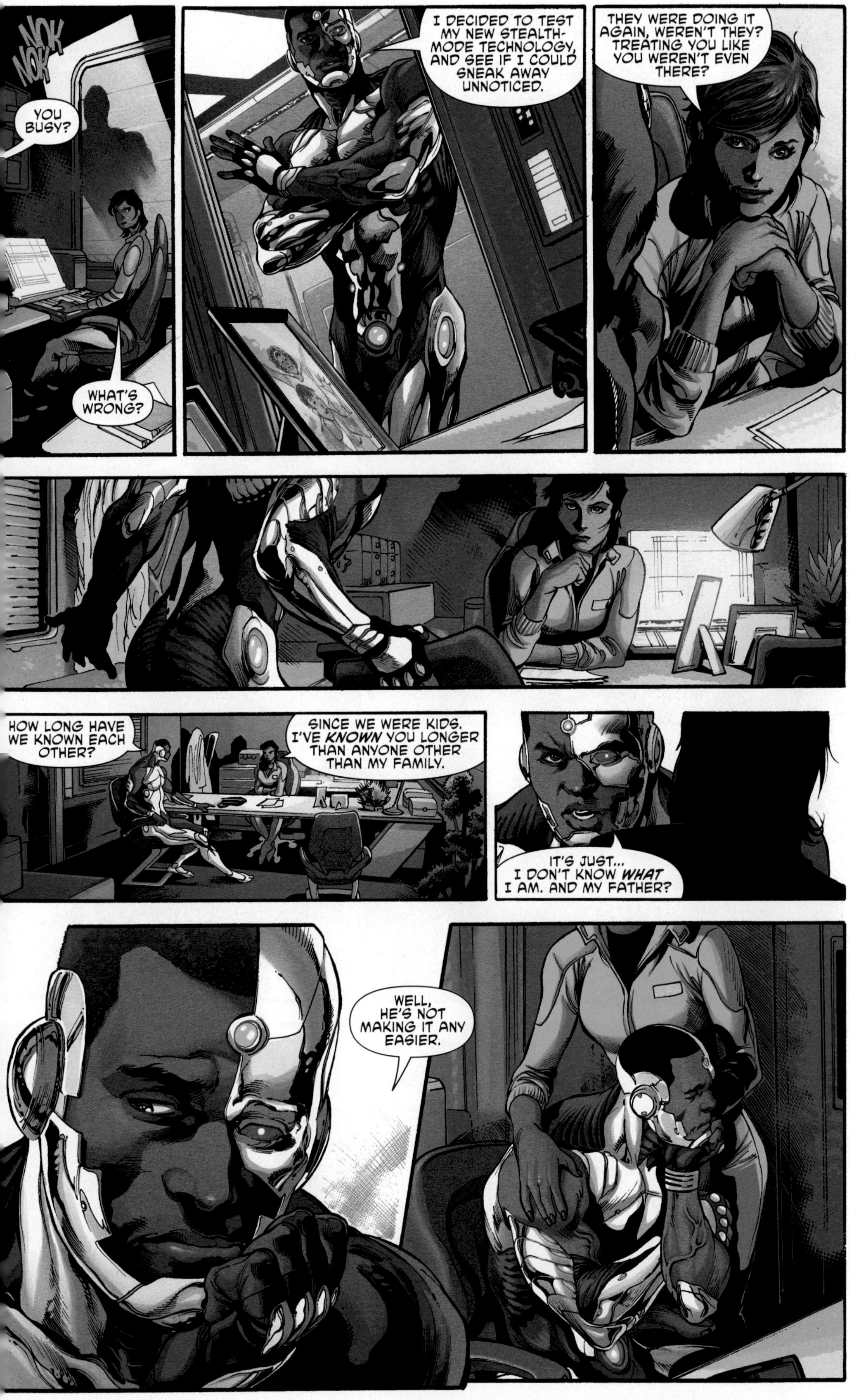
NOK NOK
YOU BUSY?
WHAT'S WRONG?
I DECIDED TO TEST MY NEW STEALTH-MODE TECHNOLOGY, AND SEE IF I COULD SNEAK AWAY UNNOTICED.
THEY WERE DOING IT AGAIN, WEREN'T THEY? TREATING YOU LIKE YOU WEREN'T EVEN THERE?
HOW LONG HAVE WE KNOWN EACH OTHER?
SINCE WE WERE KIDS. I'VE KNOWN YOU LONGER THAN ANYONE OTHER THAN MY FAMILY.
IT'S JUST... I DON'T KNOW WHAT I AM. AND MY FATHER?
WELL, HE'S NOT MAKING IT ANY EASIER.

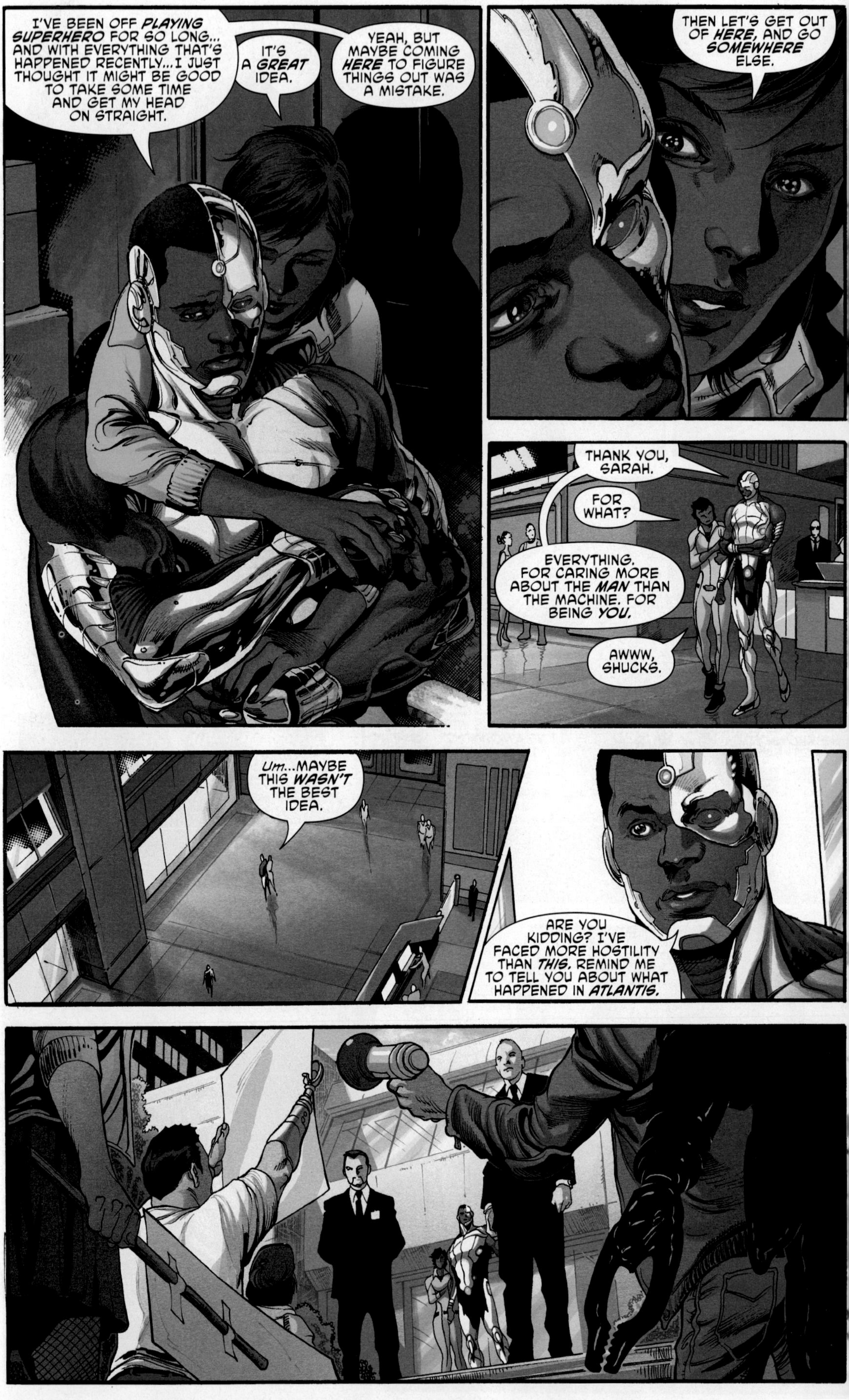
I'VE BEEN OFF PLAYING SUPERHERO FOR SO LONG... AND WITH EVERYTHING THAT'S HAPPENED RECENTLY...I JUST THOUGHT IT MIGHT BE GOOD TO TAKE SOME TIME AND GET MY HEAD ON STRAIGHT.
IT'S A GREAT IDEA.
YEAH, BUT MAYBE COMING HERE TO FIGURE THINGS OUT WAS A MISTAKE.
THEN LET'S GET OUT OF HERE, AND GO SOMEWHERE ELSE.
THANK YOU, SARAH.
FOR WHAT?
EVERYTHING. FOR CARING MORE ABOUT THE MAN THAN THE MACHINE. FOR BEING YOU.
AWWW, SHUCKS.
Um...MAYBE THIS WASN'T THE BEST IDEA.
ARE YOU KIDDING? I'VE FACED MORE HOSTILITY THAN THIS. REMIND ME TO TELL YOU ABOUT WHAT HAPPENED IN ATLANTIS.

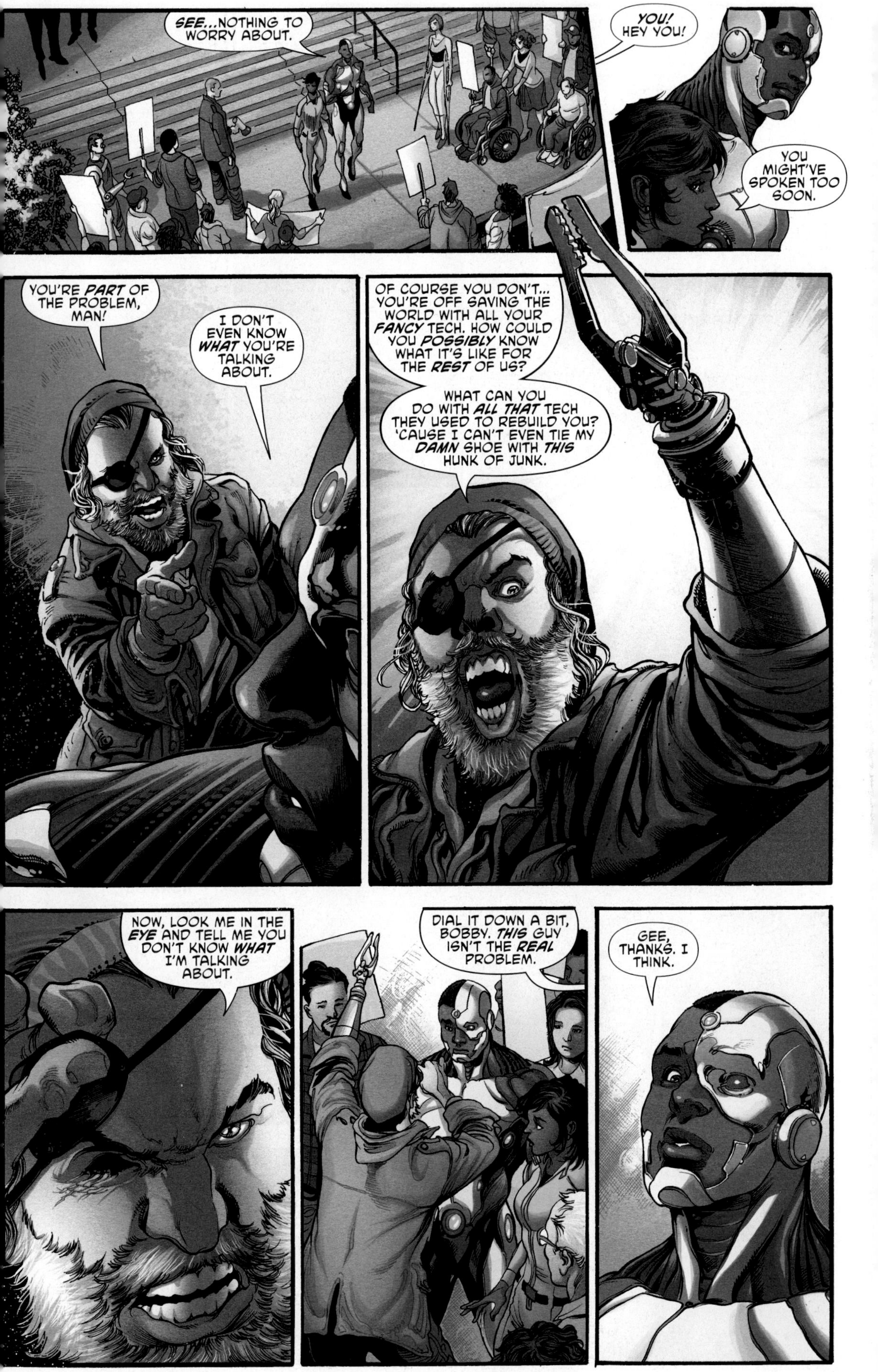
SEE... NOTHING TO WORRY ABOUT.
YOU! HEY YOU!
YOU MIGHT'VE SPOKEN TOO SOON.
YOU'RE PART OF THE PROBLEM, MAN!
I DON'T EVEN KNOW WHAT YOU'RE TALKING ABOUT.
OF COURSE YOU DON'T... YOU'RE OFF SAVING THE WORLD WITH ALL YOUR FANCY TECH. HOW COULD YOU POSSIBLY KNOW WHAT IT'S LIKE FOR THE REST OF US?
WHAT CAN YOU DO WITH ALL THAT TECH THEY USED TO REBUILD YOU? 'CAUSE I CAN'T EVEN TIE MY DAMN SHOE WITH THIS HUNK OF JUNK.
NOW, LOOK ME IN THE EYE AND TELL ME YOU DON'T KNOW WHAT I'M TALKING ABOUT.
DIAL IT DOWN A BIT, BOBBY. THIS GUY ISN'T THE REAL PROBLEM.
GEE, THANKS. I THINK.

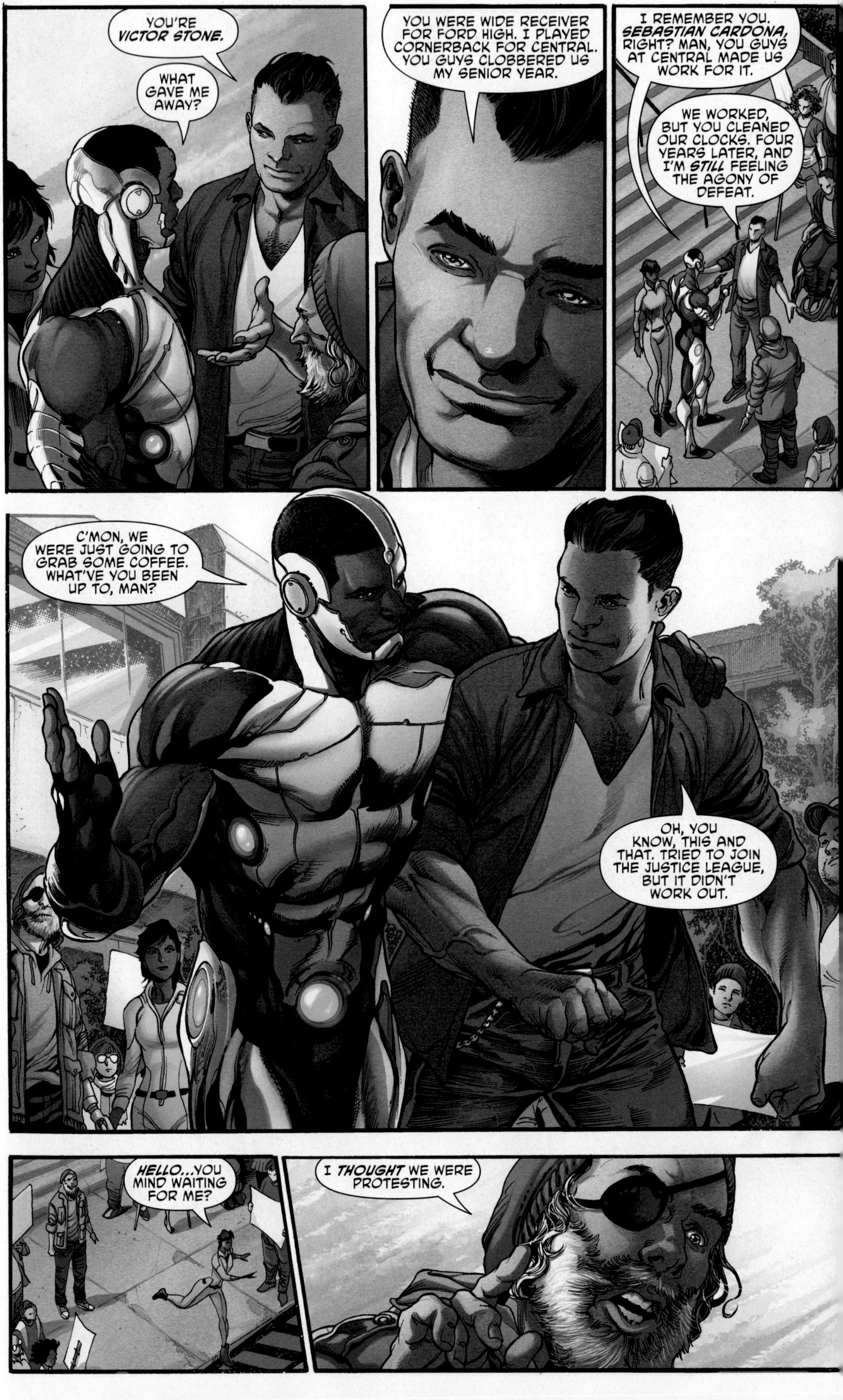
YOU'RE *VICTOR STONE.*
WHAT GAVE ME AWAY?
YOU WERE WIDE RECEIVER FOR FORD HIGH. I PLAYED CORNERBACK FOR CENTRAL. YOU GUYS CLOBBERED US MY SENIOR YEAR.
I REMEMBER YOU. *SEBASTIAN CARDONA,* RIGHT? MAN, YOU GUYS AT CENTRAL MADE US WORK FOR IT.
WE WORKED, BUT YOU CLEANED OUR CLOCKS. FOUR YEARS LATER, AND I'M *STILL* FEELING THE AGONY OF DEFEAT.
C'MON, WE WERE JUST GOING TO GRAB SOME COFFEE. WHAT'VE YOU BEEN UP TO, MAN?
OH, YOU KNOW, THIS AND THAT. TRIED TO JOIN THE JUSTICE LEAGUE, BUT IT DIDN'T WORK OUT.
*HELLO*...YOU MIND WAITING FOR ME?
I *THOUGHT* WE WERE PROTESTING.

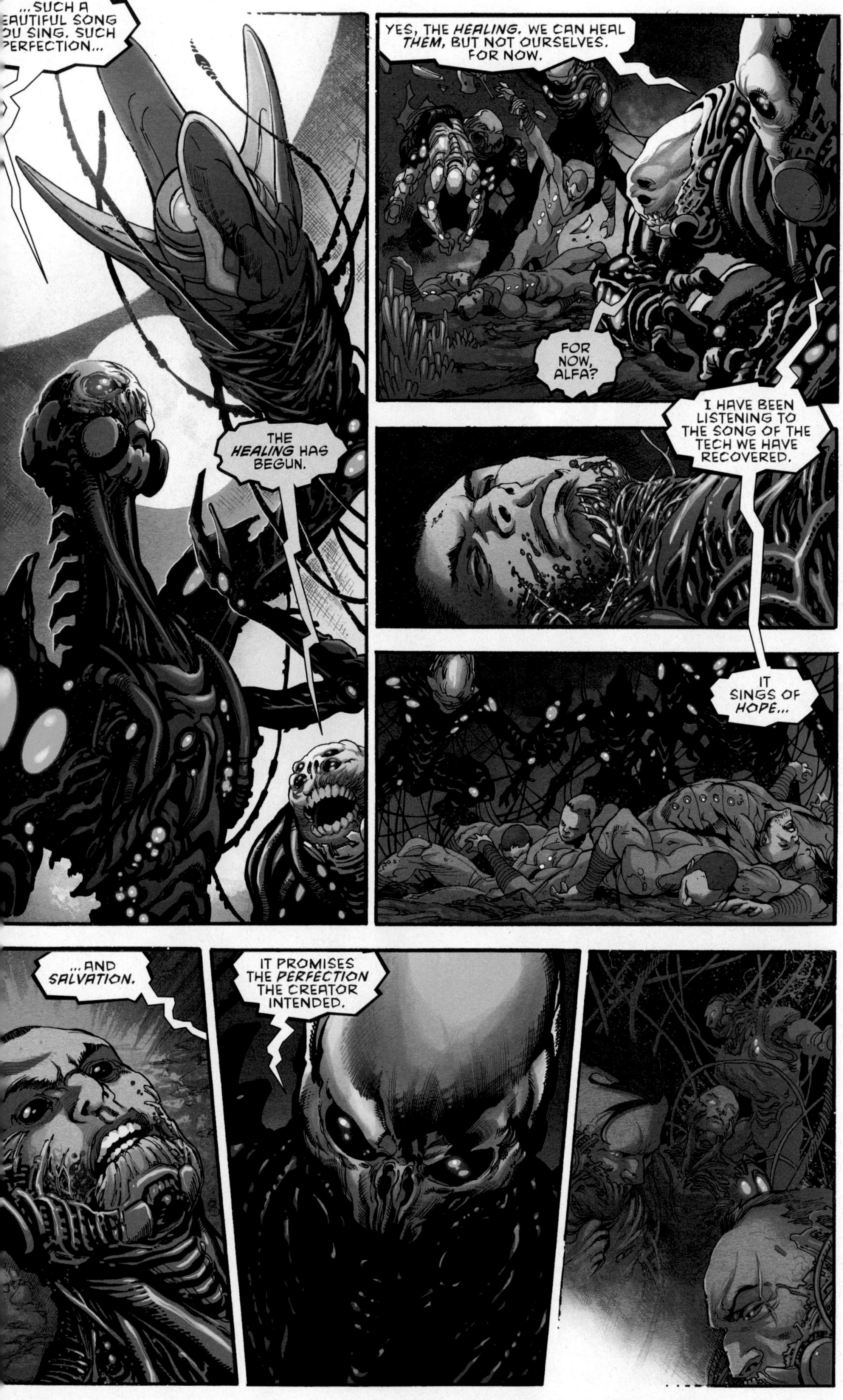
...SUCH A
EAUTIFUL SONG
OU SING. SUCH
PERFECTION...
THE HEALING HAS BEGUN.
YES, THE HEALING. WE CAN HEAL THEM, BUT NOT OURSELVES. FOR NOW.
FOR NOW, ALFA?
I HAVE BEEN LISTENING TO THE SONG OF THE TECH WE HAVE RECOVERED.
IT SINGS OF HOPE...
...AND SALVATION.
IT PROMISES THE PERFECTION THE CREATOR INTENDED.

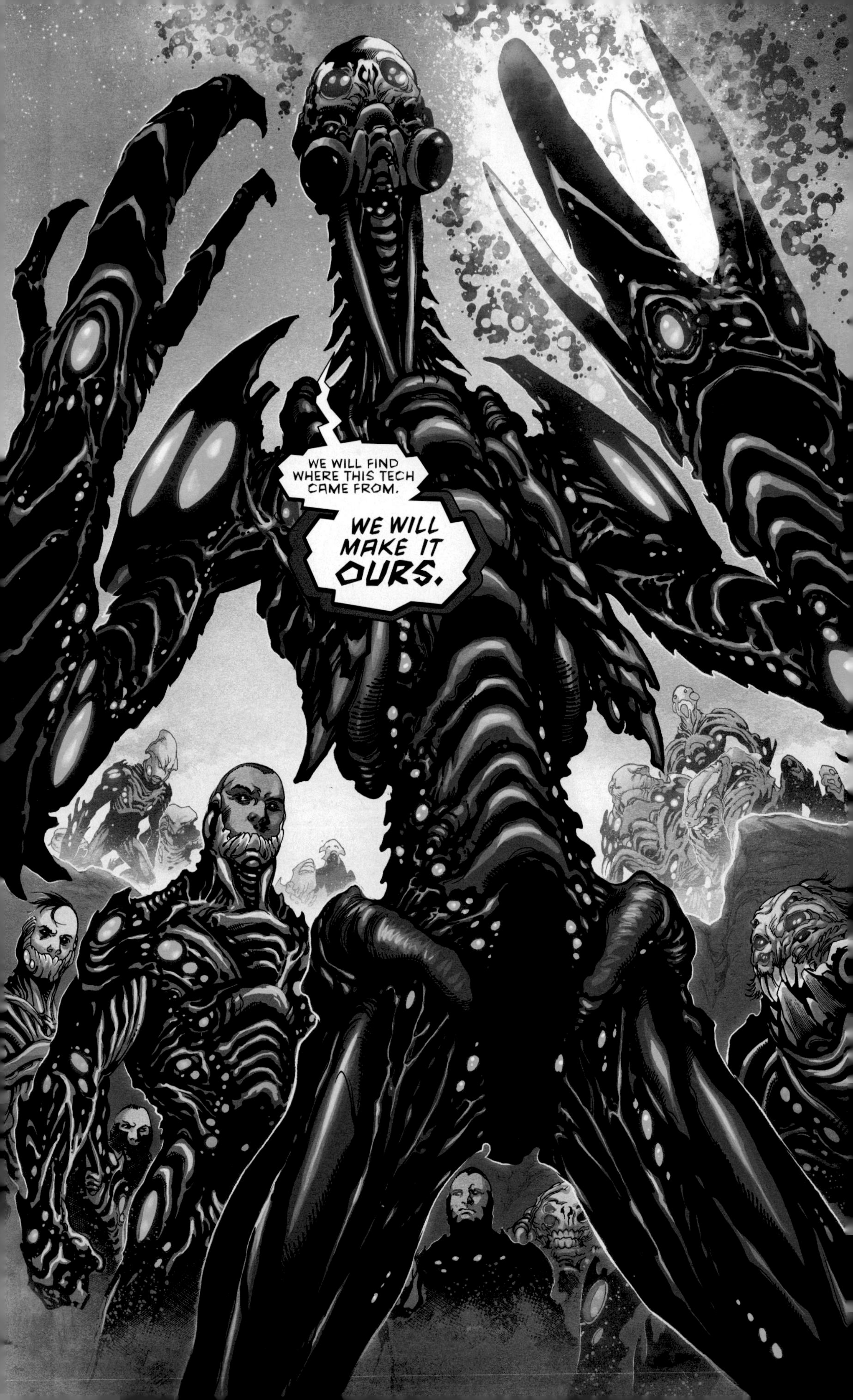
WE WILL FIND WHERE THIS TECH CAME FROM.
WE WILL MAKE IT OURS.

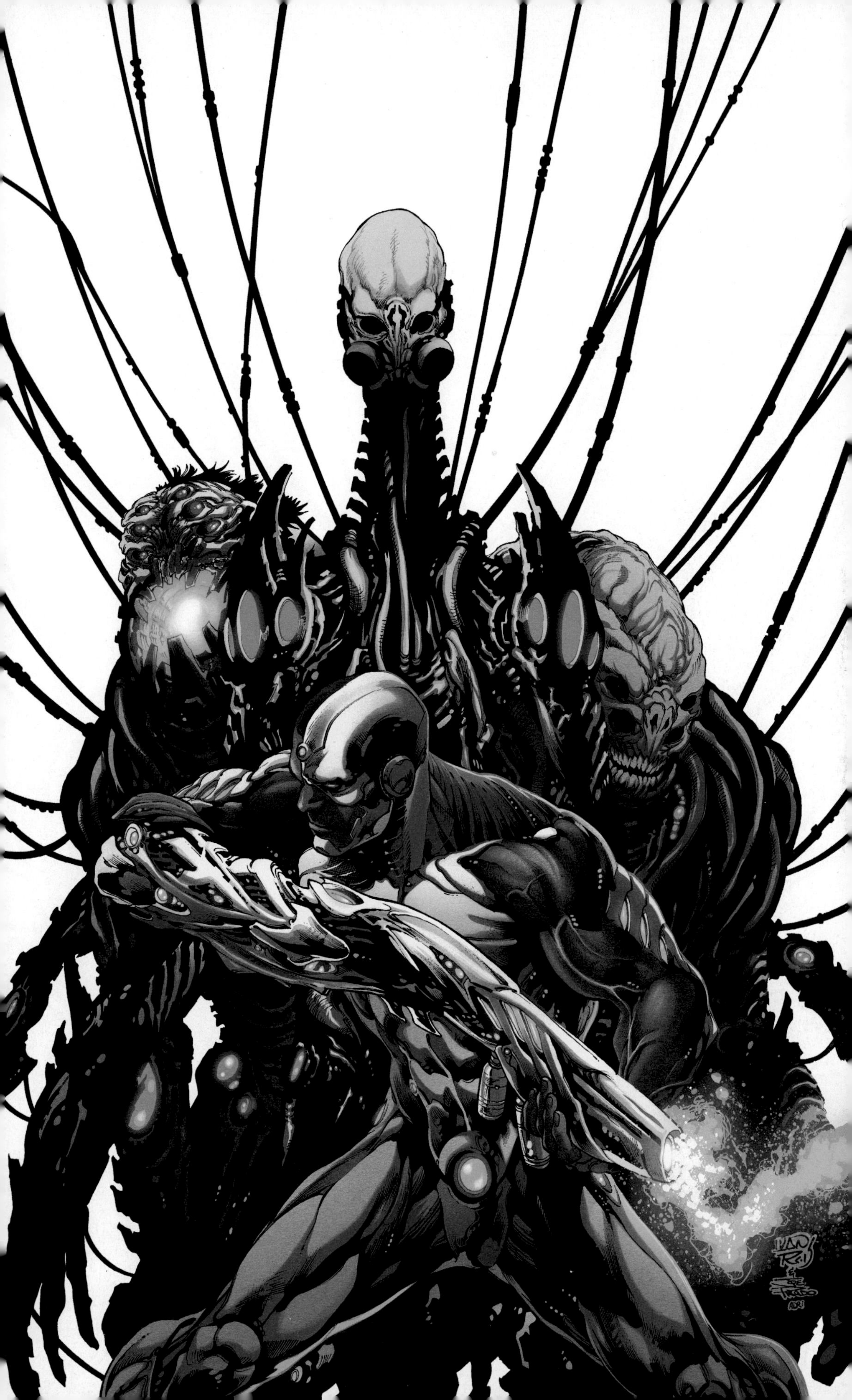

**TARGET: VICTOR STONE**

**IVAN REIS** penciller **JOE PRADO, RAY McCARTHY** and **SCOTT HANNA** inkers **ADRIANO LUCAS** colorist **ROB LEIGH** letterer
**IVAN REIS, JOE PRADO** and **ADRIANO LUCAS** cover art

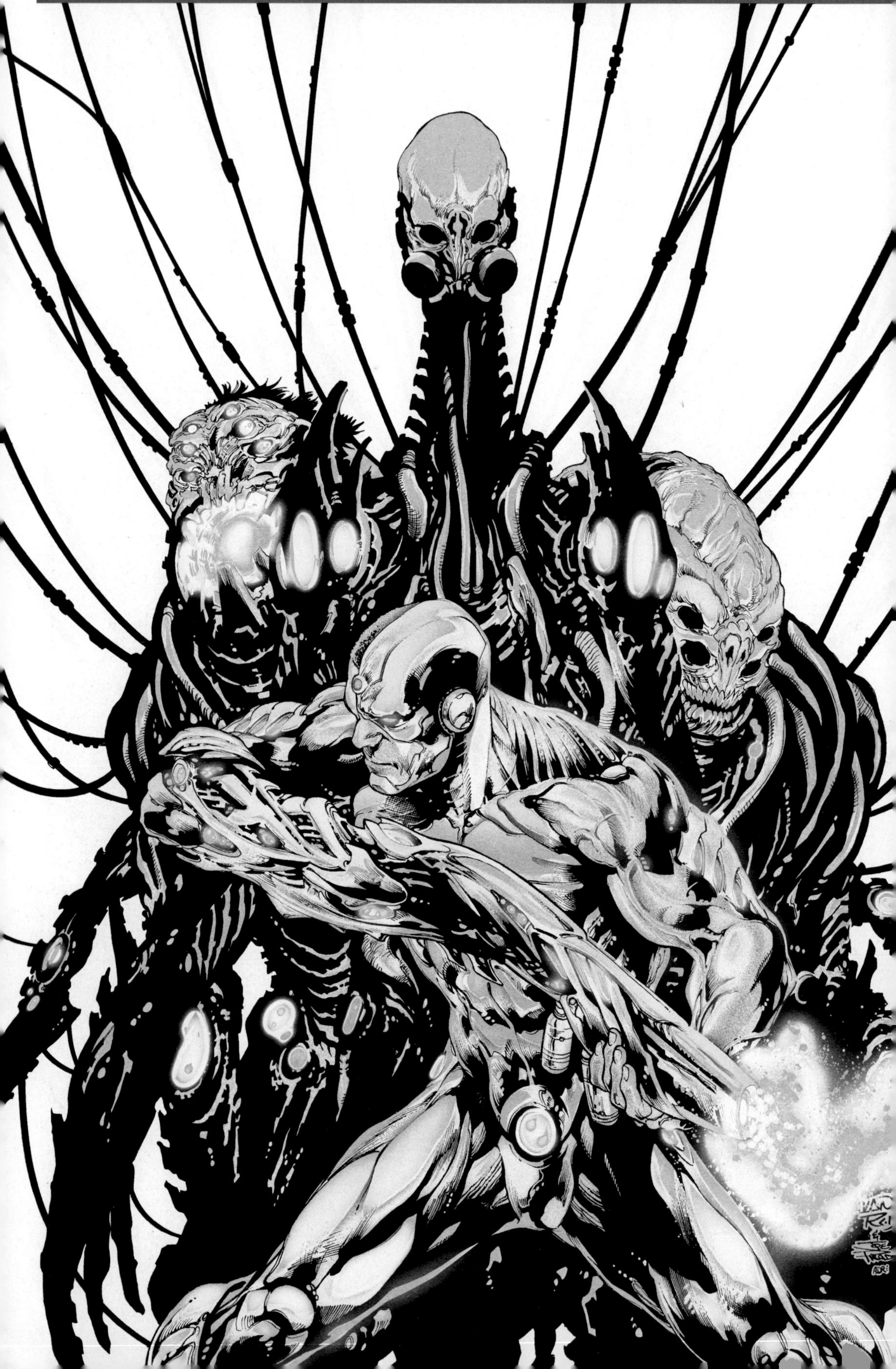

WHERE ARE THE OTHERS?

IT'S JUST US.

WHAT?

"THEY FOUND US. IT WAS A MASSACRE."

GET HIM TO THE INFIRMARY.

I TRIED TO WARN YOU. YOU WOULDN'T LISTEN.

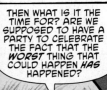

NOW ISN'T THE TIME FOR I-TOLD-YOU-SO.

THEN WHAT IS IT THE TIME FOR? ARE WE SUPPOSED TO HAVE A PARTY TO CELEBRATE THE FACT THAT THE WORST THING THAT COULD HAPPEN HAS HAPPENED?

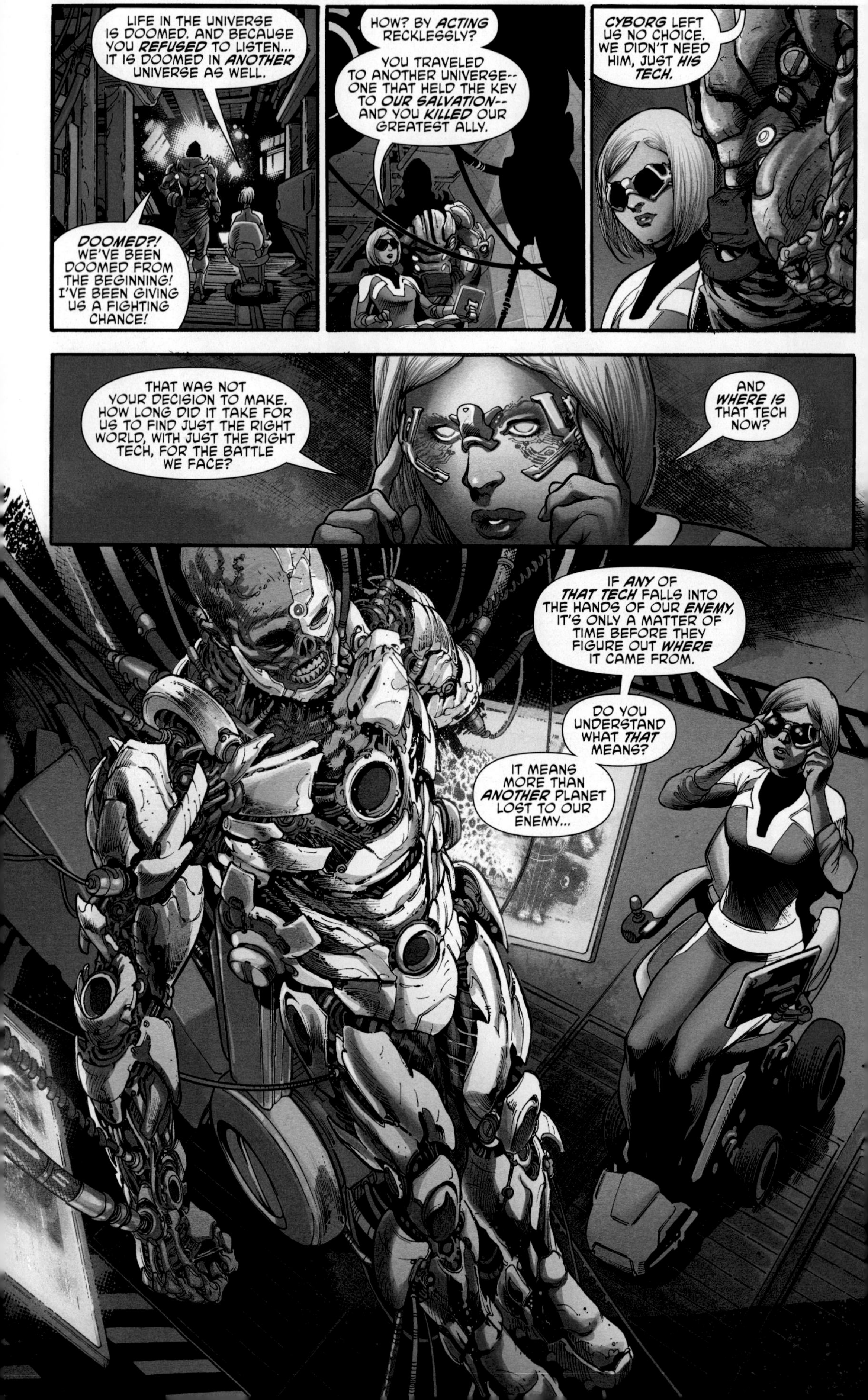

LIFE IN THE UNIVERSE IS DOOMED. AND BECAUSE YOU *REFUSED* TO LISTEN... IT IS DOOMED IN *ANOTHER* UNIVERSE AS WELL.
*DOOMED?!* WE'VE BEEN DOOMED FROM THE BEGINNING! I'VE BEEN GIVING US A FIGHTING CHANCE!
HOW? BY *ACTING* RECKLESSLY?
YOU TRAVELED TO ANOTHER UNIVERSE--ONE THAT HELD THE KEY TO *OUR SALVATION*--AND YOU *KILLED* OUR GREATEST ALLY.
*CYBORG* LEFT US NO CHOICE. WE DIDN'T NEED HIM, JUST *HIS TECH.*
THAT WAS NOT YOUR DECISION TO MAKE. HOW LONG DID IT TAKE FOR US TO FIND JUST THE RIGHT WORLD, WITH JUST THE RIGHT TECH, FOR THE BATTLE WE FACE?
AND *WHERE IS* THAT TECH NOW?
IF *ANY* OF *THAT TECH* FALLS INTO THE HANDS OF OUR *ENEMY*, IT'S ONLY A MATTER OF TIME BEFORE THEY FIGURE OUT *WHERE* IT CAME FROM.
DO YOU UNDERSTAND WHAT *THAT* MEANS?
IT MEANS MORE THAN *ANOTHER* PLANET LOST TO OUR ENEMY...

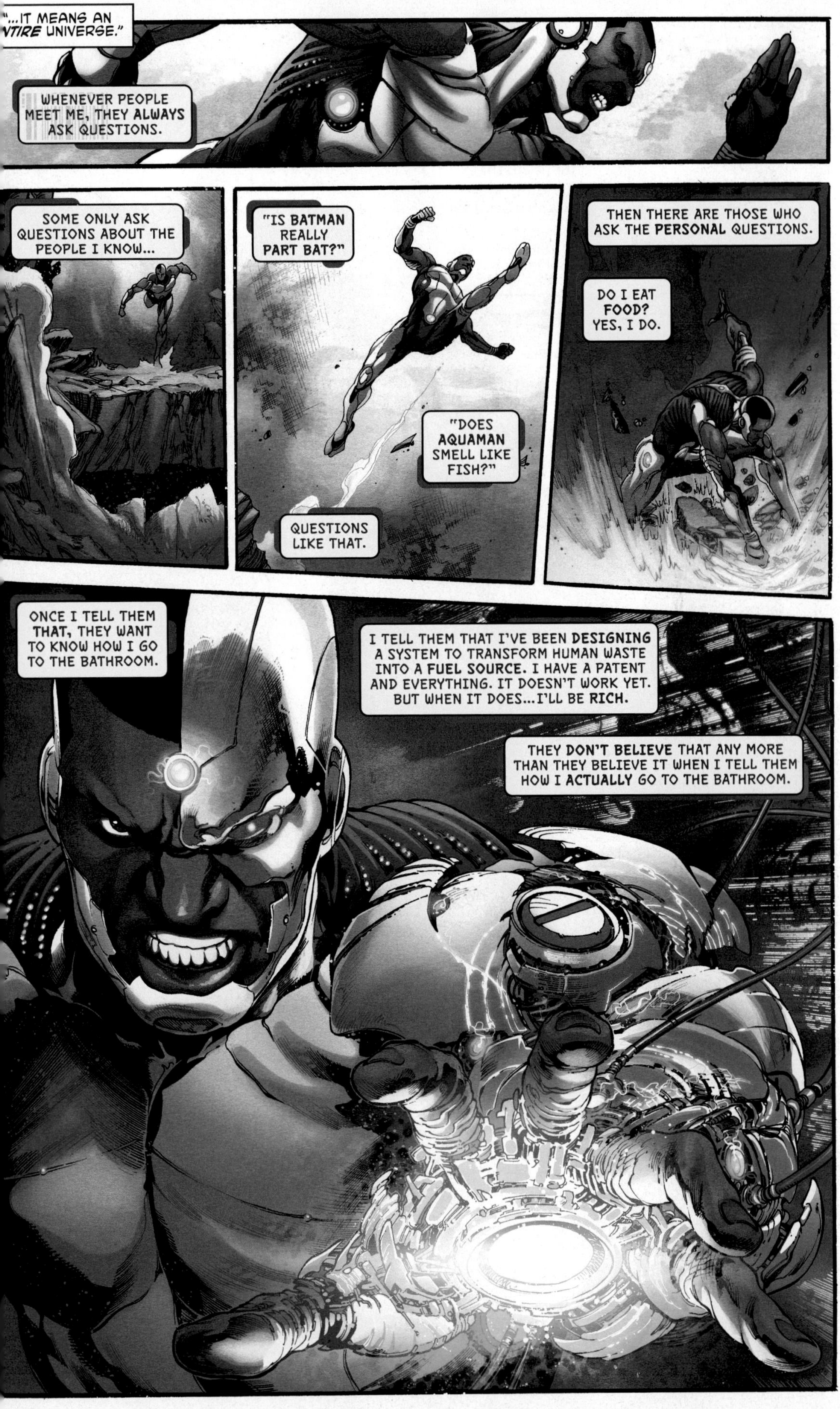
"...IT MEANS AN
NTIRE UNIVERSE."
WHENEVER PEOPLE MEET ME, THEY ALWAYS ASK QUESTIONS.
SOME ONLY ASK QUESTIONS ABOUT THE PEOPLE I KNOW...
"IS BATMAN REALLY PART BAT?"
"DOES AQUAMAN SMELL LIKE FISH?"
QUESTIONS LIKE THAT.
THEN THERE ARE THOSE WHO ASK THE PERSONAL QUESTIONS.
DO I EAT FOOD? YES, I DO.
ONCE I TELL THEM THAT, THEY WANT TO KNOW HOW I GO TO THE BATHROOM.
I TELL THEM THAT I'VE BEEN DESIGNING A SYSTEM TO TRANSFORM HUMAN WASTE INTO A FUEL SOURCE. I HAVE A PATENT AND EVERYTHING. IT DOESN'T WORK YET. BUT WHEN IT DOES...I'LL BE RICH.
THEY DON'T BELIEVE THAT ANY MORE THAN THEY BELIEVE IT WHEN I TELL THEM HOW I ACTUALLY GO TO THE BATHROOM.

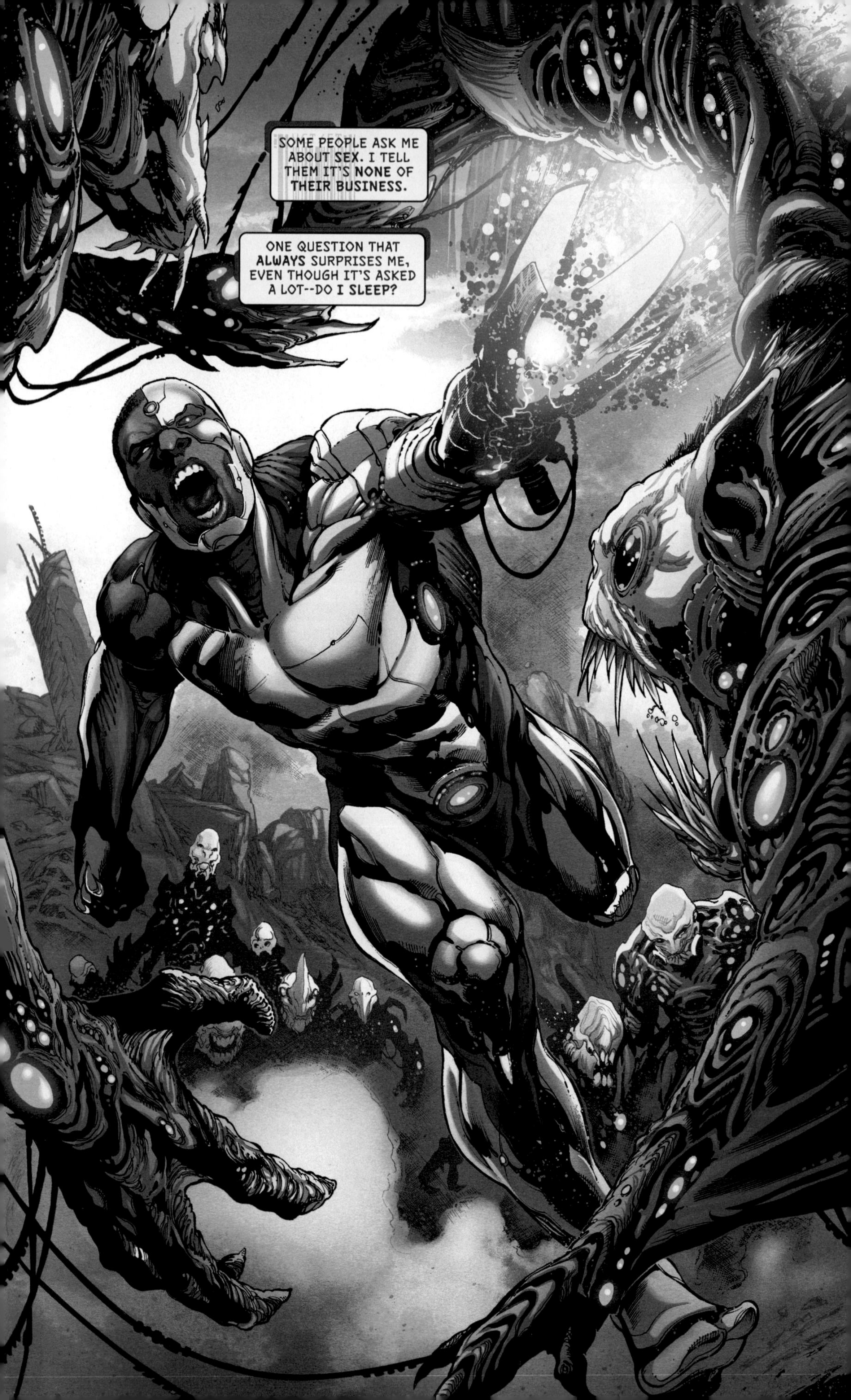
SOME PEOPLE ASK ME ABOUT SEX. I TELL THEM IT'S NONE OF THEIR BUSINESS.
ONE QUESTION THAT ALWAYS SURPRISES ME, EVEN THOUGH IT'S ASKED A LOT--DO I SLEEP?

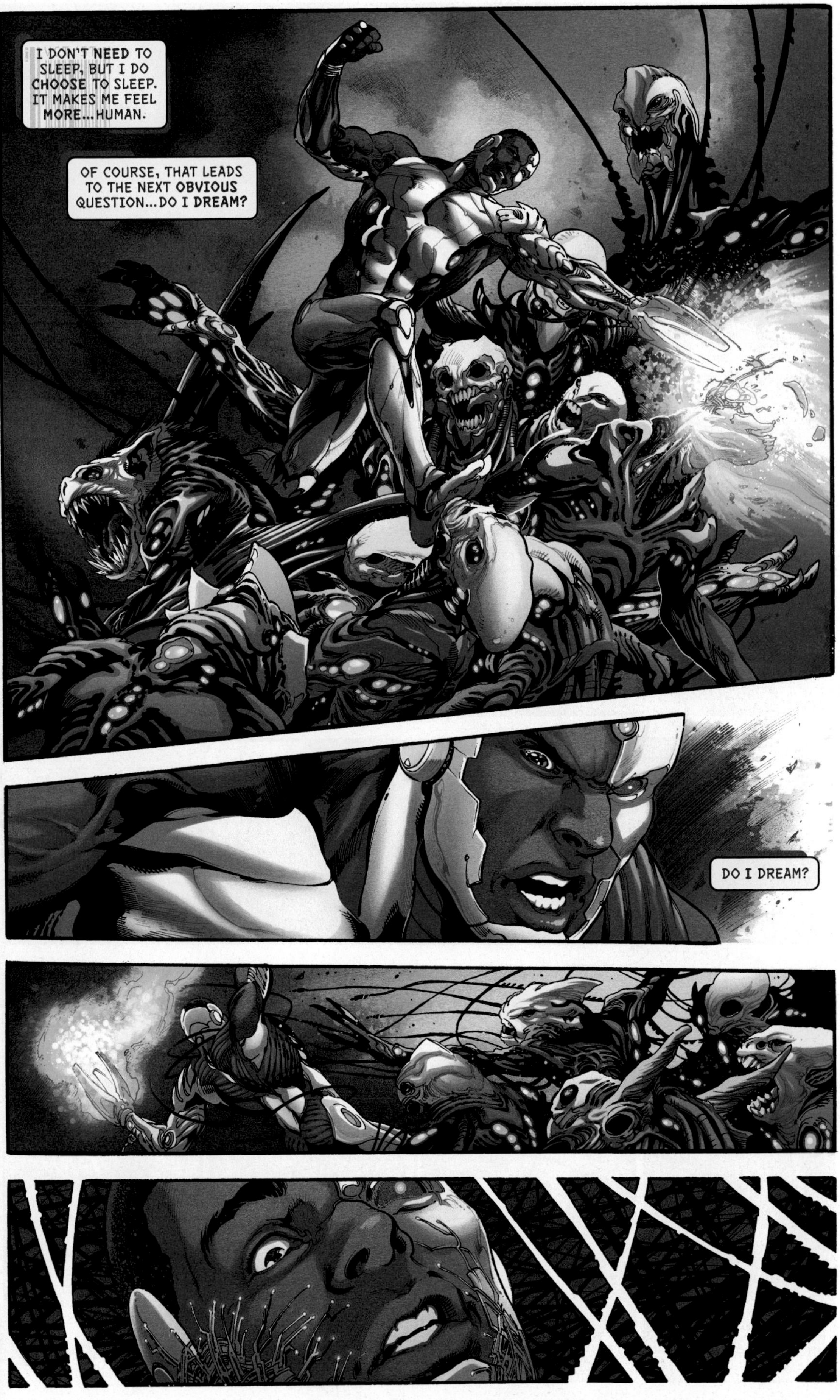
I DON'T NEED TO SLEEP, BUT I DO CHOOSE TO SLEEP. IT MAKES ME FEEL MORE...HUMAN.
OF COURSE, THAT LEADS TO THE NEXT OBVIOUS QUESTION...DO I DREAM?
DO I DREAM?

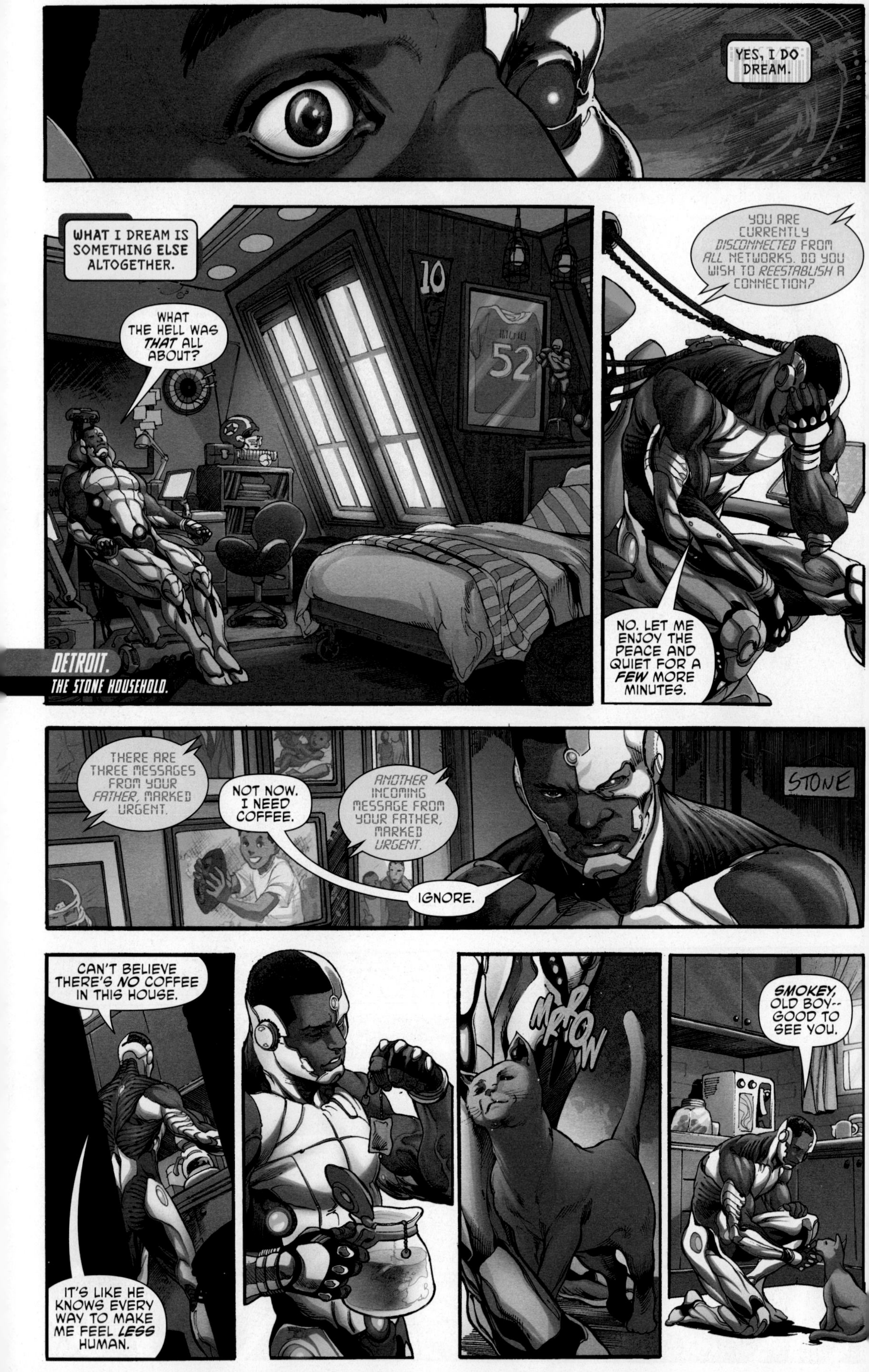
YES, I DO DREAM.
WHAT I DREAM IS SOMETHING ELSE ALTOGETHER.
WHAT THE HELL WAS THAT ALL ABOUT?
DETROIT. THE STONE HOUSEHOLD.
YOU ARE CURRENTLY DISCONNECTED FROM ALL NETWORKS. DO YOU WISH TO REESTABLISH A CONNECTION?
NO. LET ME ENJOY THE PEACE AND QUIET FOR A FEW MORE MINUTES.
THERE ARE THREE MESSAGES FROM YOUR FATHER, MARKED URGENT.
NOT NOW. I NEED COFFEE.
ANOTHER INCOMING MESSAGE FROM YOUR FATHER, MARKED URGENT.
IGNORE.
STONE
CAN'T BELIEVE THERE'S NO COFFEE IN THIS HOUSE.
IT'S LIKE HE KNOWS EVERY WAY TO MAKE ME FEEL LESS HUMAN.
MRROW
SMOKEY, OLD BOY-- GOOD TO SEE YOU.

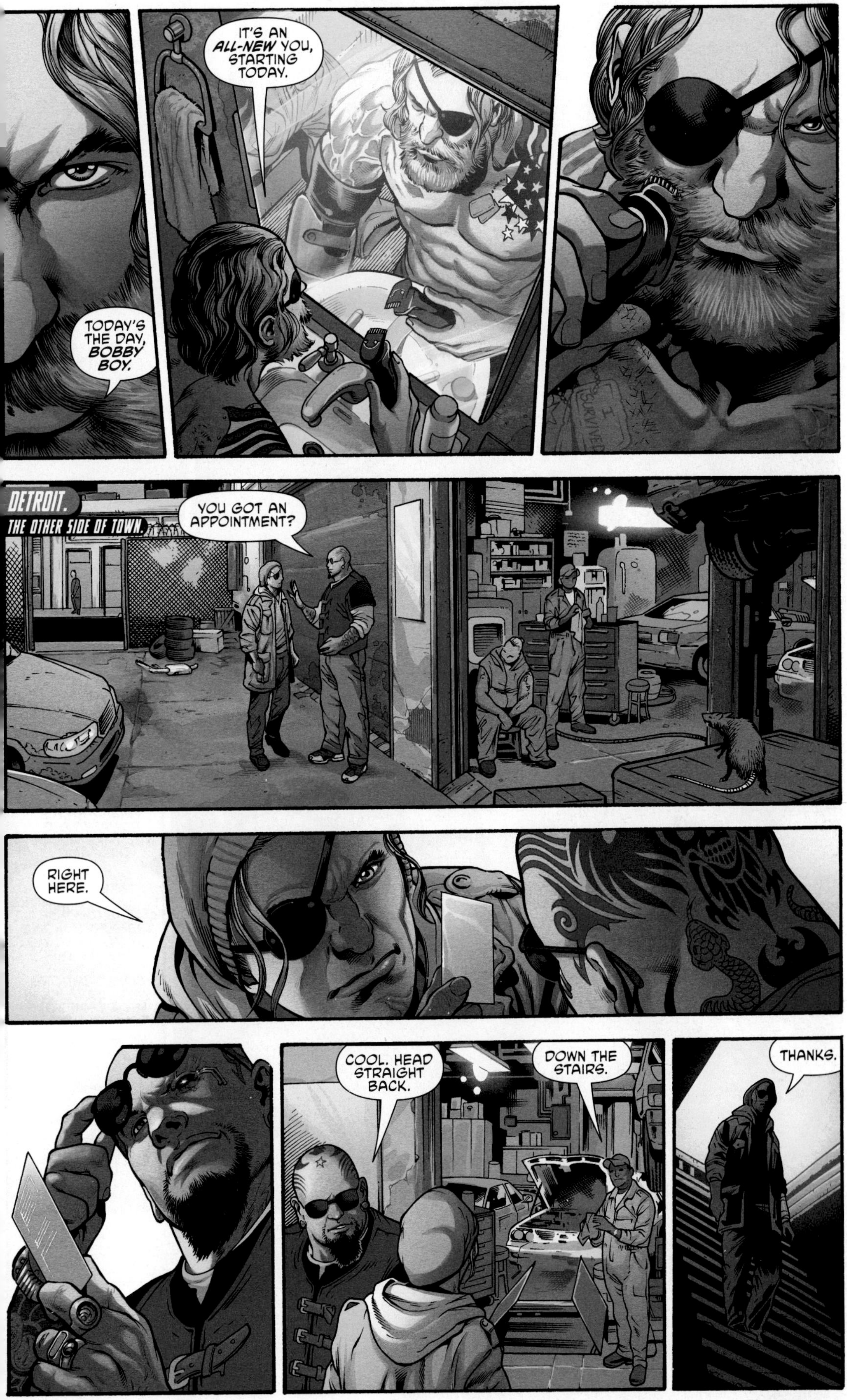

TODAY'S THE DAY, BOBBY BOY.
IT'S AN ALL-NEW YOU, STARTING TODAY.
I SURVIVED
DETROIT.
THE OTHER SIDE OF TOWN.
YOU GOT AN APPOINTMENT?
RIGHT HERE.
COOL. HEAD STRAIGHT BACK.
DOWN THE STAIRS.
THANKS.

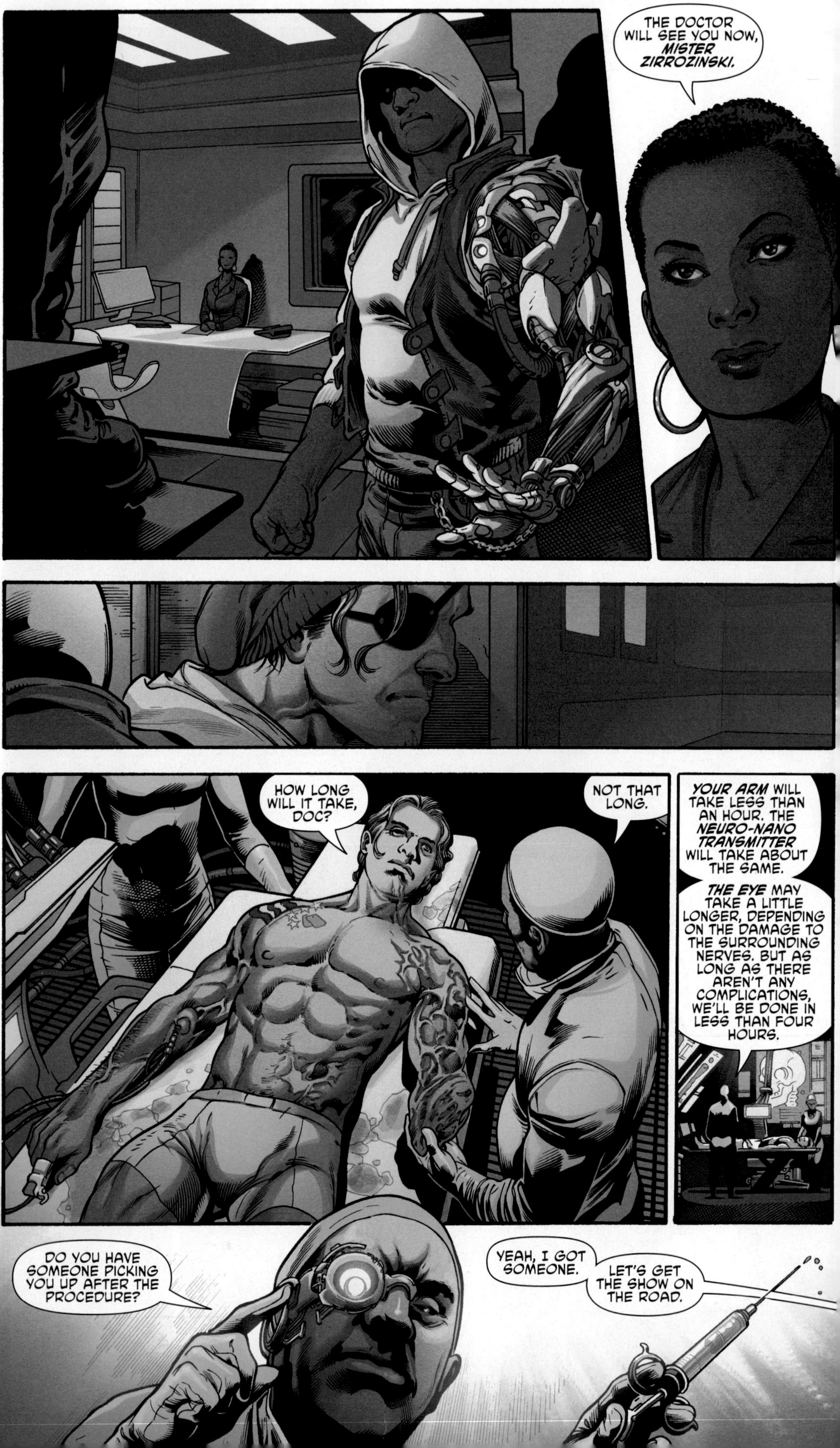
THE DOCTOR WILL SEE YOU NOW, *MISTER ZIRROZINSKI.*
HOW LONG WILL IT TAKE, DOC?
NOT THAT LONG.
*YOUR ARM* WILL TAKE LESS THAN AN HOUR. THE *NEURO-NANO TRANSMITTER* WILL TAKE ABOUT THE SAME.
*THE EYE* MAY TAKE A LITTLE LONGER, DEPENDING ON THE DAMAGE TO THE SURROUNDING NERVES. BUT AS LONG AS THERE AREN'T ANY COMPLICATIONS, WE'LL BE DONE IN LESS THAN FOUR HOURS.
DO YOU HAVE SOMEONE PICKING YOU UP AFTER THE PROCEDURE?
YEAH, I GOT SOMEONE.
LET'S GET THE SHOW ON THE ROAD.

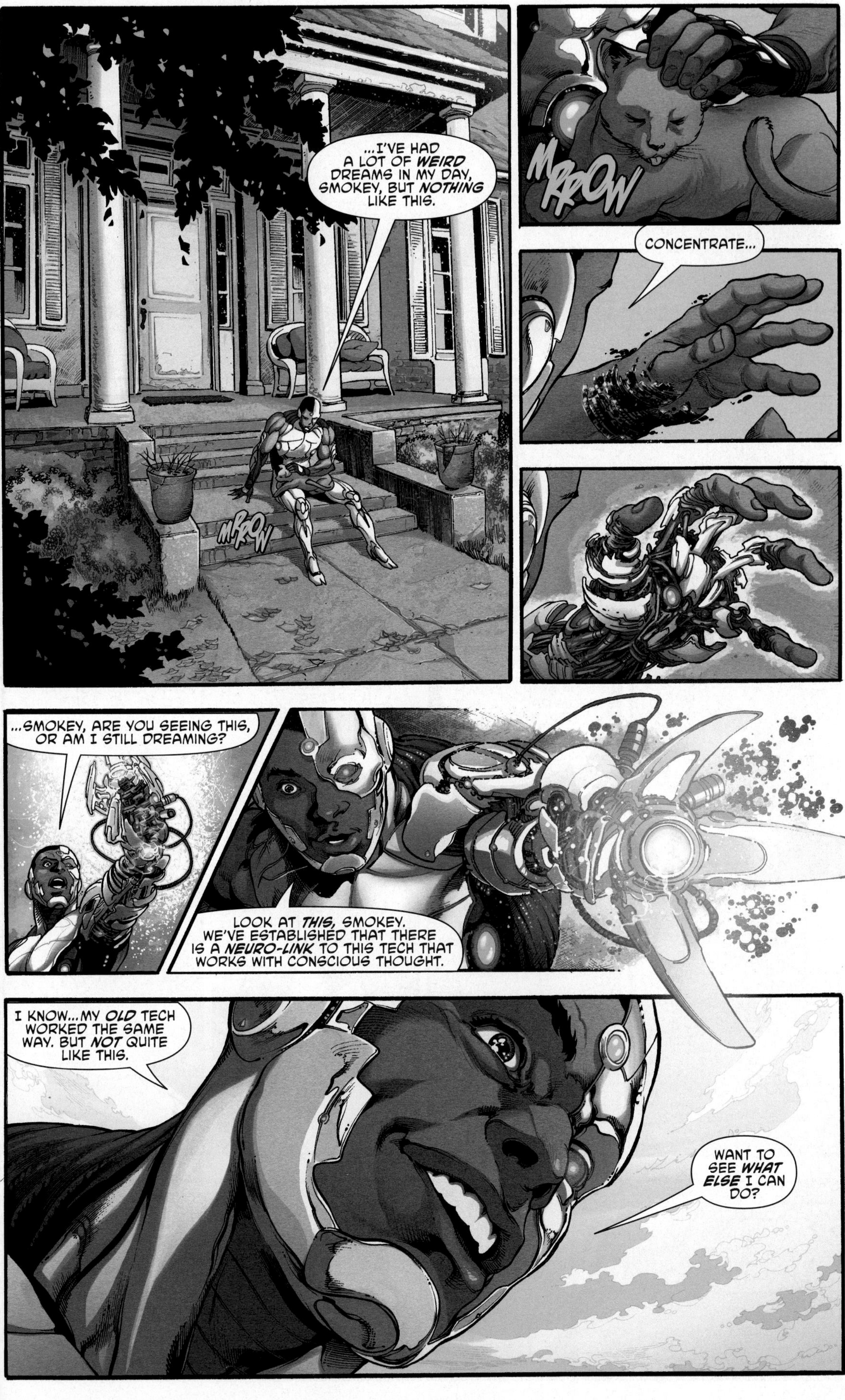
...I'VE HAD A LOT OF WEIRD DREAMS IN MY DAY, SMOKEY, BUT NOTHING LIKE THIS.
MRROW
MRROW
CONCENTRATE...
...SMOKEY, ARE YOU SEEING THIS, OR AM I STILL DREAMING?
LOOK AT THIS, SMOKEY. WE'VE ESTABLISHED THAT THERE IS A NEURO-LINK TO THIS TECH THAT WORKS WITH CONSCIOUS THOUGHT.
I KNOW...MY OLD TECH WORKED THE SAME WAY. BUT NOT QUITE LIKE THIS.
WANT TO SEE WHAT ELSE I CAN DO?

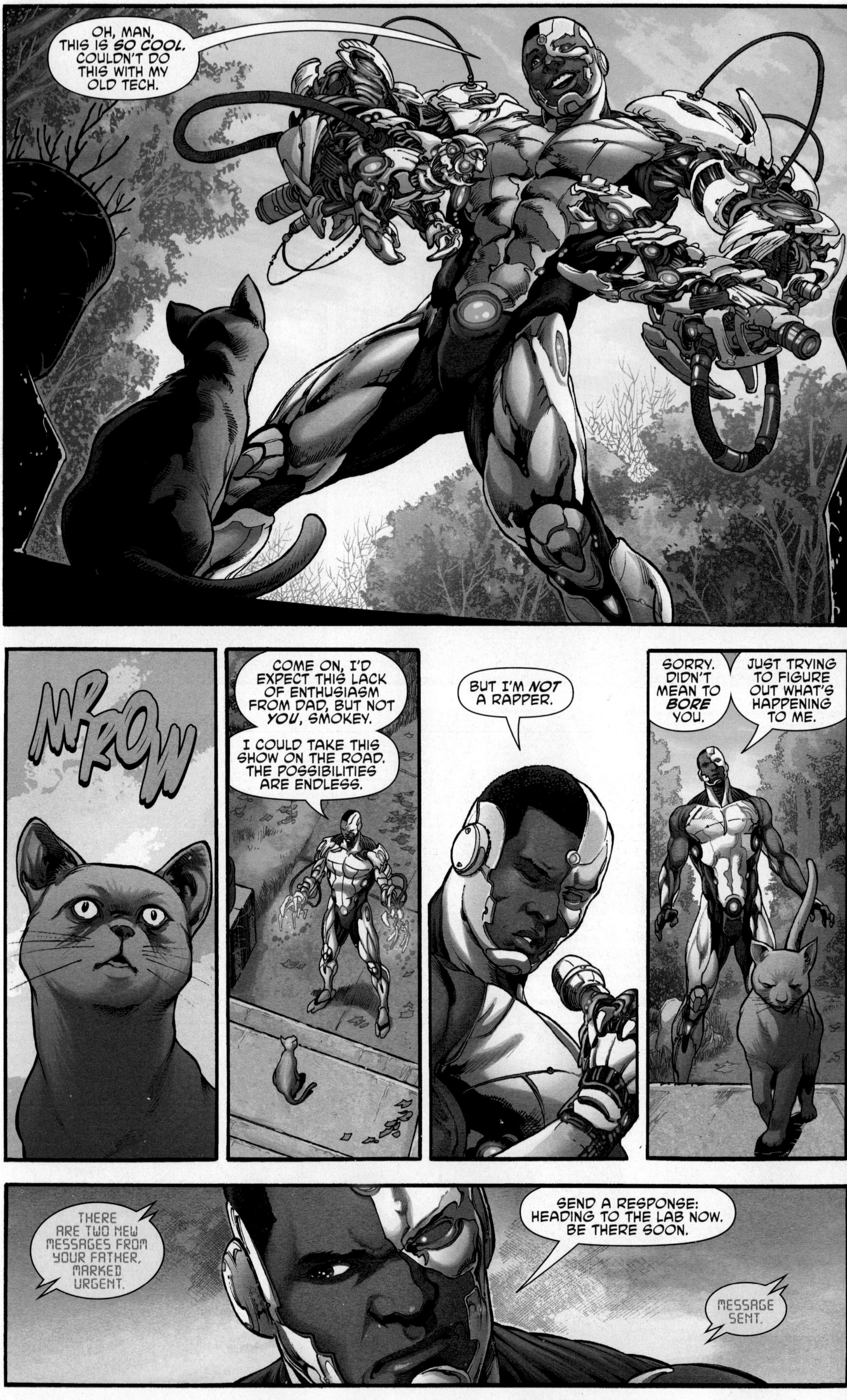
OH, MAN, THIS IS SO COOL. COULDN'T DO THIS WITH MY OLD TECH.
MRROW
COME ON, I'D EXPECT THIS LACK OF ENTHUSIASM FROM DAD, BUT NOT YOU, SMOKEY.
I COULD TAKE THIS SHOW ON THE ROAD. THE POSSIBILITIES ARE ENDLESS.
BUT I'M NOT A RAPPER.
SORRY. DIDN'T MEAN TO BORE YOU.
JUST TRYING TO FIGURE OUT WHAT'S HAPPENING TO ME.
THERE ARE TWO NEW MESSAGES FROM YOUR FATHER, MARKED URGENT.
SEND A RESPONSE: HEADING TO THE LAB NOW. BE THERE SOON.
MESSAGE SENT.

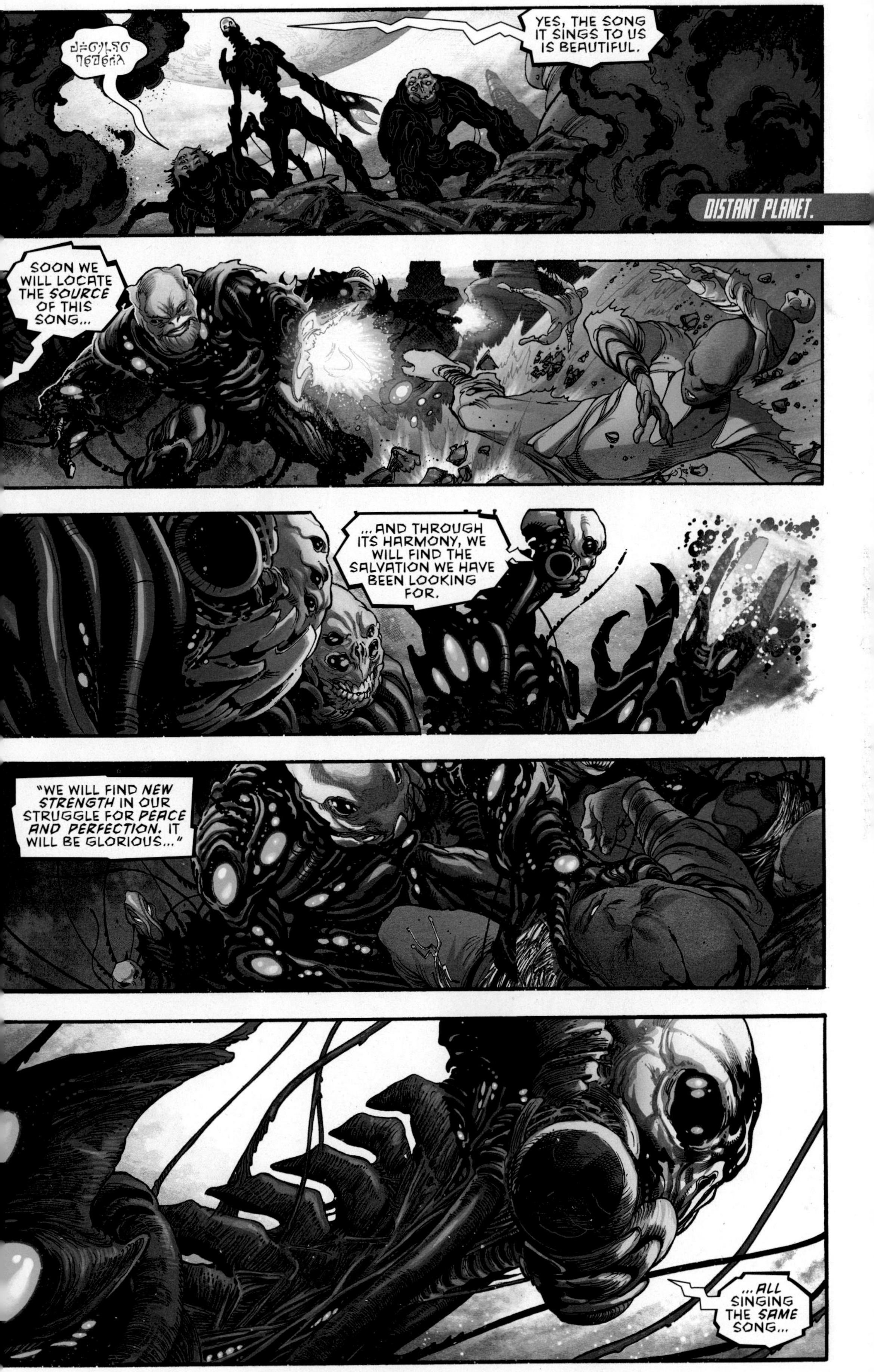YES, THE SONG IT SINGS TO US IS BEAUTIFUL.
DISTANT PLANET.
SOON WE WILL LOCATE THE SOURCE OF THIS SONG...
...AND THROUGH ITS HARMONY, WE WILL FIND THE SALVATION WE HAVE BEEN LOOKING FOR.
"WE WILL FIND NEW STRENGTH IN OUR STRUGGLE FOR PEACE AND PERFECTION. IT WILL BE GLORIOUS..."
...ALL SINGING THE SAME SONG...

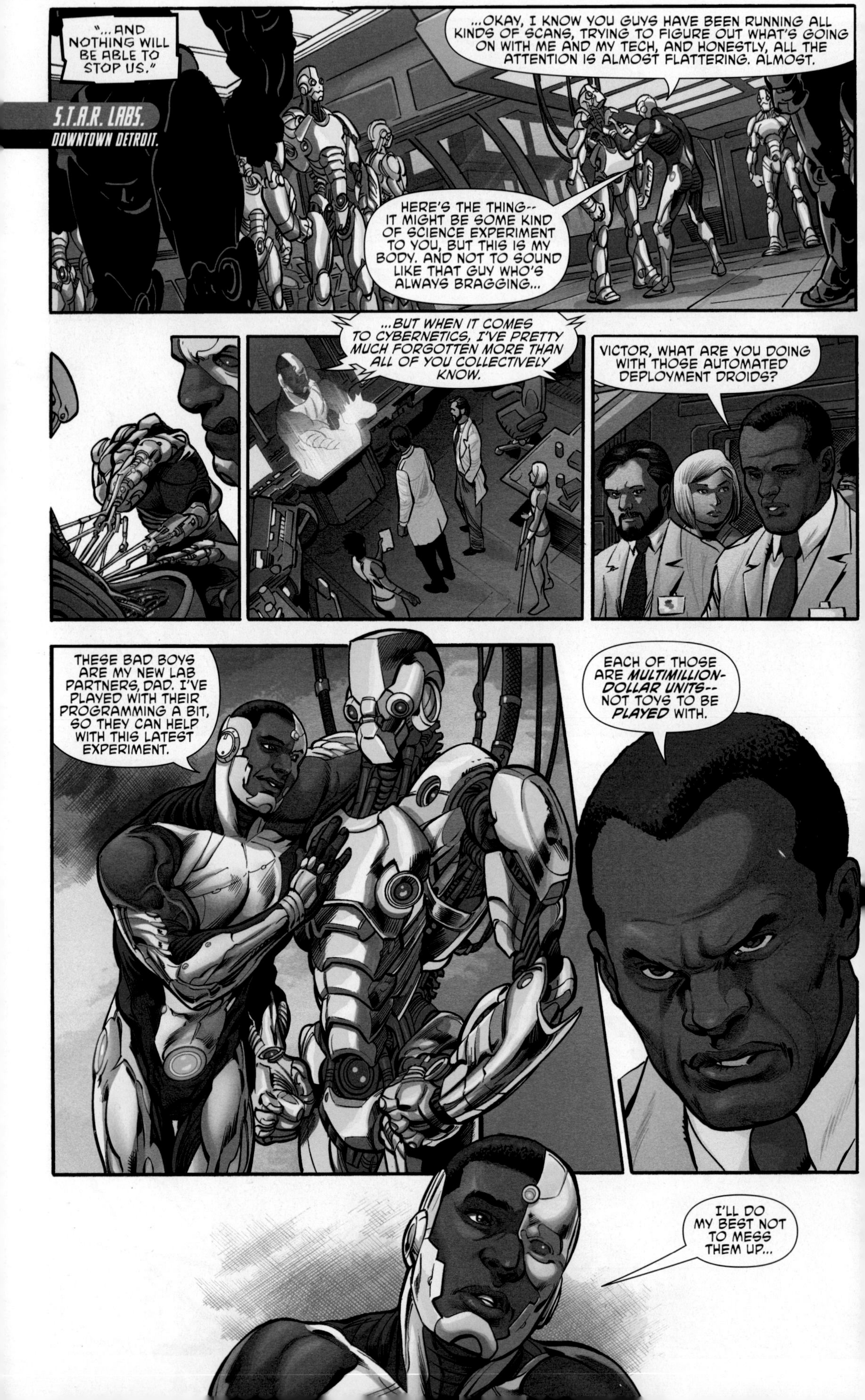
"...AND NOTHING WILL BE ABLE TO STOP US."
S.T.A.R. LABS. DOWNTOWN DETROIT.
...OKAY, I KNOW YOU GUYS HAVE BEEN RUNNING ALL KINDS OF SCANS, TRYING TO FIGURE OUT WHAT'S GOING ON WITH ME AND MY TECH, AND HONESTLY, ALL THE ATTENTION IS ALMOST FLATTERING. ALMOST.
HERE'S THE THING-- IT MIGHT BE SOME KIND OF SCIENCE EXPERIMENT TO YOU, BUT THIS IS MY BODY. AND NOT TO SOUND LIKE THAT GUY WHO'S ALWAYS BRAGGING...
...BUT WHEN IT COMES TO CYBERNETICS, I'VE PRETTY MUCH FORGOTTEN MORE THAN ALL OF YOU COLLECTIVELY KNOW.
VICTOR, WHAT ARE YOU DOING WITH THOSE AUTOMATED DEPLOYMENT DROIDS?
THESE BAD BOYS ARE MY NEW LAB PARTNERS, DAD. I'VE PLAYED WITH THEIR PROGRAMMING A BIT, SO THEY CAN HELP WITH THIS LATEST EXPERIMENT.
EACH OF THOSE ARE MULTIMILLION-DOLLAR UNITS-- NOT TOYS TO BE PLAYED WITH.
I'LL DO MY BEST NOT TO MESS THEM UP...

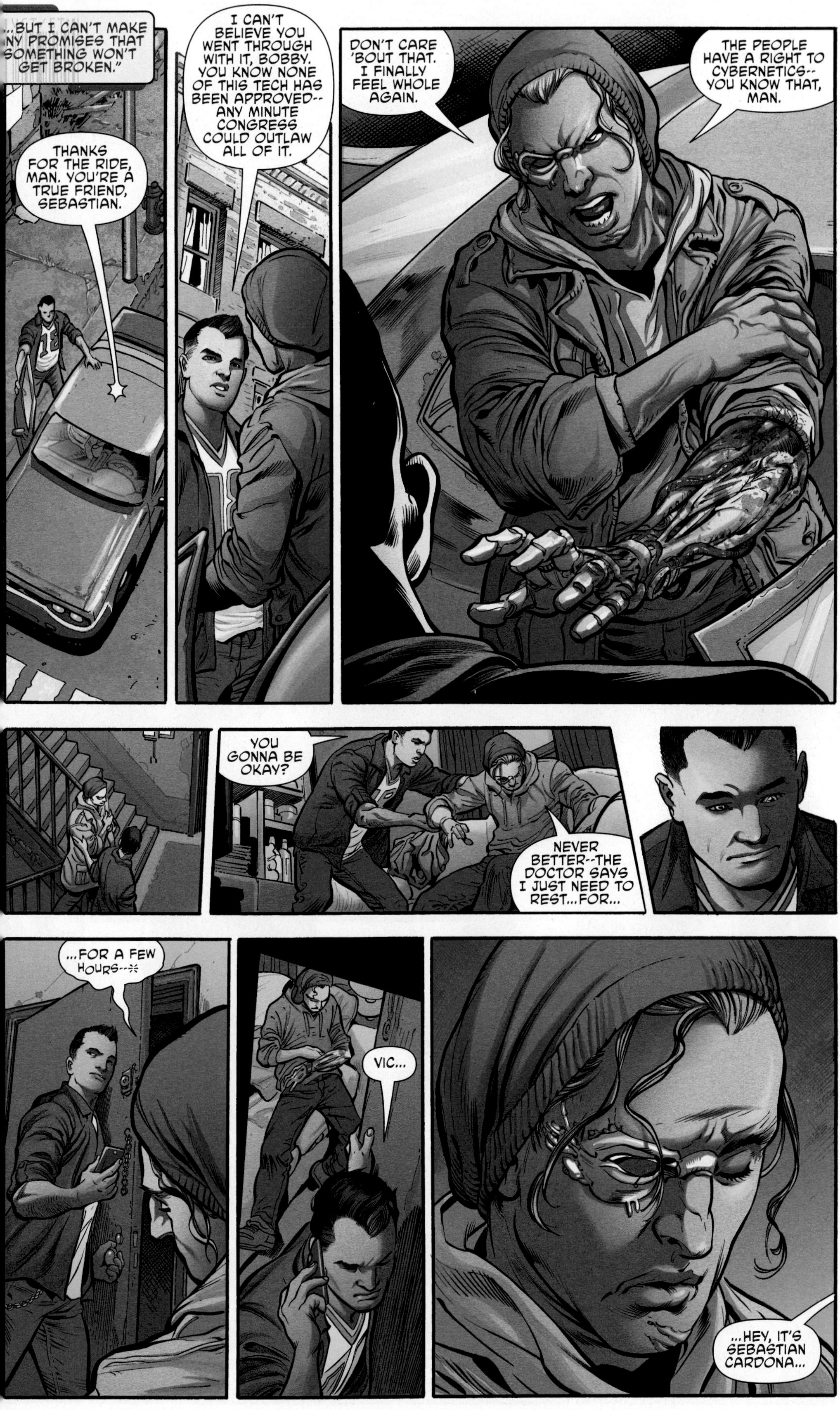
...BUT I CAN'T MAKE ANY PROMISES THAT SOMETHING WON'T GET BROKEN."
THANKS FOR THE RIDE, MAN. YOU'RE A TRUE FRIEND, SEBASTIAN.
I CAN'T BELIEVE YOU WENT THROUGH WITH IT, BOBBY. YOU KNOW NONE OF THIS TECH HAS BEEN APPROVED--ANY MINUTE CONGRESS COULD OUTLAW ALL OF IT.
DON'T CARE 'BOUT THAT. I FINALLY FEEL WHOLE AGAIN.
THE PEOPLE HAVE A RIGHT TO CYBERNETICS--YOU KNOW THAT, MAN.
YOU GONNA BE OKAY?
NEVER BETTER--THE DOCTOR SAYS I JUST NEED TO REST...FOR...
...FOR A FEW HOURS--
VIC...
...HEY, IT'S SEBASTIAN CARDONA...

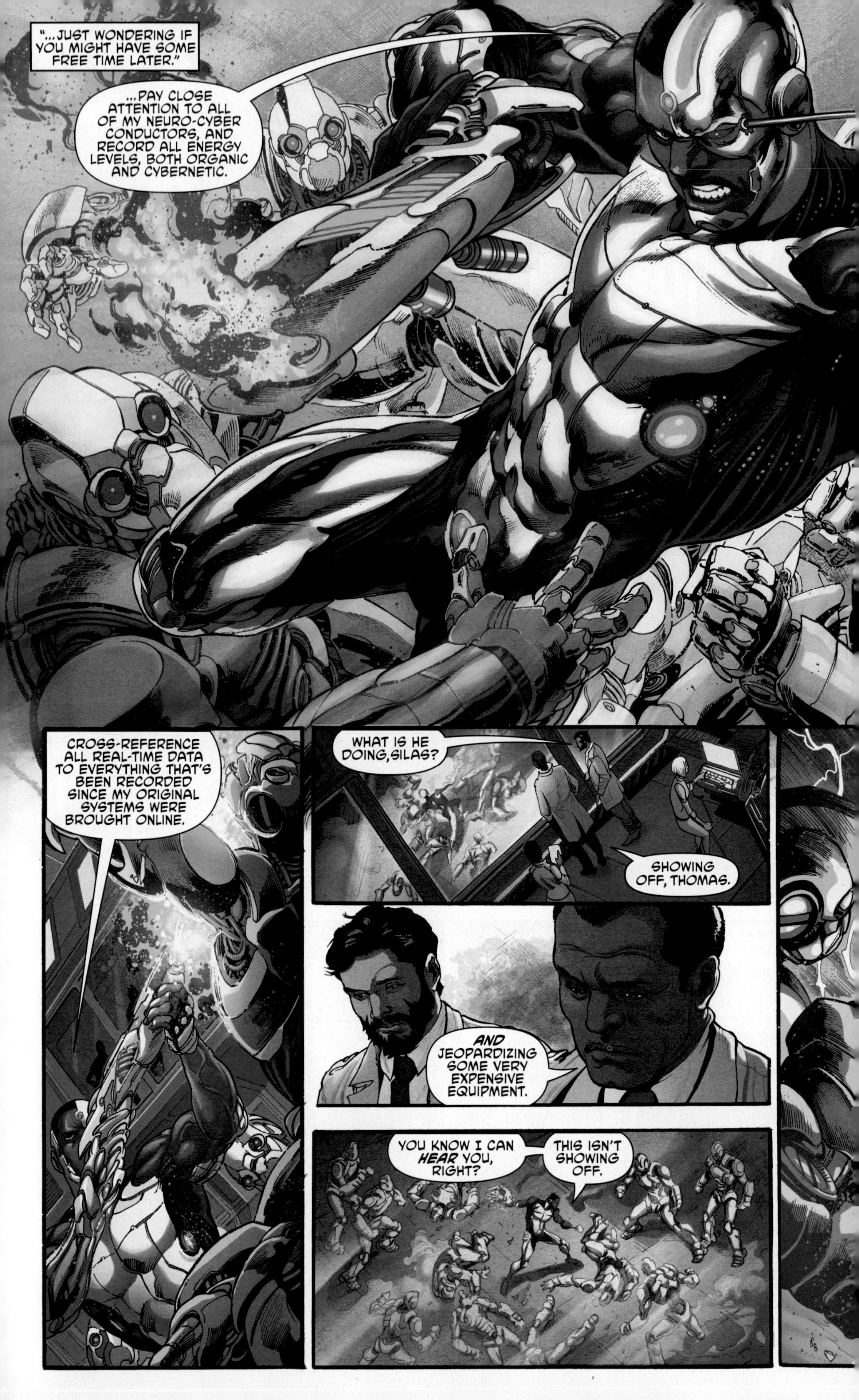
"...JUST WONDERING IF YOU MIGHT HAVE SOME FREE TIME LATER."
...PAY CLOSE ATTENTION TO ALL OF MY NEURO-CYBER CONDUCTORS, AND RECORD ALL ENERGY LEVELS, BOTH ORGANIC AND CYBERNETIC.
CROSS-REFERENCE ALL REAL-TIME DATA TO EVERYTHING THAT'S BEEN RECORDED SINCE MY ORIGINAL SYSTEMS WERE BROUGHT ONLINE.
WHAT IS HE DOING, SILAS?
SHOWING OFF, THOMAS.
*AND* JEOPARDIZING SOME VERY EXPENSIVE EQUIPMENT.
YOU KNOW I CAN *HEAR* YOU, RIGHT?
THIS ISN'T SHOWING OFF.

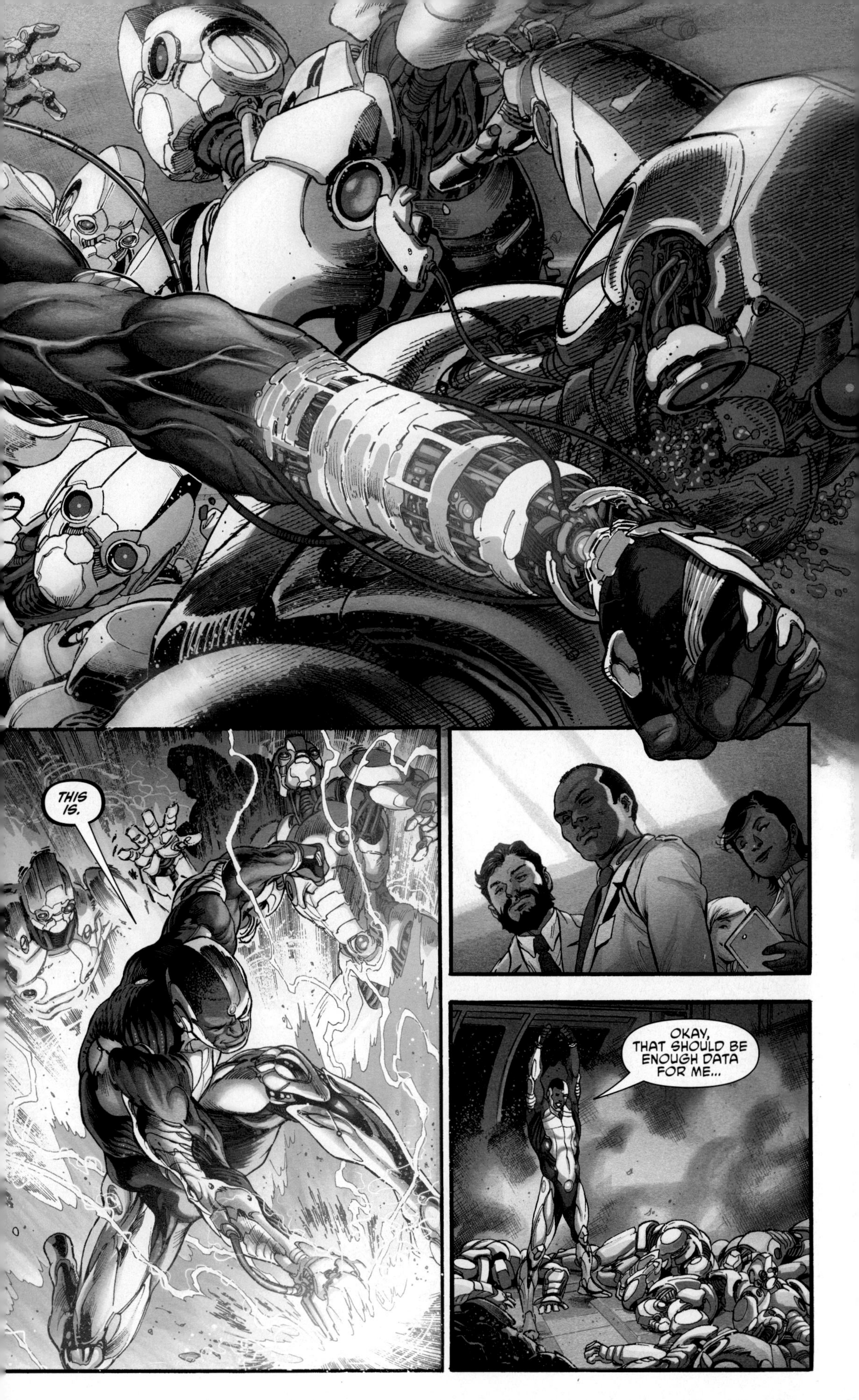
THIS IS.
OKAY, THAT SHOULD BE ENOUGH DATA FOR ME...

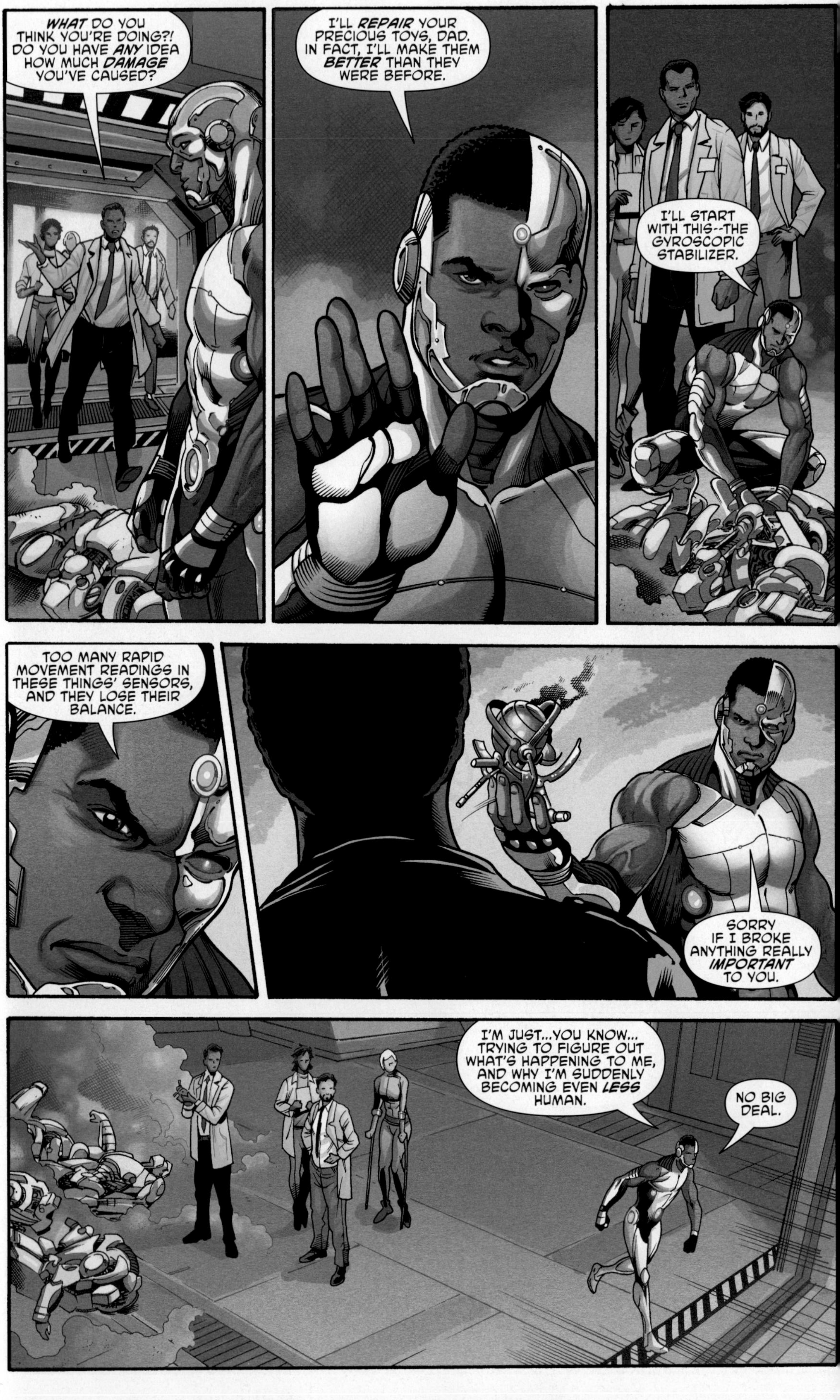

WHAT DO YOU THINK YOU'RE DOING?! DO YOU HAVE ANY IDEA HOW MUCH DAMAGE YOU'VE CAUSED?
I'LL REPAIR YOUR PRECIOUS TOYS, DAD. IN FACT, I'LL MAKE THEM BETTER THAN THEY WERE BEFORE.
I'LL START WITH THIS--THE GYROSCOPIC STABILIZER.
TOO MANY RAPID MOVEMENT READINGS IN THESE THINGS' SENSORS, AND THEY LOSE THEIR BALANCE.
SORRY IF I BROKE ANYTHING REALLY IMPORTANT TO YOU.
I'M JUST...YOU KNOW... TRYING TO FIGURE OUT WHAT'S HAPPENING TO ME, AND WHY I'M SUDDENLY BECOMING EVEN LESS HUMAN.
NO BIG DEAL.

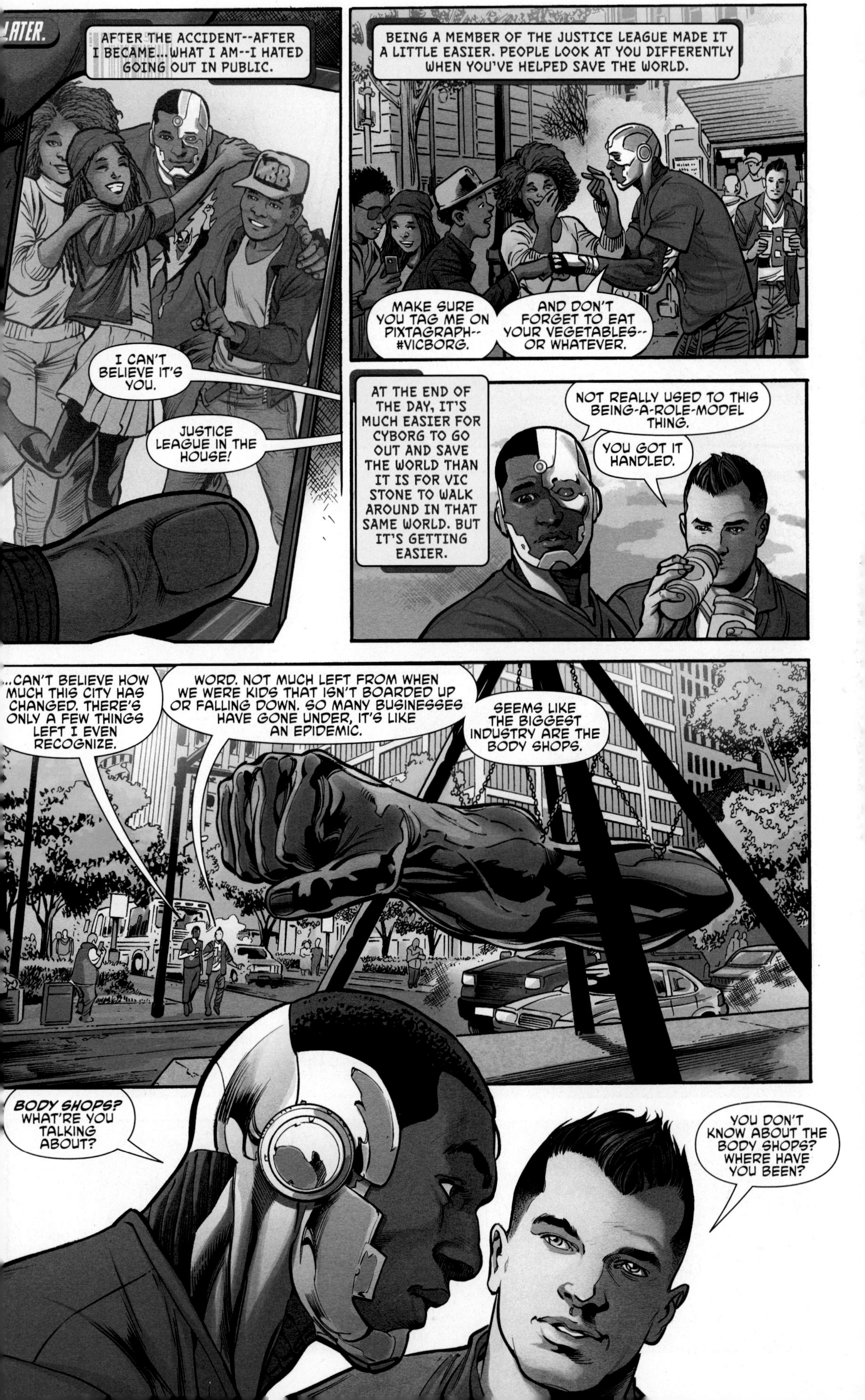
LATER.
AFTER THE ACCIDENT--AFTER I BECAME... WHAT I AM--I HATED GOING OUT IN PUBLIC.
I CAN'T BELIEVE IT'S YOU.
JUSTICE LEAGUE IN THE HOUSE!
BEING A MEMBER OF THE JUSTICE LEAGUE MADE IT A LITTLE EASIER. PEOPLE LOOK AT YOU DIFFERENTLY WHEN YOU'VE HELPED SAVE THE WORLD.
MAKE SURE YOU TAG ME ON PIXTAGRAPH-- #VICBORG.
AND DON'T FORGET TO EAT YOUR VEGETABLES-- OR WHATEVER.
AT THE END OF THE DAY, IT'S MUCH EASIER FOR CYBORG TO GO OUT AND SAVE THE WORLD THAN IT IS FOR VIC STONE TO WALK AROUND IN THAT SAME WORLD. BUT IT'S GETTING EASIER.
NOT REALLY USED TO THIS BEING-A-ROLE-MODEL THING.
YOU GOT IT HANDLED.
...CAN'T BELIEVE HOW MUCH THIS CITY HAS CHANGED. THERE'S ONLY A FEW THINGS LEFT I EVEN RECOGNIZE.
WORD. NOT MUCH LEFT FROM WHEN WE WERE KIDS THAT ISN'T BOARDED UP OR FALLING DOWN. SO MANY BUSINESSES HAVE GONE UNDER, IT'S LIKE AN EPIDEMIC.
SEEMS LIKE THE BIGGEST INDUSTRY ARE THE BODY SHOPS.
BODY SHOPS? WHAT'RE YOU TALKING ABOUT?
YOU DON'T KNOW ABOUT THE BODY SHOPS? WHERE HAVE YOU BEEN?

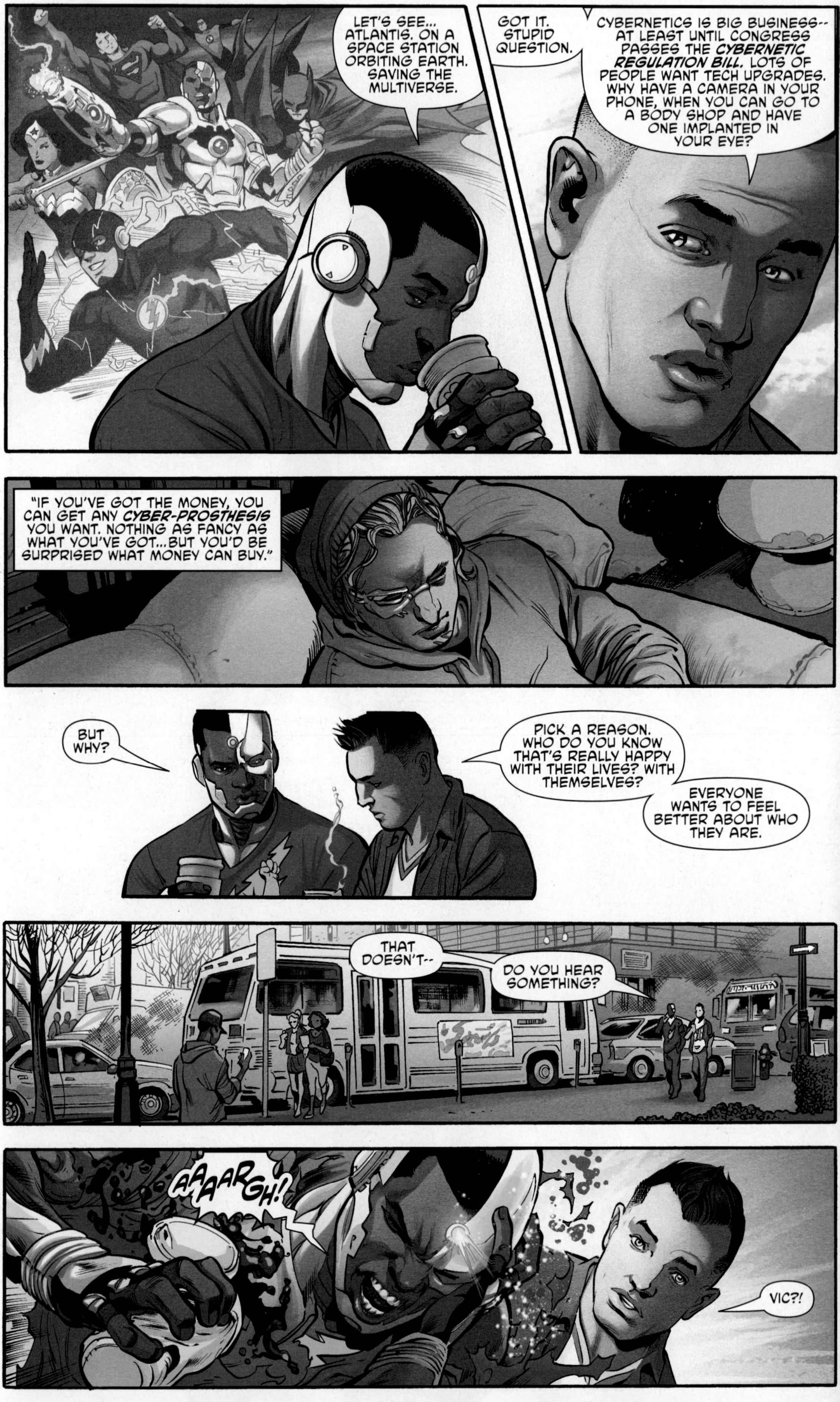
LET'S SEE... ATLANTIS. ON A SPACE STATION ORBITING EARTH. SAVING THE MULTIVERSE.
GOT IT. STUPID QUESTION.
CYBERNETICS IS BIG BUSINESS-- AT LEAST UNTIL CONGRESS PASSES THE CYBERNETIC REGULATION BILL. LOTS OF PEOPLE WANT TECH UPGRADES. WHY HAVE A CAMERA IN YOUR PHONE, WHEN YOU CAN GO TO A BODY SHOP AND HAVE ONE IMPLANTED IN YOUR EYE?
"IF YOU'VE GOT THE MONEY, YOU CAN GET ANY CYBER-PROSTHESIS YOU WANT. NOTHING AS FANCY AS WHAT YOU'VE GOT...BUT YOU'D BE SURPRISED WHAT MONEY CAN BUY."
BUT WHY?
PICK A REASON. WHO DO YOU KNOW THAT'S REALLY HAPPY WITH THEIR LIVES? WITH THEMSELVES?
EVERYONE WANTS TO FEEL BETTER ABOUT WHO THEY ARE.
THAT DOESN'T--
DO YOU HEAR SOMETHING?
AAAARGH!
VIC?!

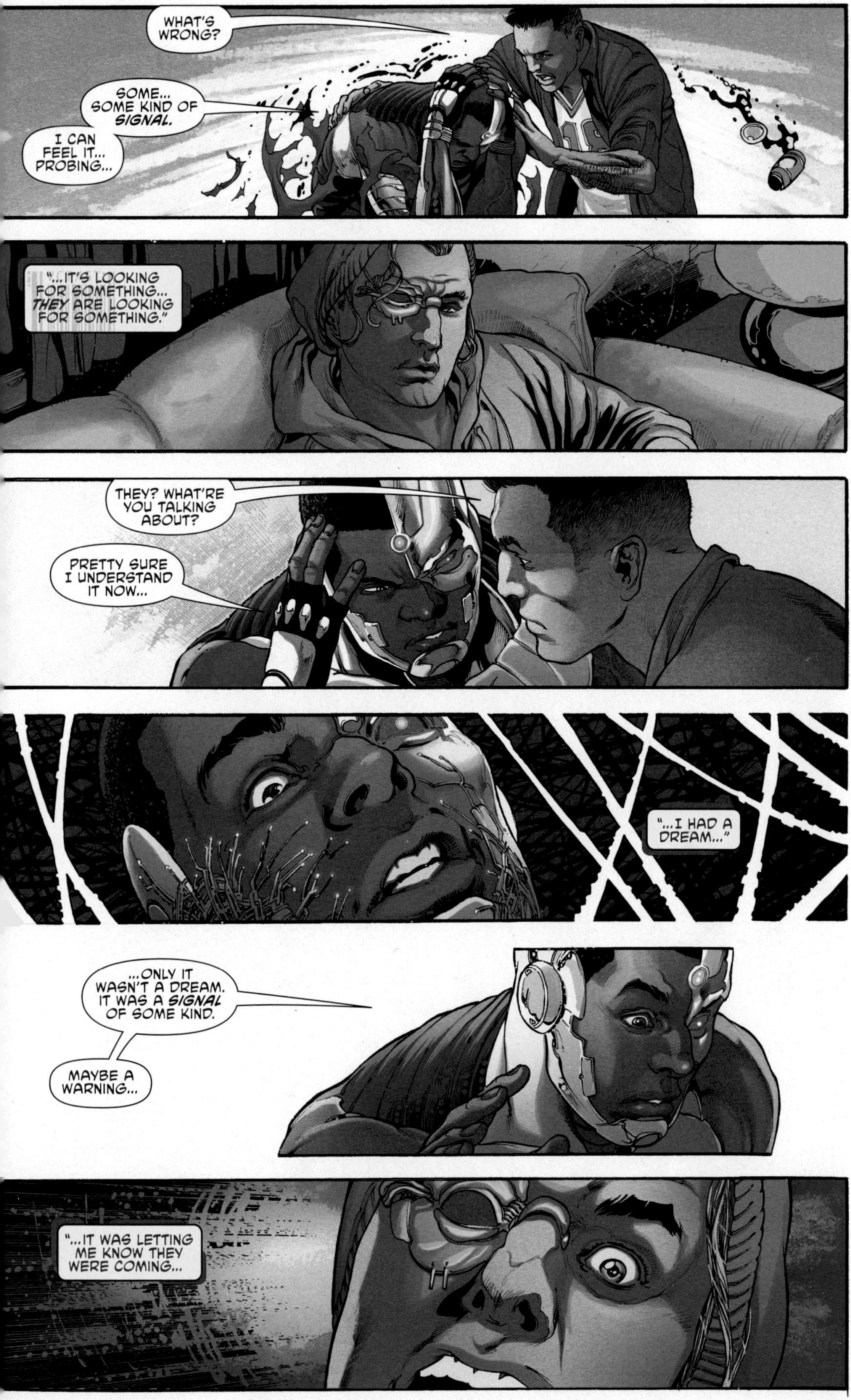

WHAT'S WRONG?
SOME... SOME KIND OF SIGNAL.
I CAN FEEL IT... PROBING...
"...IT'S LOOKING FOR SOMETHING... THEY ARE LOOKING FOR SOMETHING."
THEY? WHAT'RE YOU TALKING ABOUT?
PRETTY SURE I UNDERSTAND IT NOW...
"...I HAD A DREAM..."
...ONLY IT WASN'T A DREAM. IT WAS A SIGNAL OF SOME KIND.
MAYBE A WARNING...
"...IT WAS LETTING ME KNOW THEY WERE COMING...

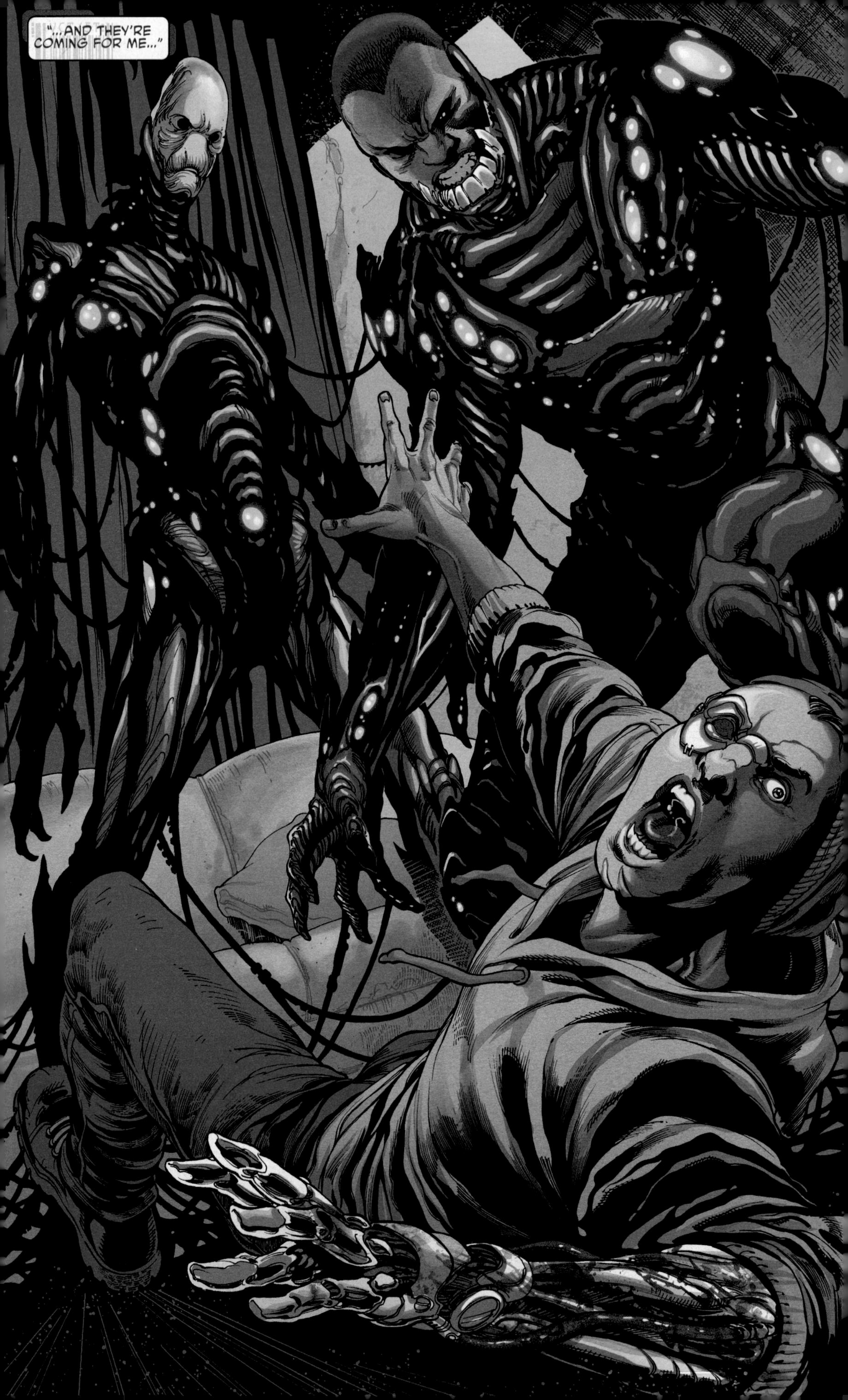
"...AND THEY'RE COMING FOR ME..."

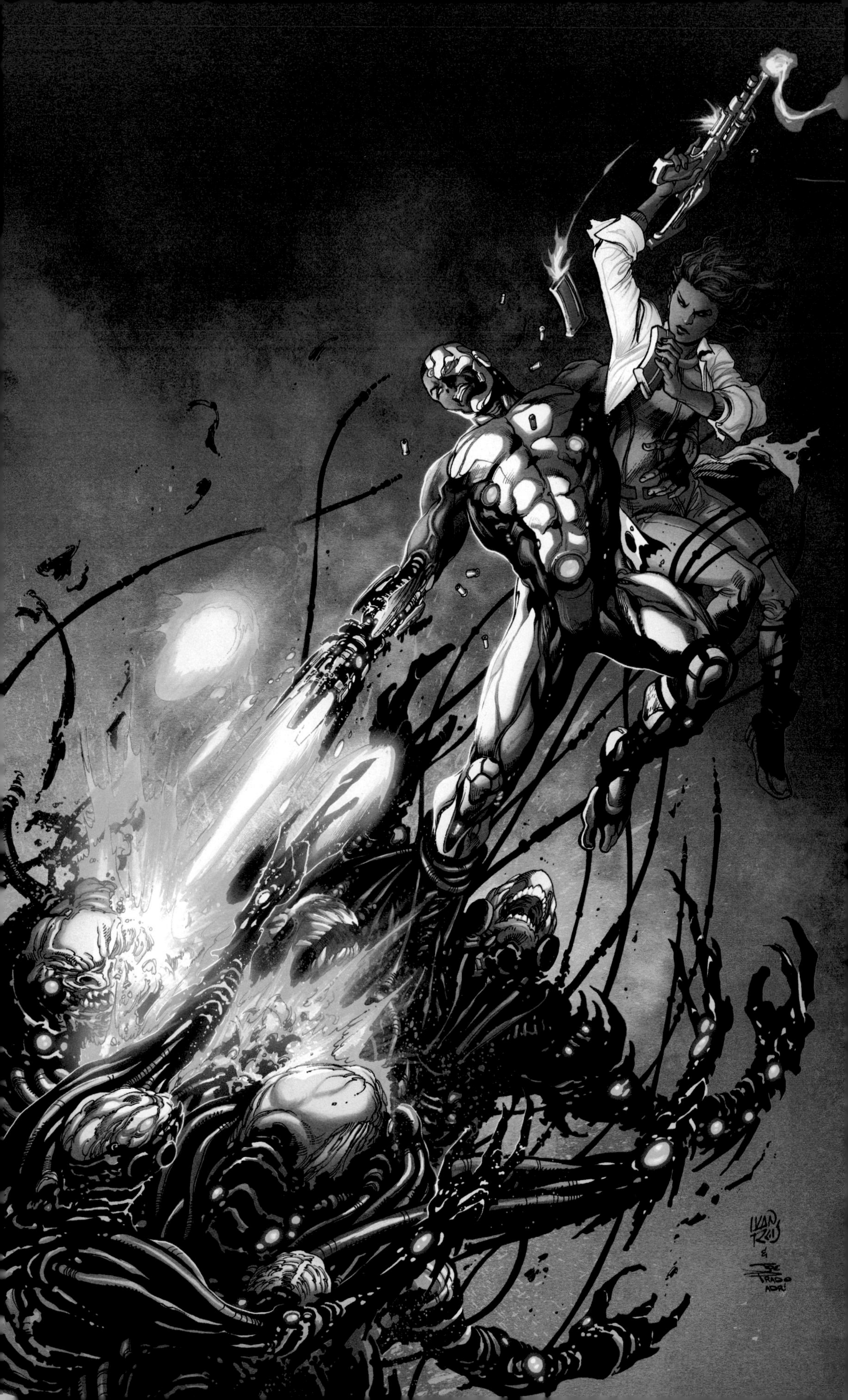

**BATTLEGROUND: DETROIT!**

**IVAN REIS EDUARDO PANSICA** pencillers **SCOTT HANNA, OCLAIR ALBERT** and **IVAN REIS** inkers **ADRIANO LUCAS** colorist **COREY BREEN** letterer
**IVAN REIS, JOE PRADO** and **ADRIANO LUCAS** cover art

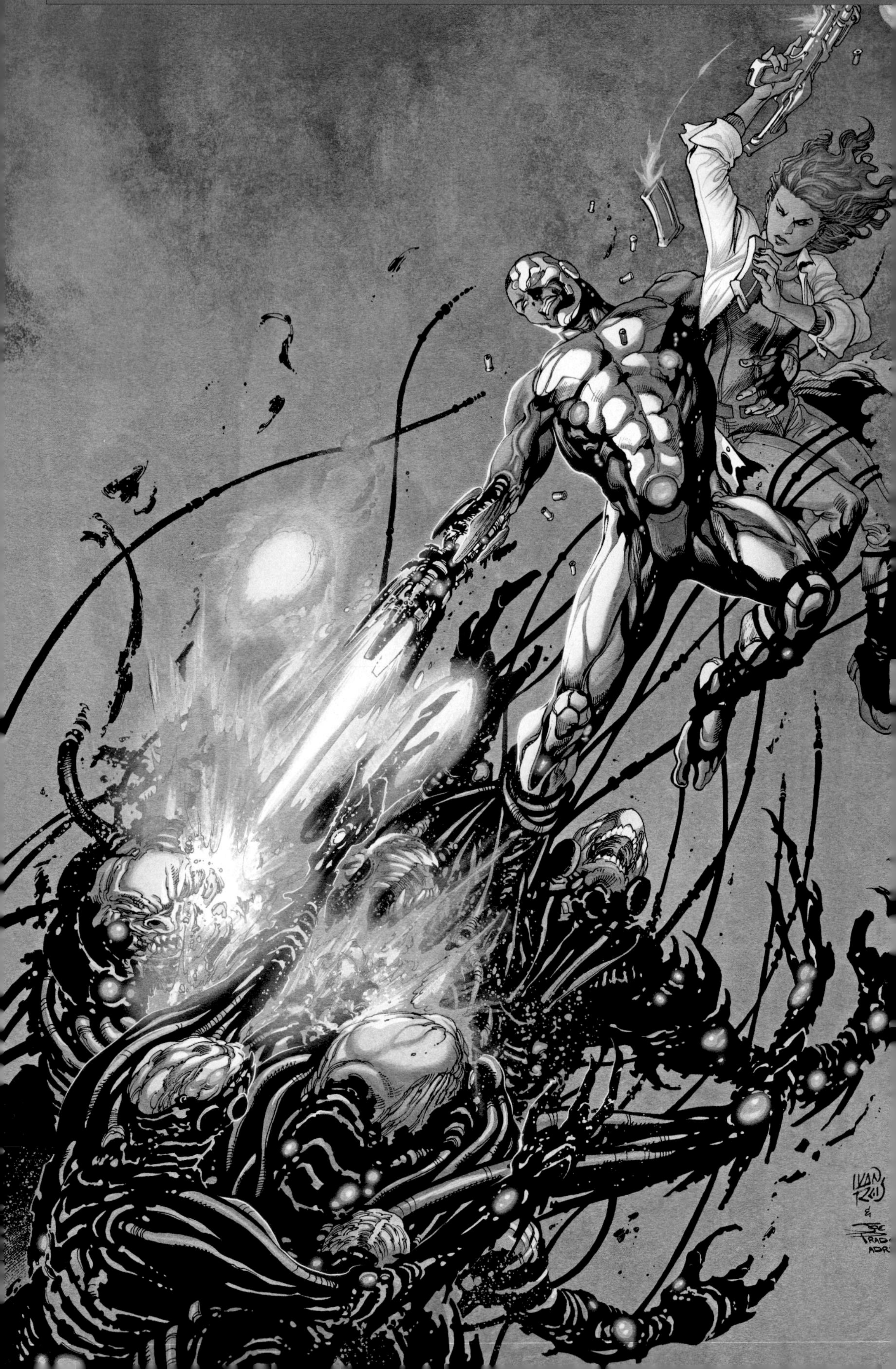

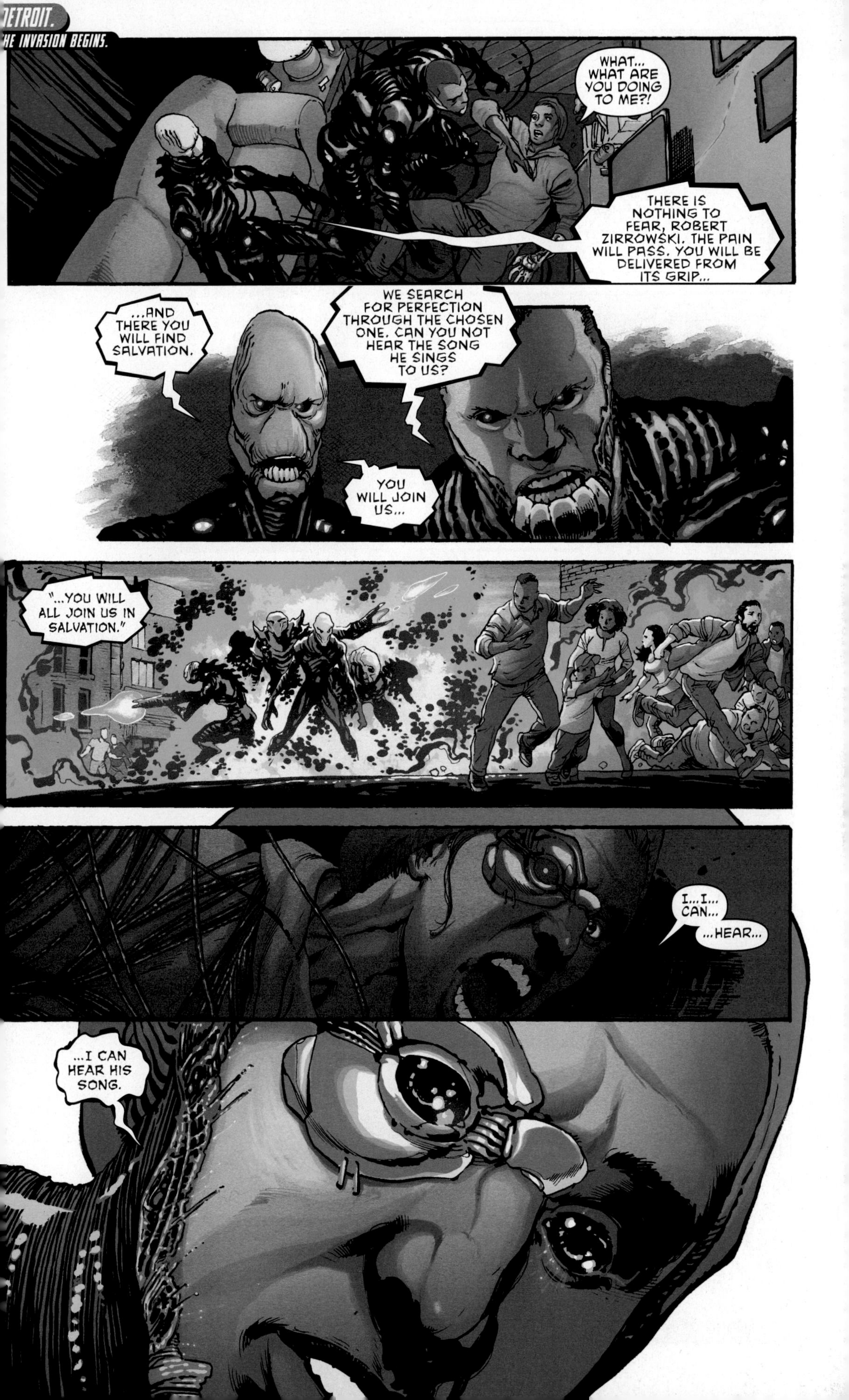
DETROIT.
THE INVASION BEGINS.
WHAT... WHAT ARE YOU DOING TO ME?!
THERE IS NOTHING TO FEAR, ROBERT ZIRROWSKI. THE PAIN WILL PASS. YOU WILL BE DELIVERED FROM ITS GRIP...
...AND THERE YOU WILL FIND SALVATION.
WE SEARCH FOR PERFECTION THROUGH THE CHOSEN ONE. CAN YOU NOT HEAR THE SONG HE SINGS TO US?
YOU WILL JOIN US...
"...YOU WILL ALL JOIN US IN SALVATION."
I...I... CAN...
...HEAR...
...I CAN HEAR HIS SONG.

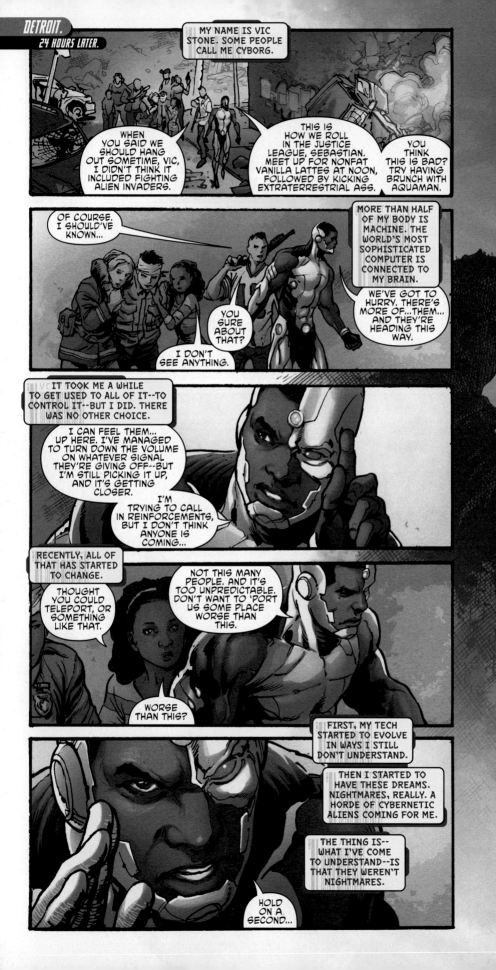

MY NAME IS VIC STONE. SOME PEOPLE CALL ME CYBORG.

WHEN YOU SAID WE SHOULD HANG OUT SOMETIME, VIC, I DIDN'T THINK IT INCLUDED FIGHTING ALIEN INVADERS.

THIS IS HOW WE ROLL IN THE JUSTICE LEAGUE, SEBASTIAN. MEET UP FOR NONFAT VANILLA LATTES AT NOON, FOLLOWED BY KICKING EXTRATERRESTRIAL ASS.

YOU THINK THIS IS BAD? TRY HAVING BRUNCH WITH AQUAMAN.

OF COURSE. I SHOULD'VE KNOWN...

YOU SURE ABOUT THAT?

I DON'T SEE ANYTHING.

MORE THAN HALF OF MY BODY IS MACHINE. THE WORLD'S MOST SOPHISTICATED COMPUTER IS CONNECTED TO MY BRAIN.

WE'VE GOT TO HURRY. THERE'S MORE OF...THEM... AND THEY'RE HEADING THIS WAY.

IT TOOK ME A WHILE TO GET USED TO ALL OF IT--TO CONTROL IT--BUT I DID. THERE WAS NO OTHER CHOICE.

I CAN FEEL THEM... UP HERE. I'VE MANAGED TO TURN DOWN THE VOLUME ON WHATEVER SIGNAL THEY'RE GIVING OFF--BUT I'M STILL PICKING IT UP, AND IT'S GETTING CLOSER.

I'M TRYING TO CALL IN REINFORCEMENTS, BUT I DON'T THINK ANYONE IS COMING...

RECENTLY, ALL OF THAT HAS STARTED TO CHANGE.

THOUGHT YOU COULD TELEPORT, OR SOMETHING LIKE THAT.

NOT THIS MANY PEOPLE. AND IT'S TOO UNPREDICTABLE. DON'T WANT TO 'PORT US SOME PLACE WORSE THAN THIS.

WORSE THAN THIS?

FIRST, MY TECH STARTED TO EVOLVE IN WAYS I STILL DON'T UNDERSTAND.

THEN I STARTED TO HAVE THESE DREAMS. NIGHTMARES, REALLY. A HORDE OF CYBERNETIC ALIENS COMING FOR ME.

THE THING IS-- WHAT I'VE COME TO UNDERSTAND--IS THAT THEY WEREN'T NIGHTMARES.

HOLD ON A SECOND...

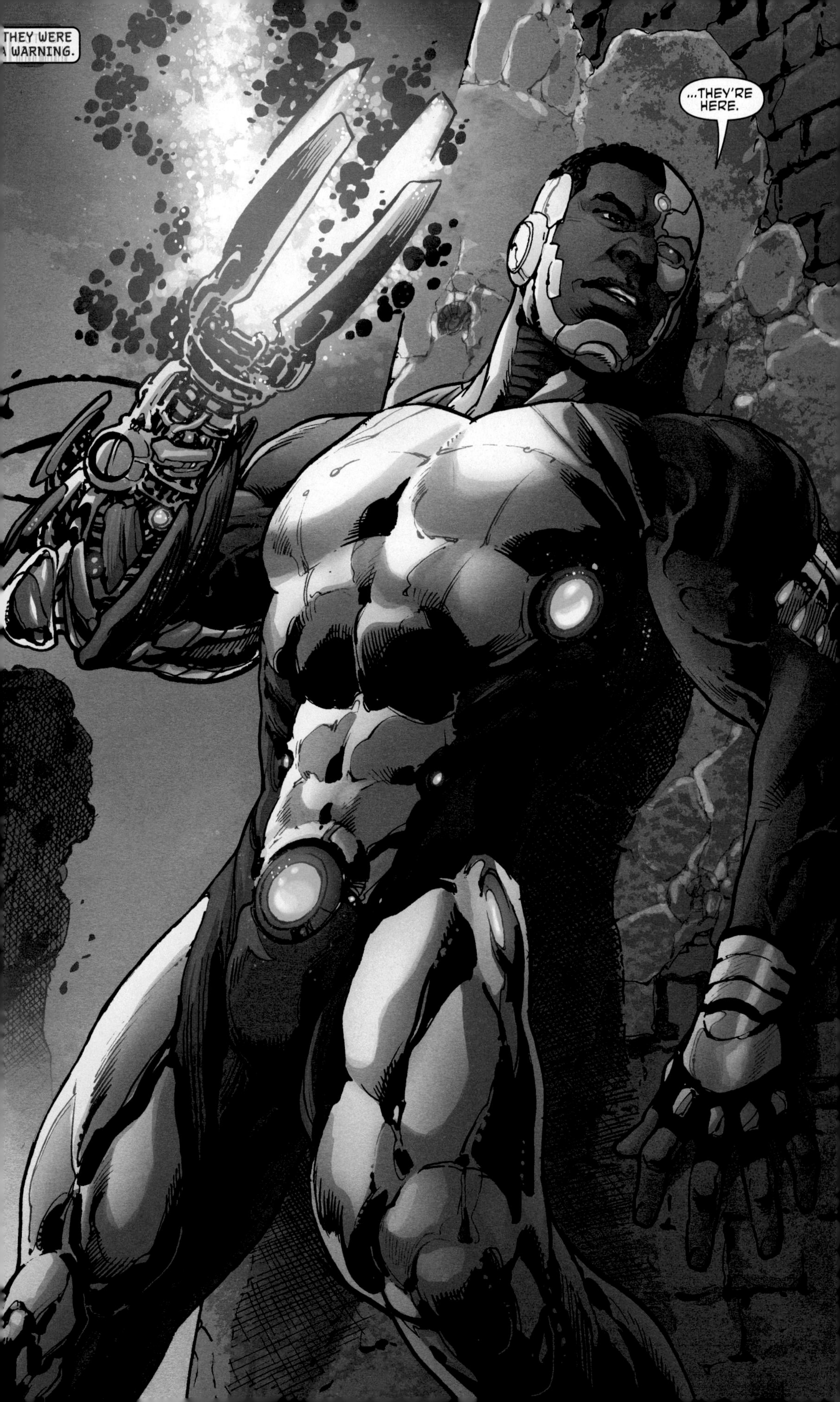

THEY WERE A WARNING.
...THEY'RE HERE.

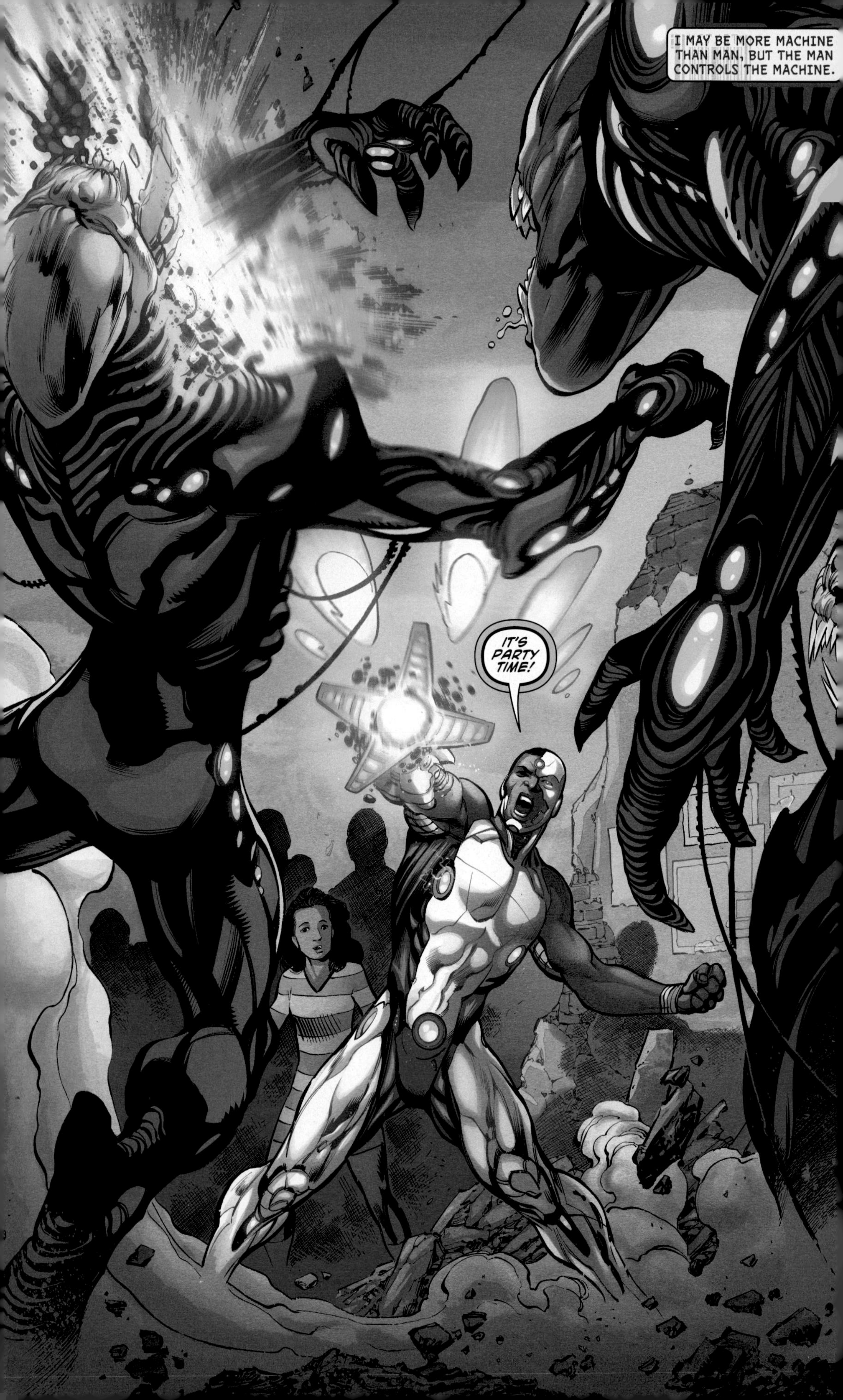
I MAY BE MORE MACHINE THAN MAN, BUT THE MAN CONTROLS THE MACHINE.
IT'S PARTY TIME!

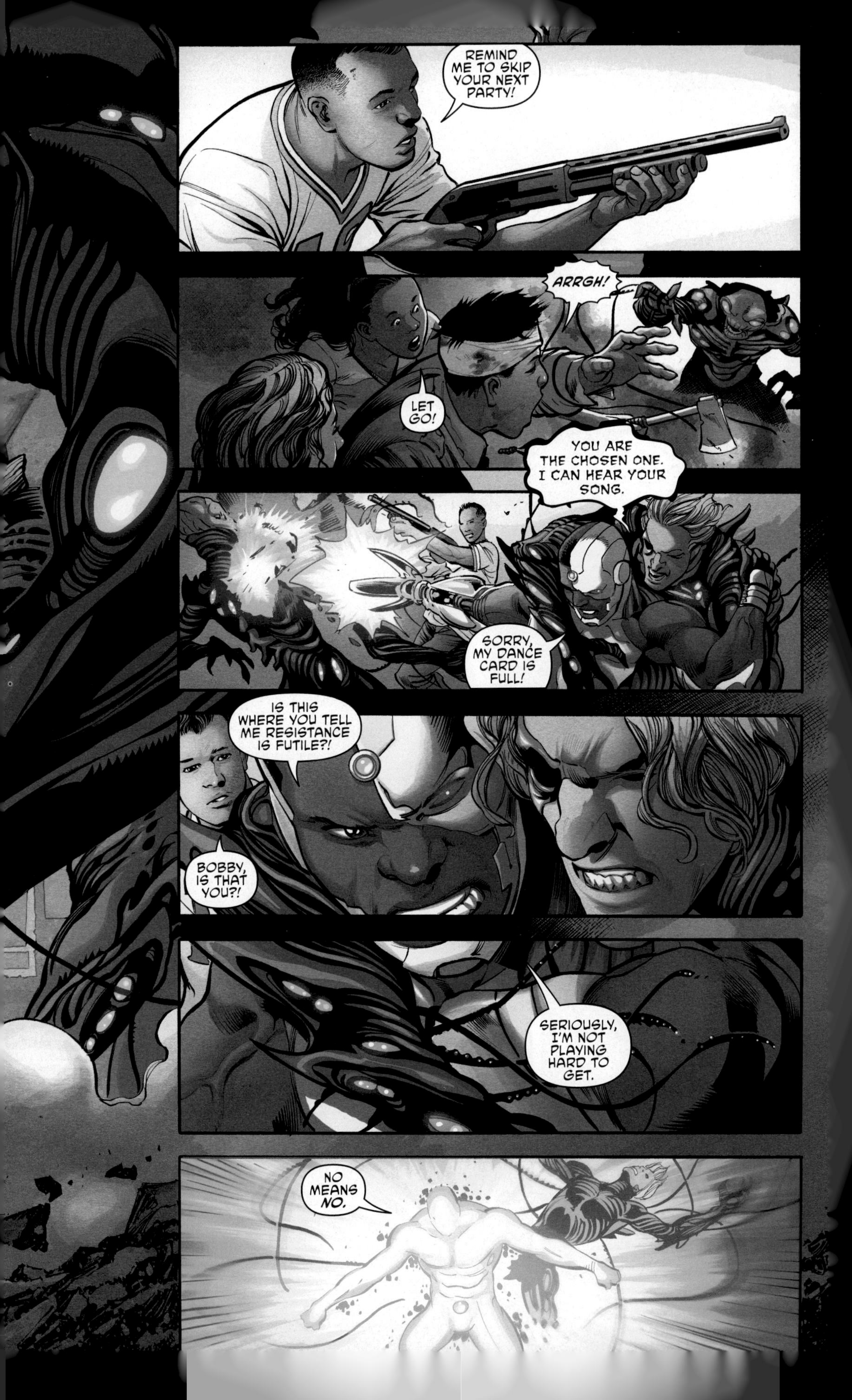
REMIND ME TO SKIP YOUR NEXT PARTY!
ARRGH!
LET GO!
YOU ARE THE CHOSEN ONE. I CAN HEAR YOUR SONG.
SORRY, MY DANCE CARD IS FULL!
IS THIS WHERE YOU TELL ME RESISTANCE IS FUTILE?!
BOBBY, IS THAT YOU?!
SERIOUSLY, I'M NOT PLAYING HARD TO GET.
NO MEANS NO.

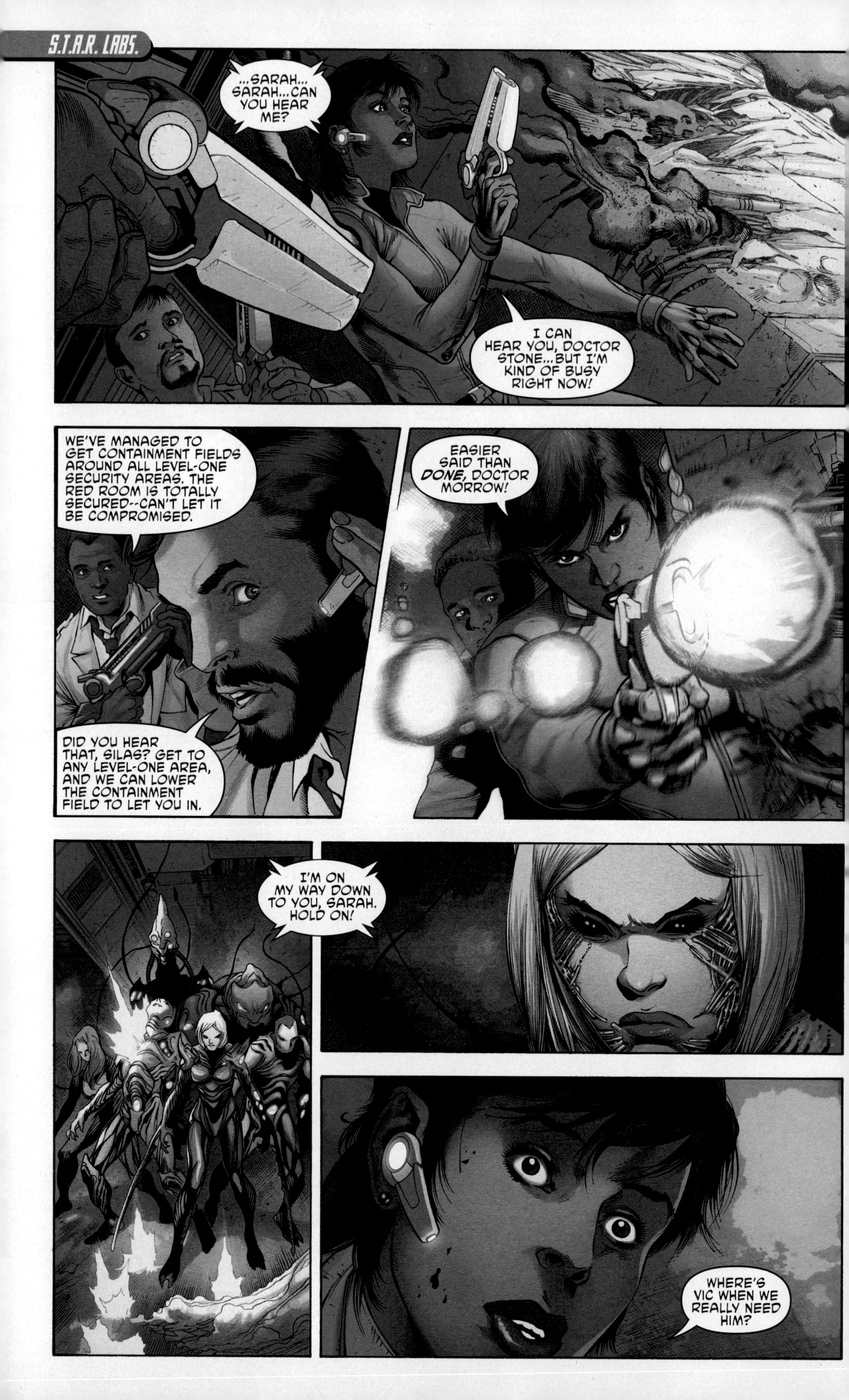
S.T.A.R. LABS.
...SARAH... SARAH...CAN YOU HEAR ME?
I CAN HEAR YOU, DOCTOR STONE...BUT I'M KIND OF BUSY RIGHT NOW!
WE'VE MANAGED TO GET CONTAINMENT FIELDS AROUND ALL LEVEL-ONE SECURITY AREAS. THE RED ROOM IS TOTALLY SECURED--CAN'T LET IT BE COMPROMISED.
DID YOU HEAR THAT, SILAS? GET TO ANY LEVEL-ONE AREA, AND WE CAN LOWER THE CONTAINMENT FIELD TO LET YOU IN.
EASIER SAID THAN *DONE*, DOCTOR MORROW!
I'M ON MY WAY DOWN TO YOU, SARAH. HOLD ON!
WHERE'S VIC WHEN WE REALLY NEED HIM?

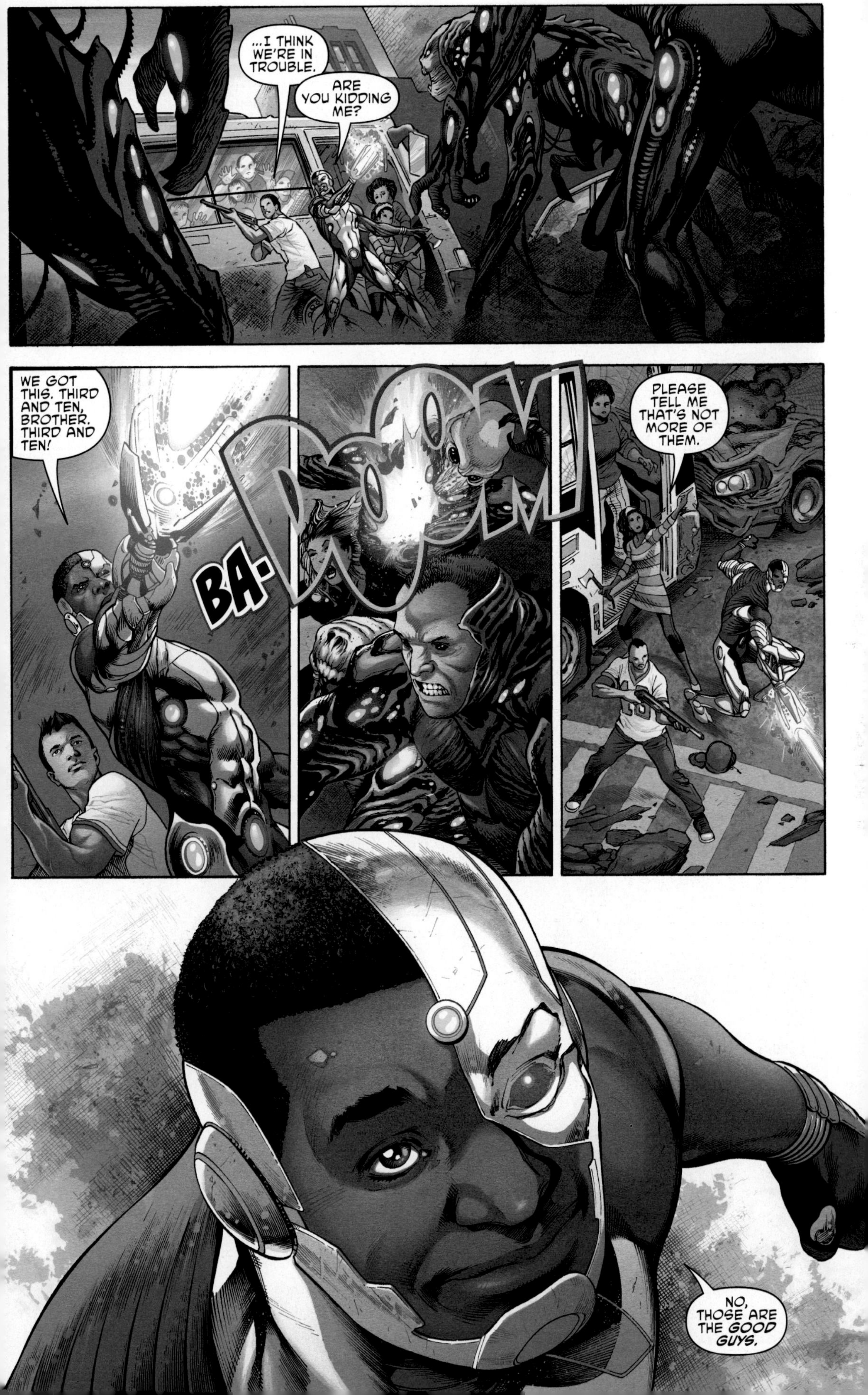
...I THINK WE'RE IN TROUBLE.
ARE YOU KIDDING ME?
WE GOT THIS. THIRD AND TEN, BROTHER. THIRD AND TEN!
BA-DOOM!
PLEASE TELL ME THAT'S NOT MORE OF THEM.
NO, THOSE ARE THE *GOOD GUYS*.

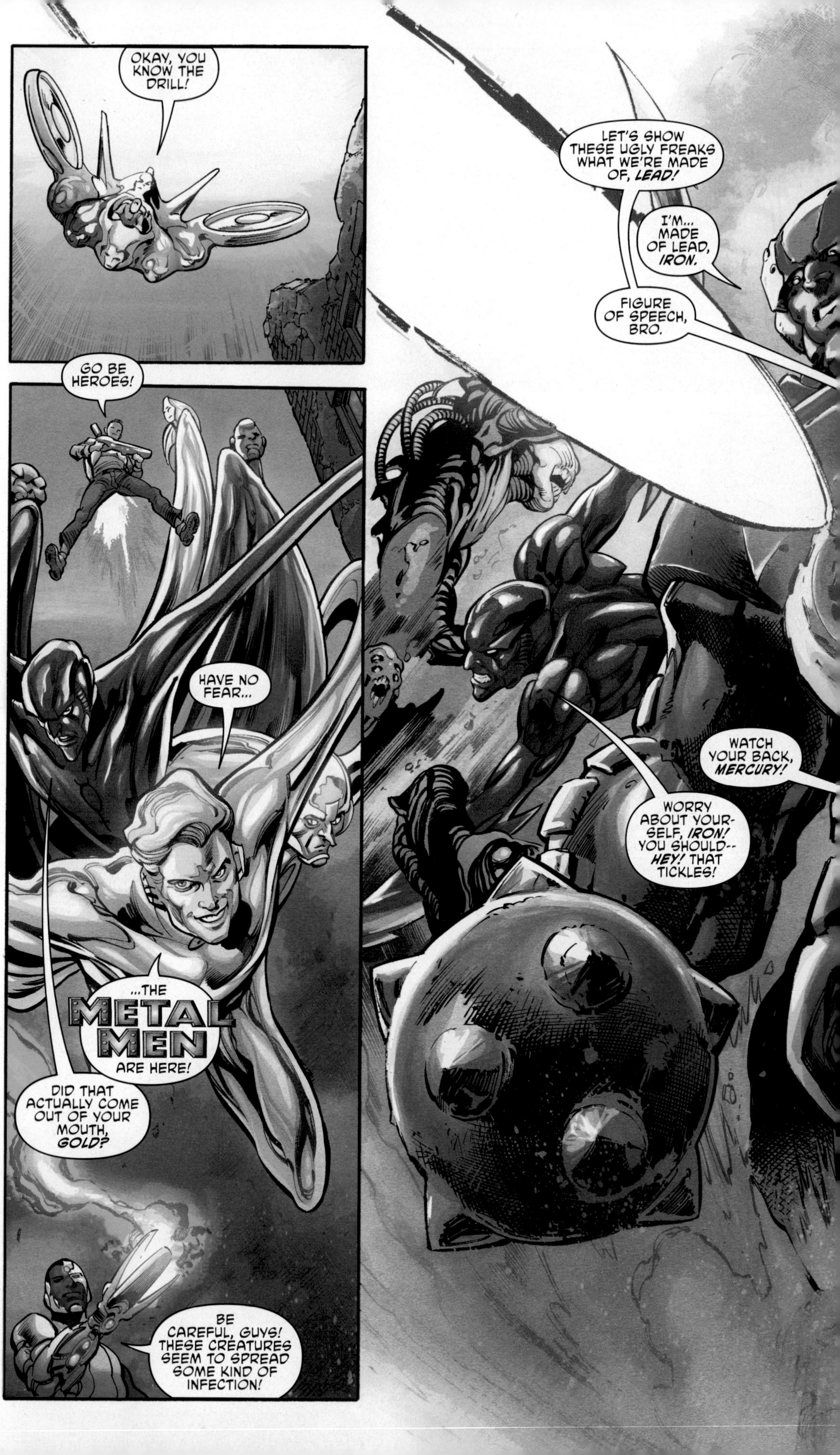

OKAY, YOU KNOW THE DRILL!
LET'S SHOW THESE UGLY FREAKS WHAT WE'RE MADE OF, *LEAD!*
I'M... MADE OF LEAD, *IRON.*
FIGURE OF SPEECH, BRO.
GO BE HEROES!
HAVE NO FEAR...
...THE METAL MEN ARE HERE!
DID THAT ACTUALLY COME OUT OF YOUR MOUTH, *GOLD?*
WATCH YOUR BACK, *MERCURY!*
WORRY ABOUT YOURSELF, *IRON!* YOU SHOULD-- *HEY!* THAT TICKLES!
BE CAREFUL, GUYS! THESE CREATURES SEEM TO SPREAD SOME KIND OF INFECTION!

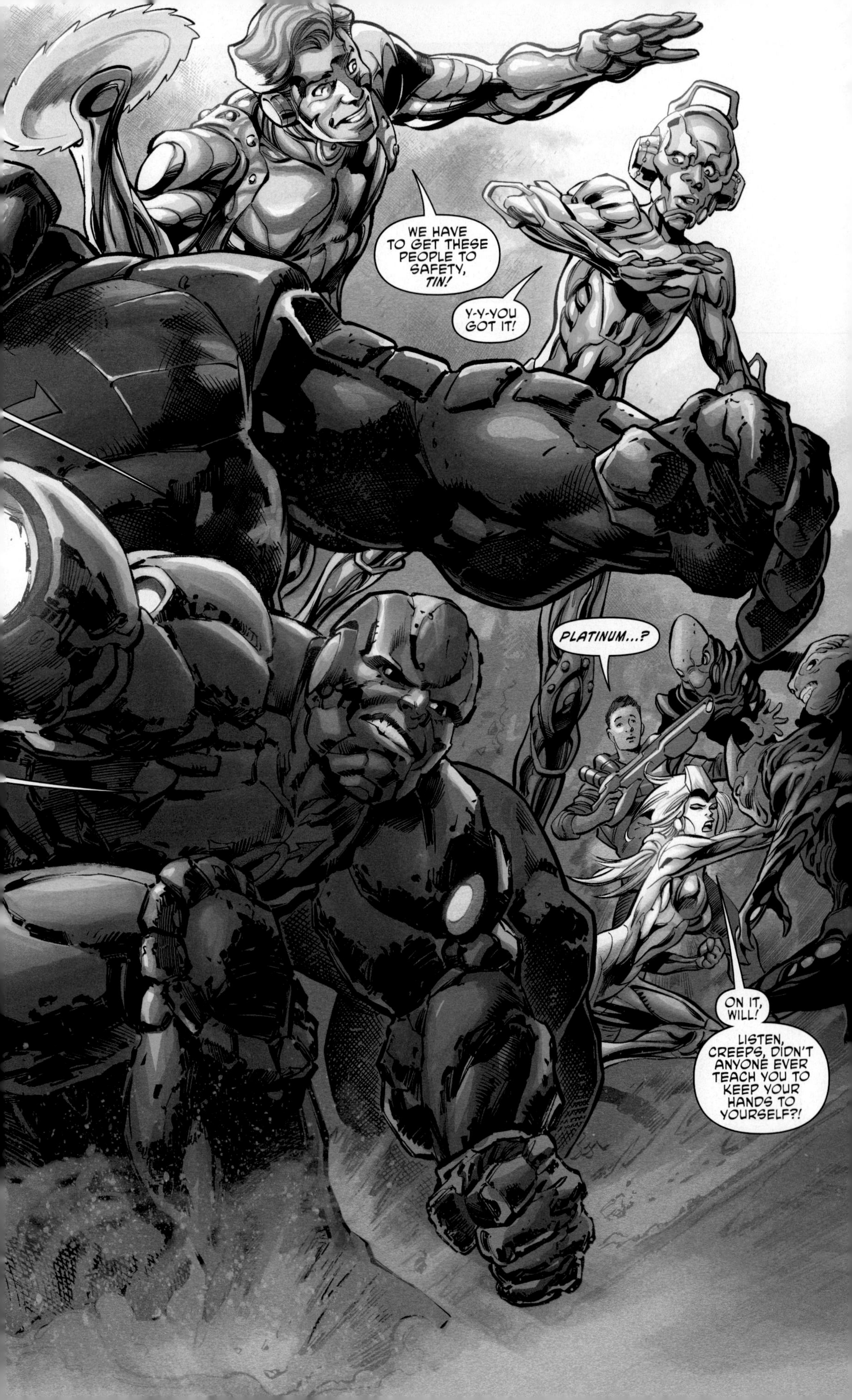
WE HAVE TO GET THESE PEOPLE TO SAFETY, *TIN!*
Y-Y-YOU GOT IT!
*PLATINUM...?*
ON IT, WILL!
LISTEN, CREEPS, DIDN'T ANYONE EVER TEACH YOU TO KEEP YOUR HANDS TO YOURSELF?!

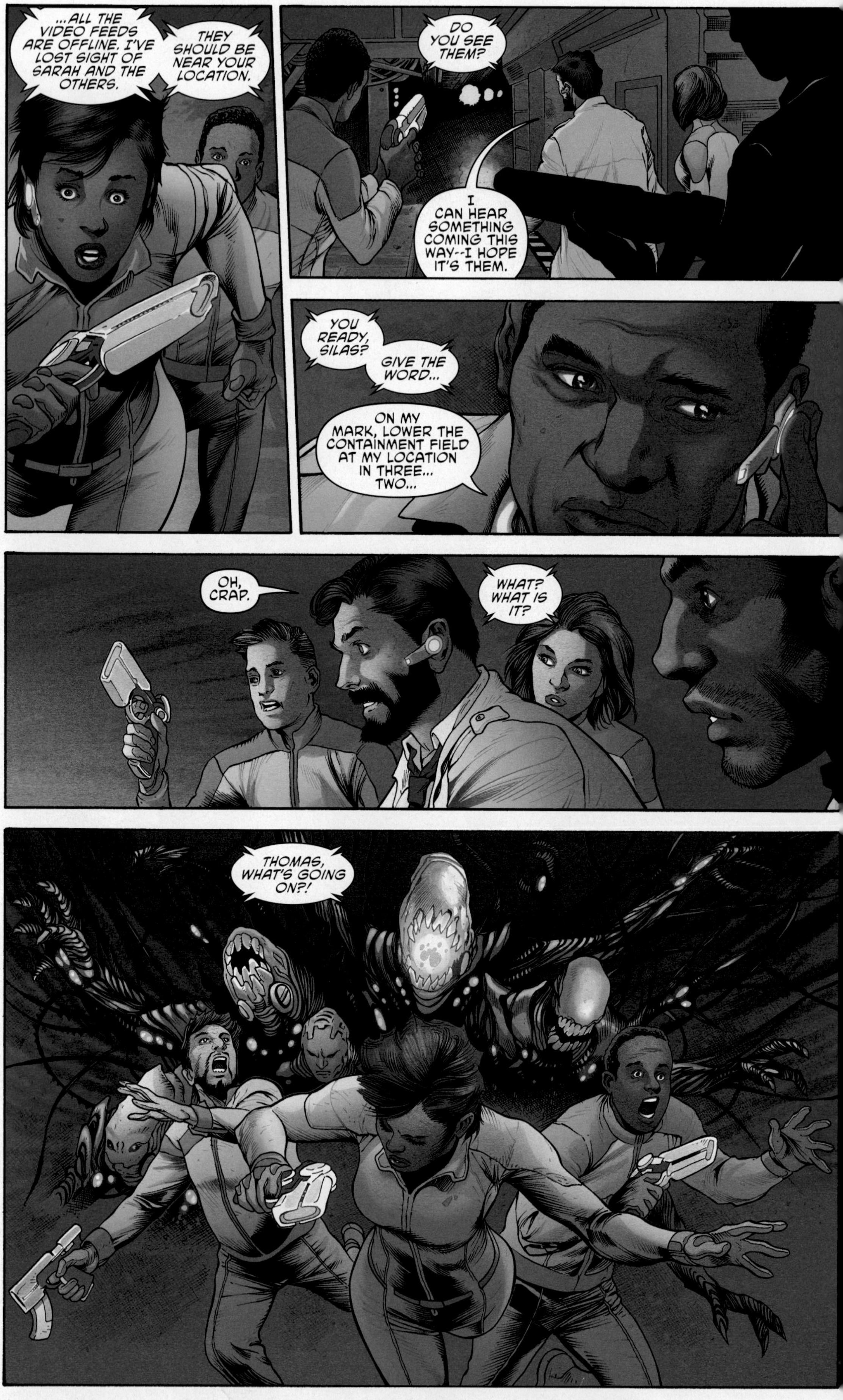
...ALL THE VIDEO FEEDS ARE OFFLINE. I'VE LOST SIGHT OF SARAH AND THE OTHERS.
THEY SHOULD BE NEAR YOUR LOCATION.
DO YOU SEE THEM?
I CAN HEAR SOMETHING COMING THIS WAY--I HOPE IT'S THEM.
YOU READY, SILAS?
GIVE THE WORD...
ON MY MARK, LOWER THE CONTAINMENT FIELD AT MY LOCATION IN THREE... TWO...
OH, CRAP.
WHAT? WHAT IS IT?
THOMAS, WHAT'S GOING ON?!

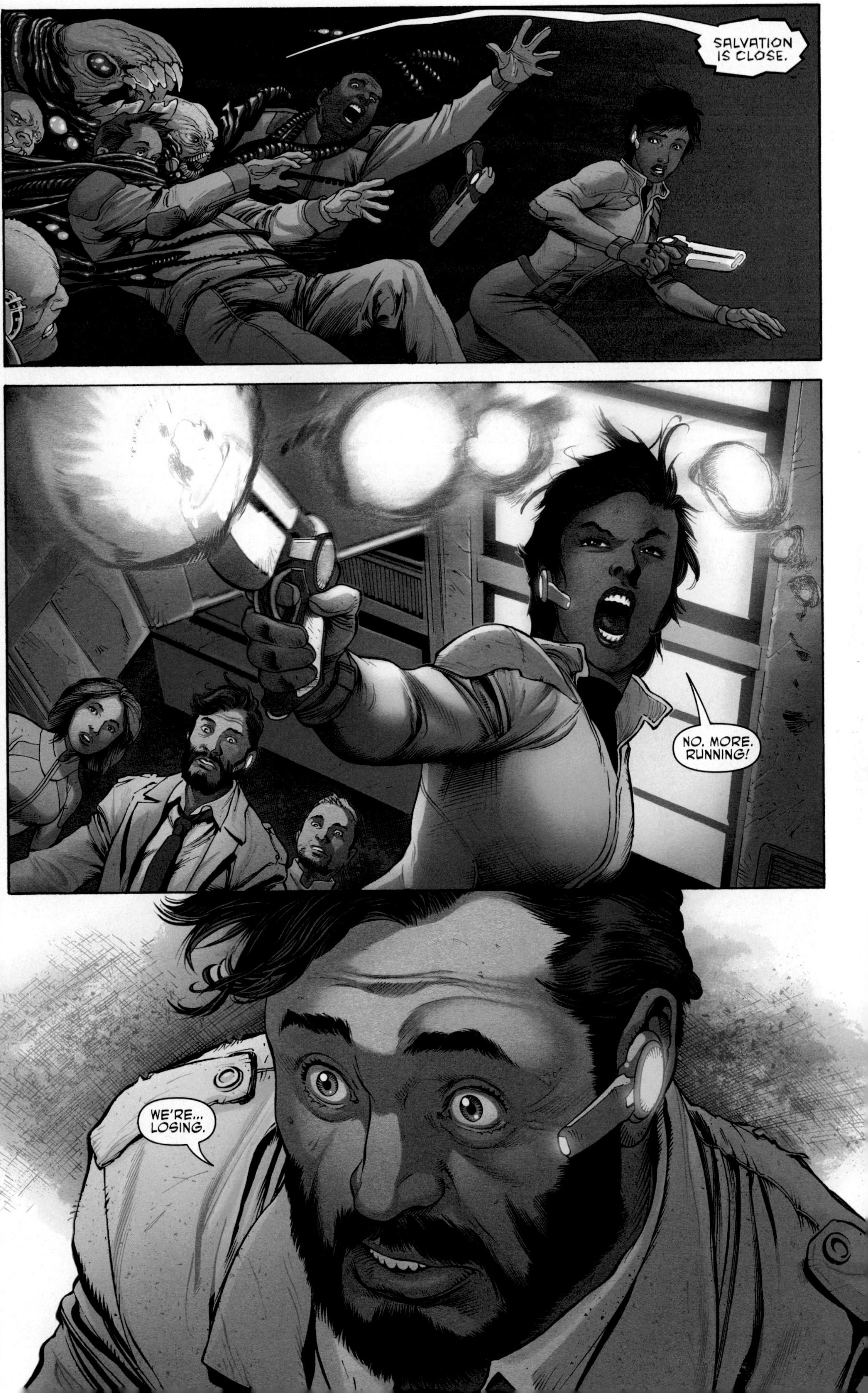
SALVATION IS CLOSE.
NO. MORE. RUNNING!
WE'RE... LOSING.

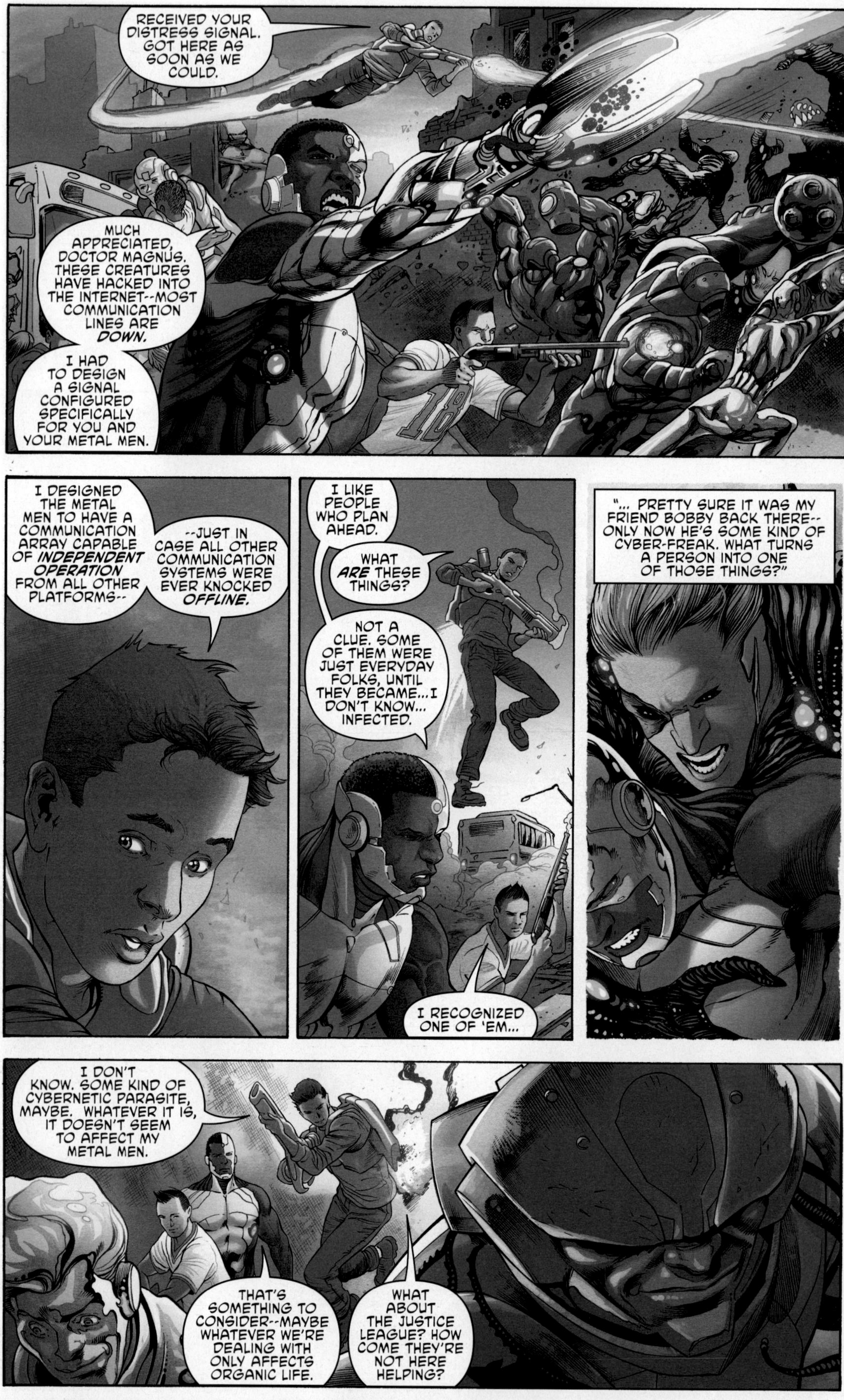
RECEIVED YOUR DISTRESS SIGNAL. GOT HERE AS SOON AS WE COULD.
MUCH APPRECIATED, DOCTOR MAGNUS. THESE CREATURES HAVE HACKED INTO THE INTERNET--MOST COMMUNICATION LINES ARE *DOWN.*
I HAD TO DESIGN A SIGNAL CONFIGURED SPECIFICALLY FOR YOU AND YOUR METAL MEN.
I DESIGNED THE METAL MEN TO HAVE A COMMUNICATION ARRAY CAPABLE OF *INDEPENDENT OPERATION* FROM ALL OTHER PLATFORMS--
--JUST IN CASE ALL OTHER COMMUNICATION SYSTEMS WERE EVER KNOCKED *OFFLINE.*
I LIKE PEOPLE WHO PLAN AHEAD.
WHAT *ARE* THESE THINGS?
NOT A CLUE. SOME OF THEM WERE JUST EVERYDAY FOLKS, UNTIL THEY BECAME...I DON'T KNOW... INFECTED.
I RECOGNIZED ONE OF 'EM...
"... PRETTY SURE IT WAS MY FRIEND BOBBY BACK THERE--ONLY NOW HE'S SOME KIND OF CYBER-FREAK. WHAT TURNS A PERSON INTO ONE OF THOSE THINGS?"
I DON'T KNOW. SOME KIND OF CYBERNETIC PARASITE, MAYBE. WHATEVER IT IS, IT DOESN'T SEEM TO AFFECT MY METAL MEN.
THAT'S SOMETHING TO CONSIDER--MAYBE WHATEVER WE'RE DEALING WITH ONLY AFFECTS ORGANIC LIFE.
WHAT ABOUT THE JUSTICE LEAGUE? HOW COME THEY'RE NOT HERE HELPING?

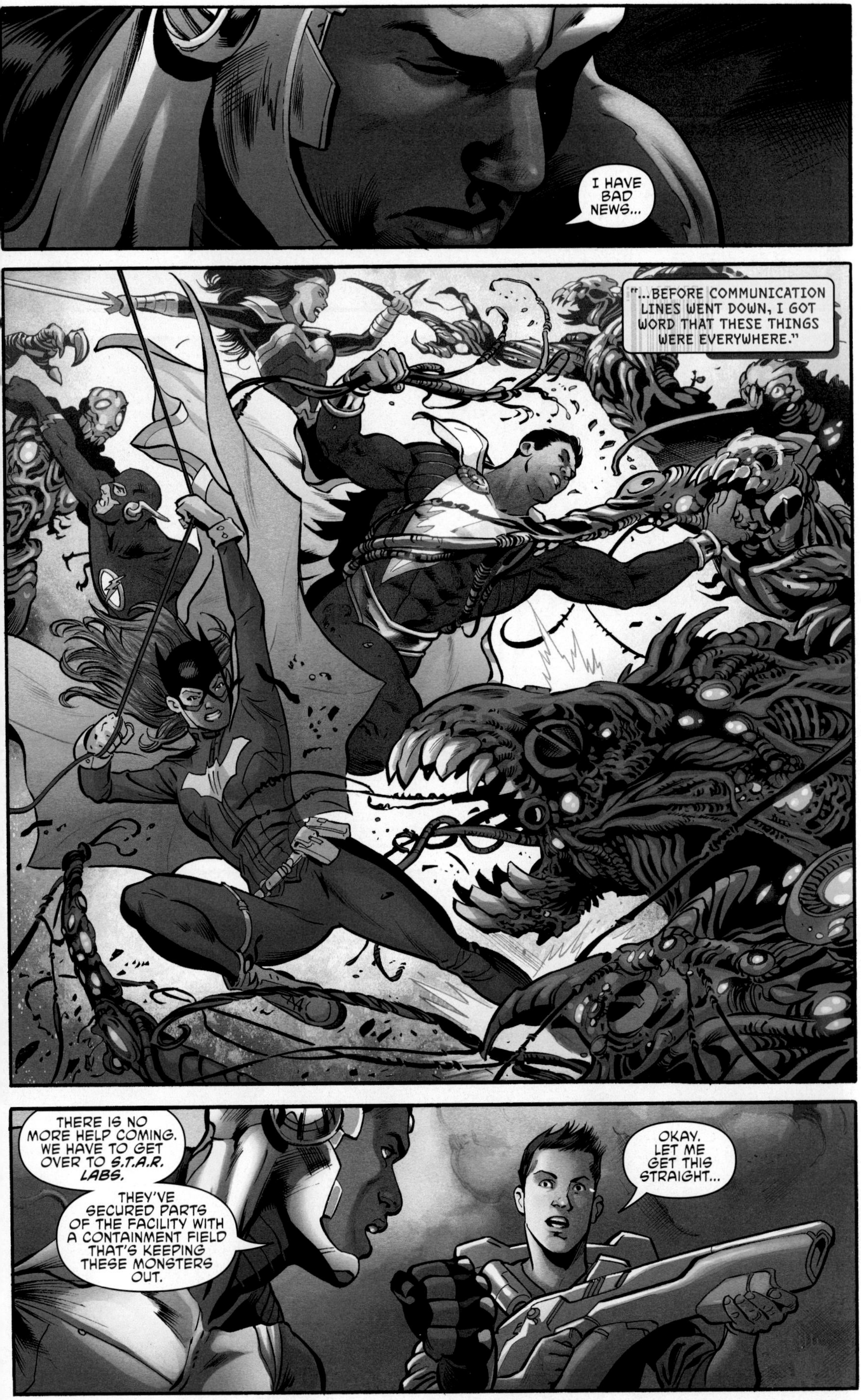
I HAVE BAD NEWS...
"...BEFORE COMMUNICATION LINES WENT DOWN, I GOT WORD THAT THESE THINGS WERE EVERYWHERE."
THERE IS NO MORE HELP COMING. WE HAVE TO GET OVER TO S.T.A.R. LABS.
THEY'VE SECURED PARTS OF THE FACILITY WITH A CONTAINMENT FIELD THAT'S KEEPING THESE MONSTERS OUT.
OKAY. LET ME GET THIS STRAIGHT...

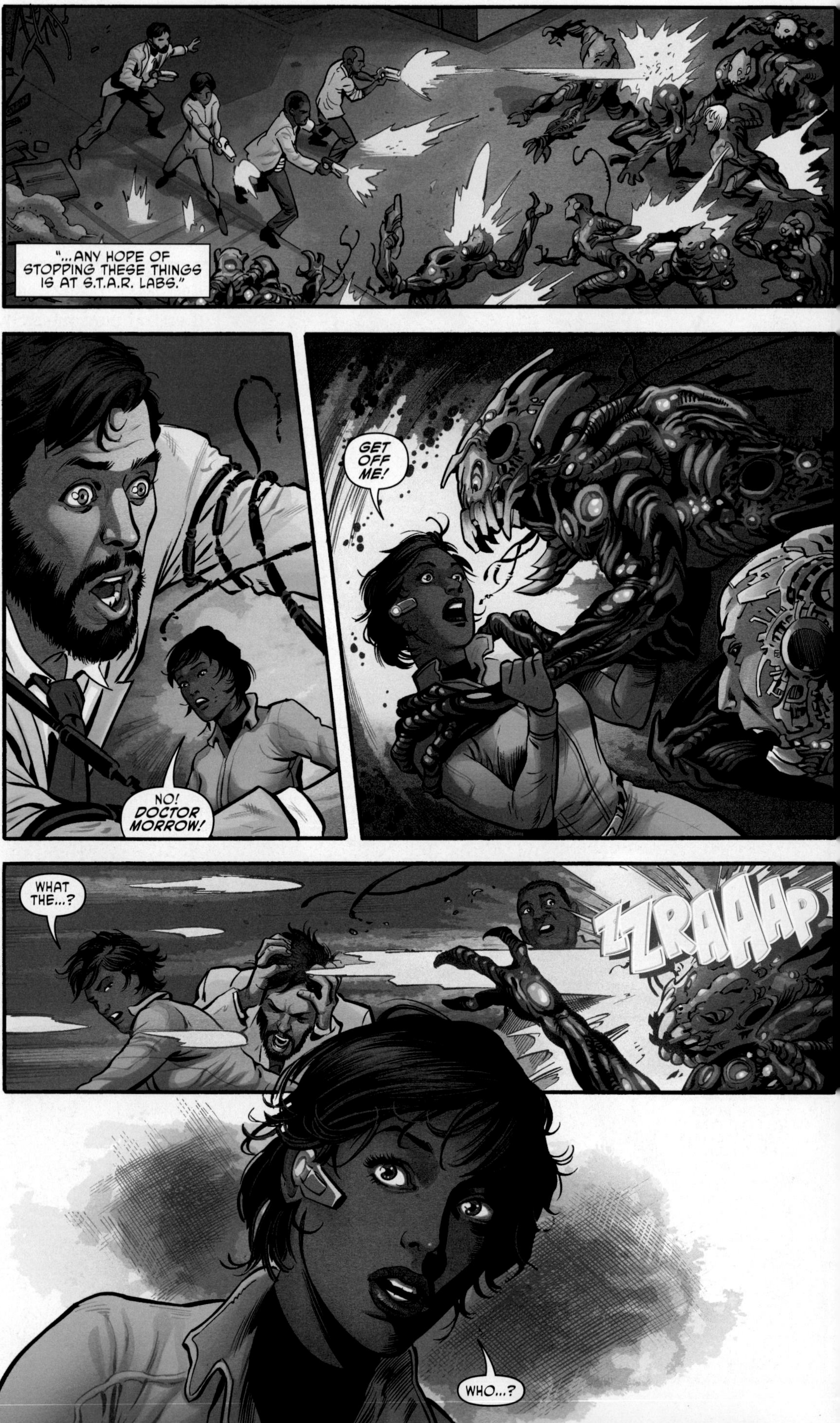
"...ANY HOPE OF STOPPING THESE THINGS IS AT S.T.A.R. LABS."
NO! DOCTOR MORROW!
GET OFF ME!
WHAT THE...?
ZZRAAAP
WHO...?

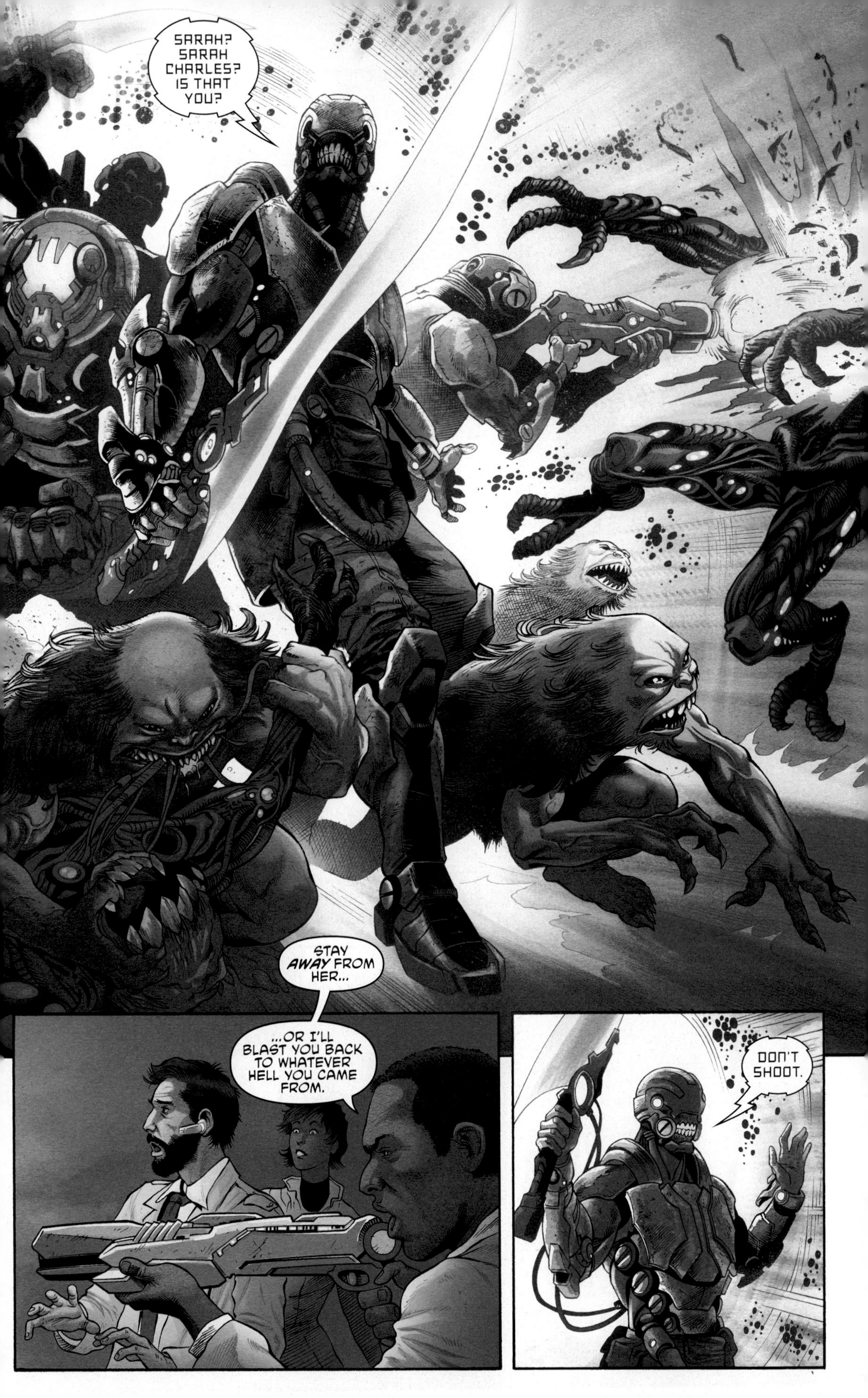
SARAH? SARAH CHARLES? IS THAT YOU?
STAY AWAY FROM HER...
...OR I'LL BLAST YOU BACK TO WHATEVER HELL YOU CAME FROM.
DON'T SHOOT.

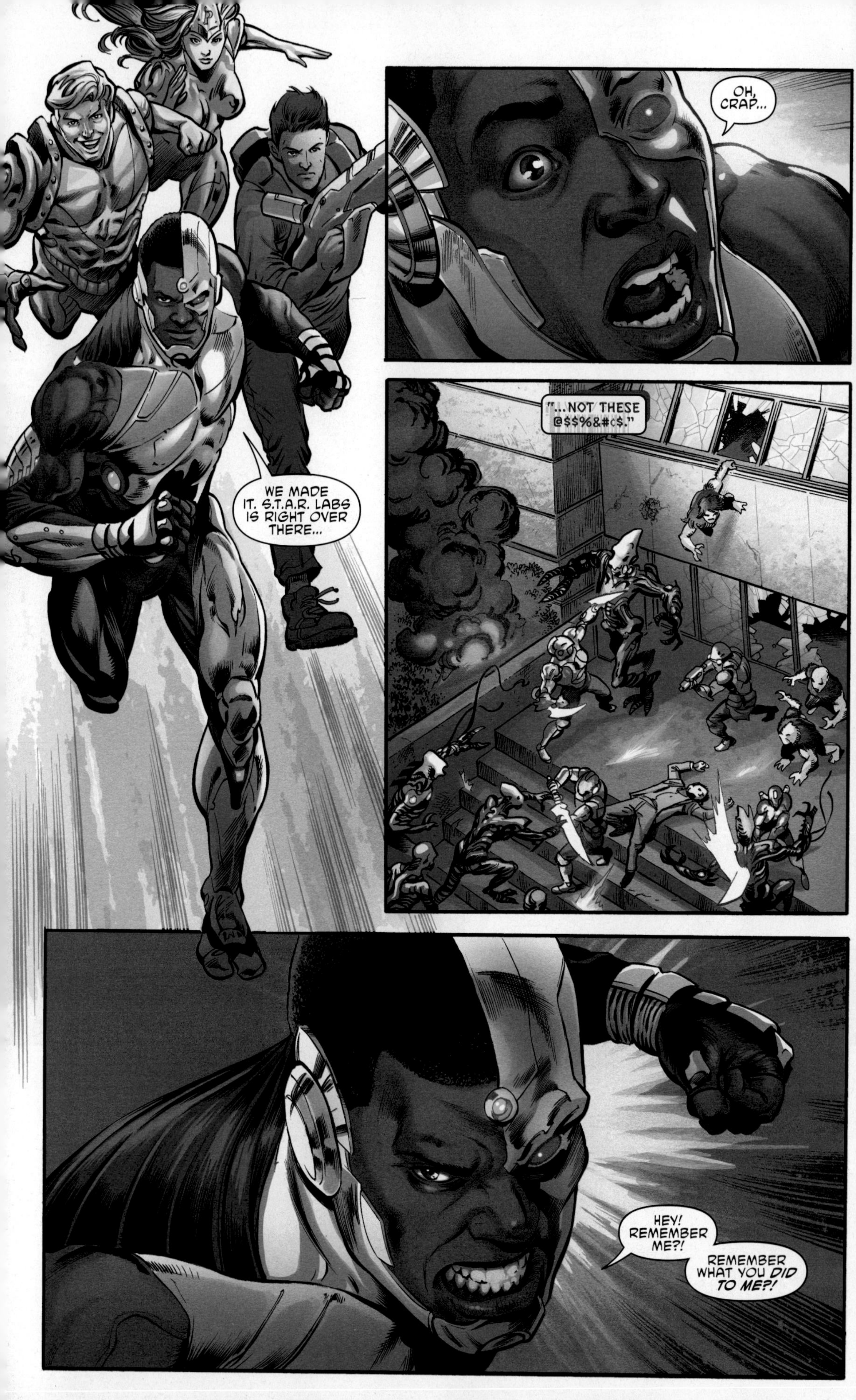
WE MADE IT. S.T.A.R. LABS IS RIGHT OVER THERE...
OH, CRAP...
"...NOT THESE @$$%&#¢$."
HEY! REMEMBER ME?!
REMEMBER WHAT YOU *DID TO ME?!*

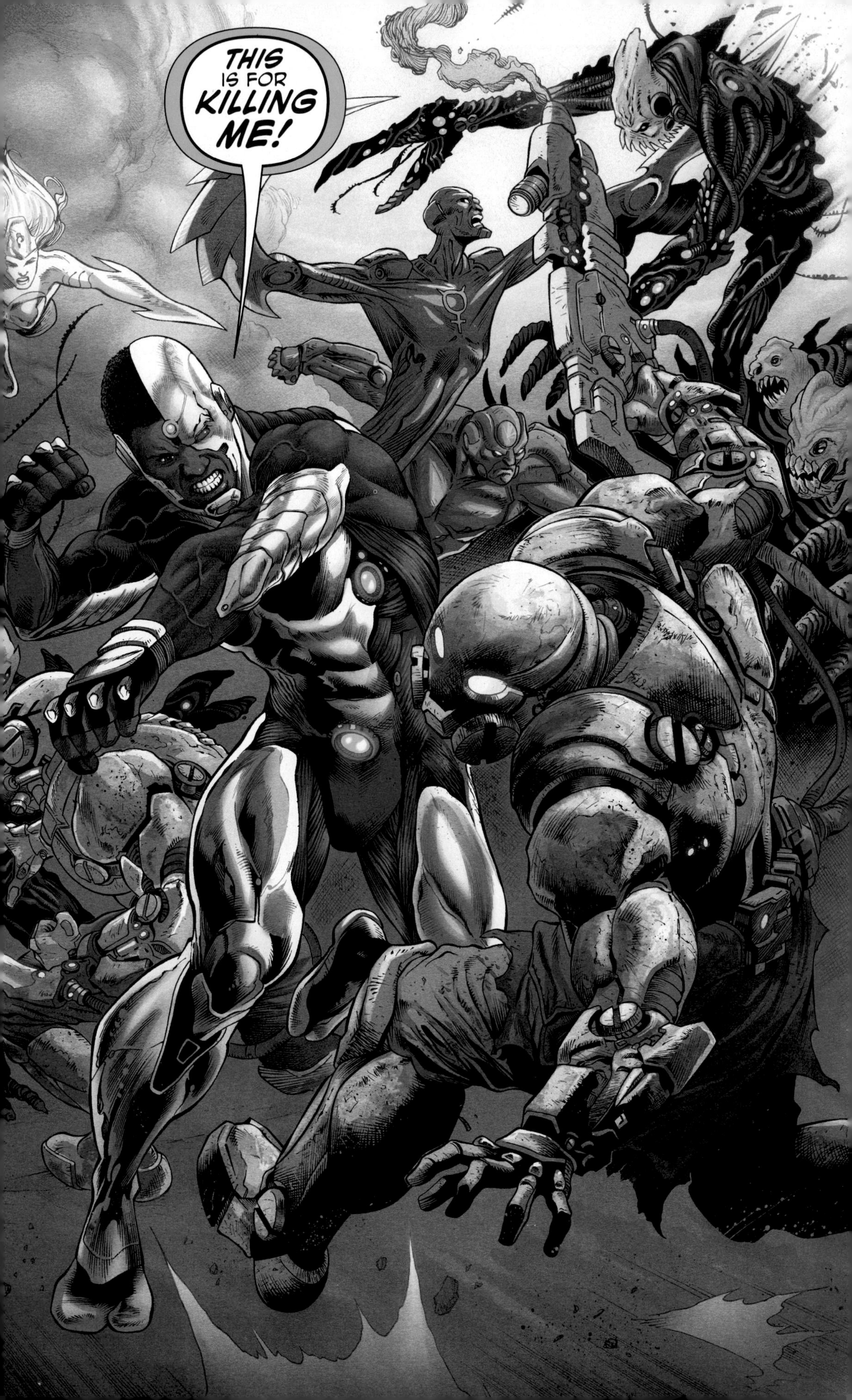
THIS IS FOR KILLING ME!

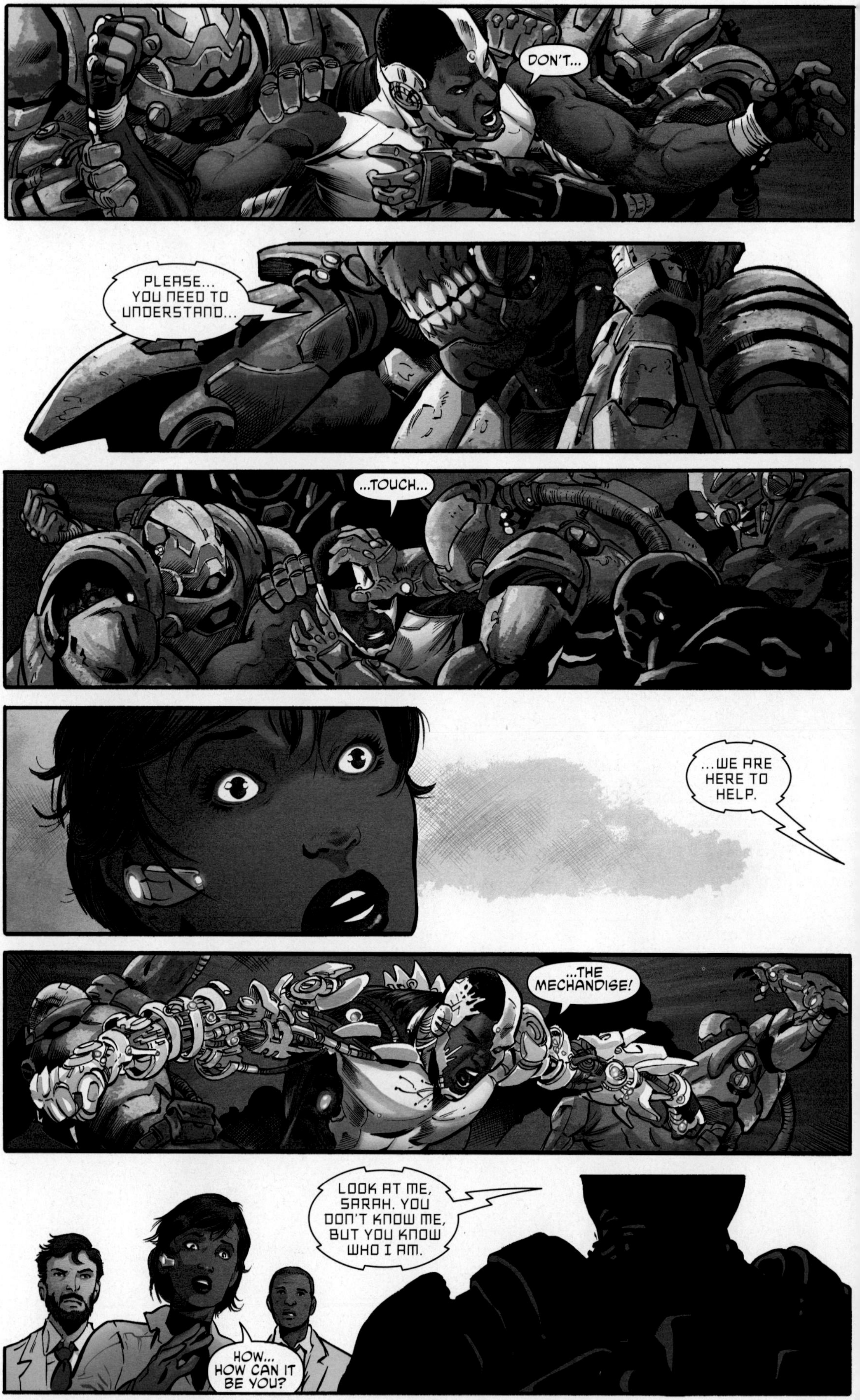
DON'T...
PLEASE... YOU NEED TO UNDERSTAND...
...TOUCH...
...WE ARE HERE TO HELP.
...THE MECHANDISE!
LOOK AT ME, SARAH. YOU DON'T KNOW ME, BUT YOU KNOW WHO I AM.
HOW... HOW CAN IT BE YOU?

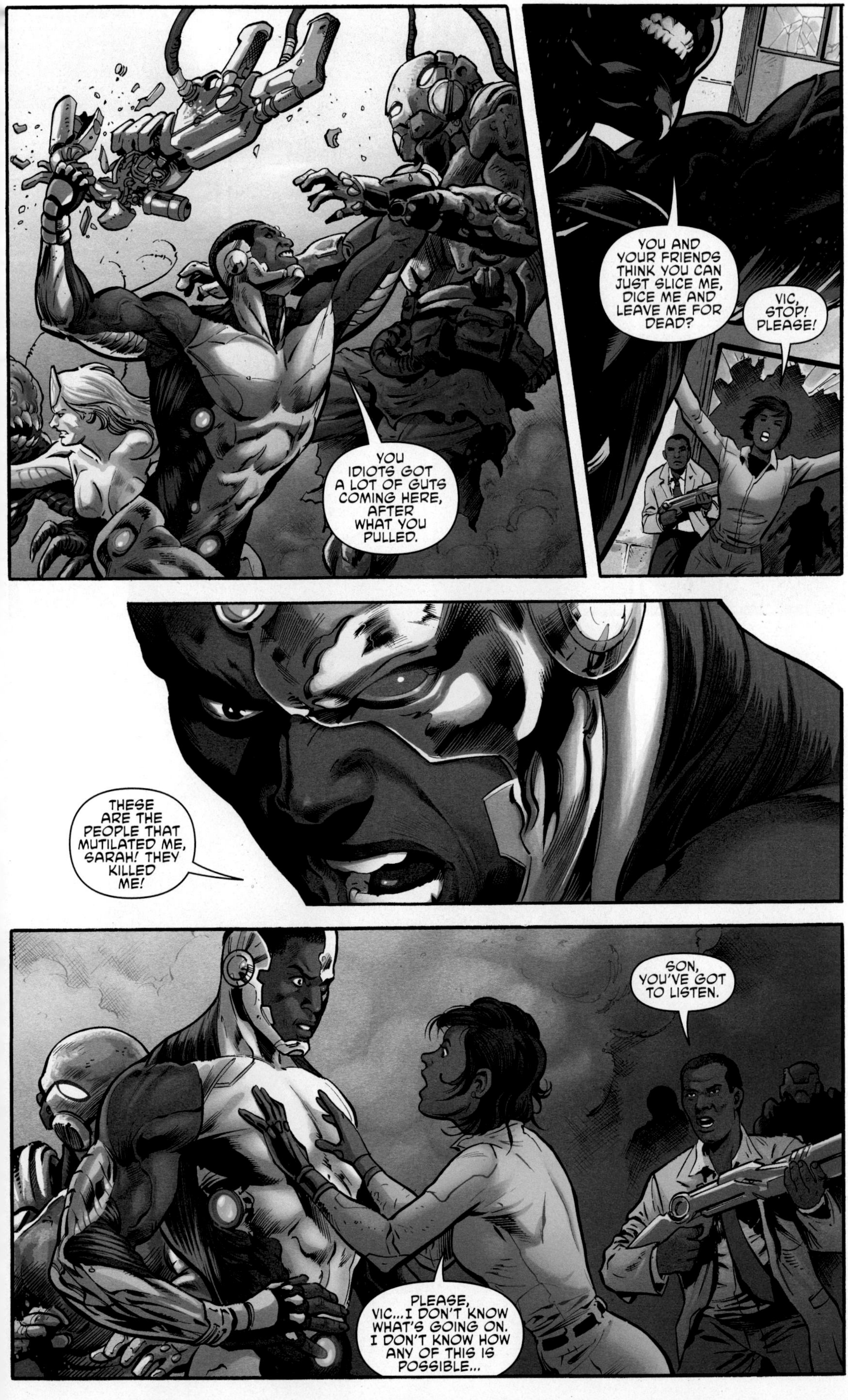
YOU IDIOTS GOT A LOT OF GUTS COMING HERE, AFTER WHAT YOU PULLED.
YOU AND YOUR FRIENDS THINK YOU CAN JUST SLICE ME, DICE ME AND LEAVE ME FOR DEAD?
VIC, STOP! PLEASE!
THESE ARE THE PEOPLE THAT MUTILATED ME, SARAH! THEY KILLED ME!
SON, YOU'VE GOT TO LISTEN.
PLEASE, VIC...I DON'T KNOW WHAT'S GOING ON. I DON'T KNOW HOW ANY OF THIS IS POSSIBLE...

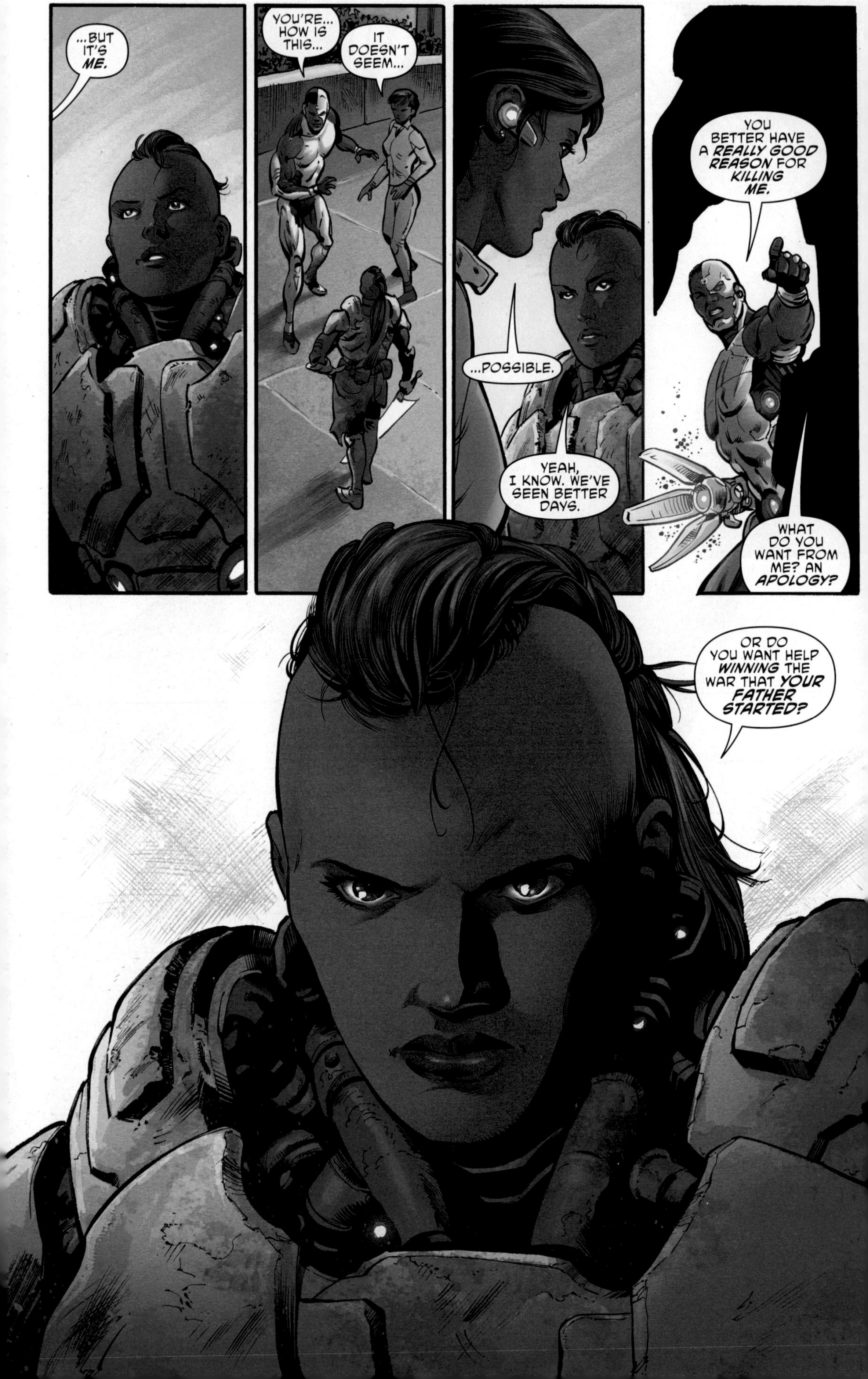
...BUT IT'S ME.
YOU'RE... HOW IS THIS...
IT DOESN'T SEEM...
...POSSIBLE.
YEAH, I KNOW. WE'VE SEEN BETTER DAYS.
YOU BETTER HAVE A REALLY GOOD REASON FOR KILLING ME.
WHAT DO YOU WANT FROM ME? AN APOLOGY?
OR DO YOU WANT HELP WINNING THE WAR THAT YOUR FATHER STARTED?

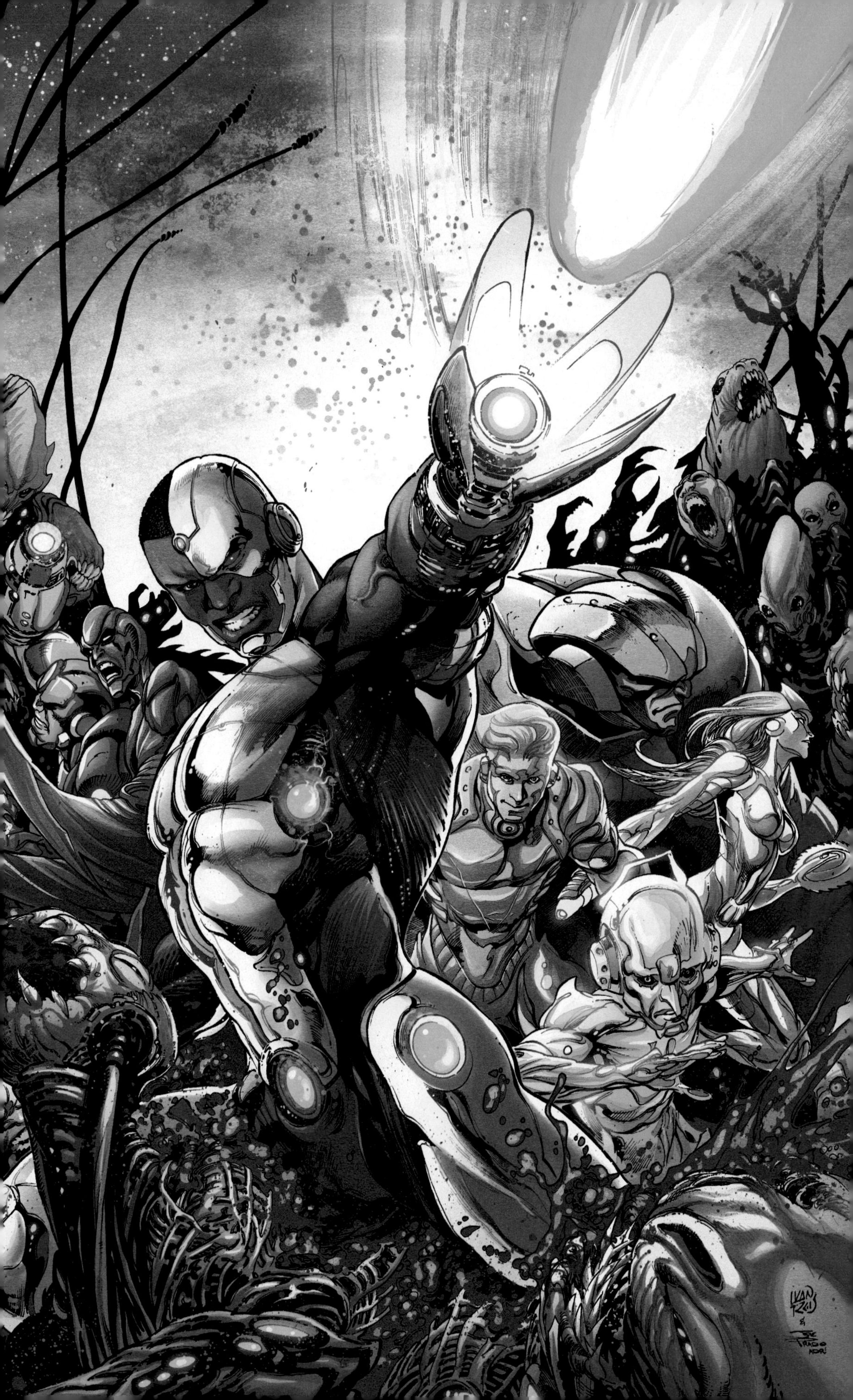

**SHATTERED REFLECTIONS**
**IVAN REIS, FELIPE WATANABE** pencillers **SCOTT HANNA, WAYNE FAUCHER** inkers **ADRIANO LUCAS, PETE PANTAZIS** colorists **ROB LEIGH** letterer
**IVAN REIS, JOE PRADO** and **ADRIANO LUCAS** cover art

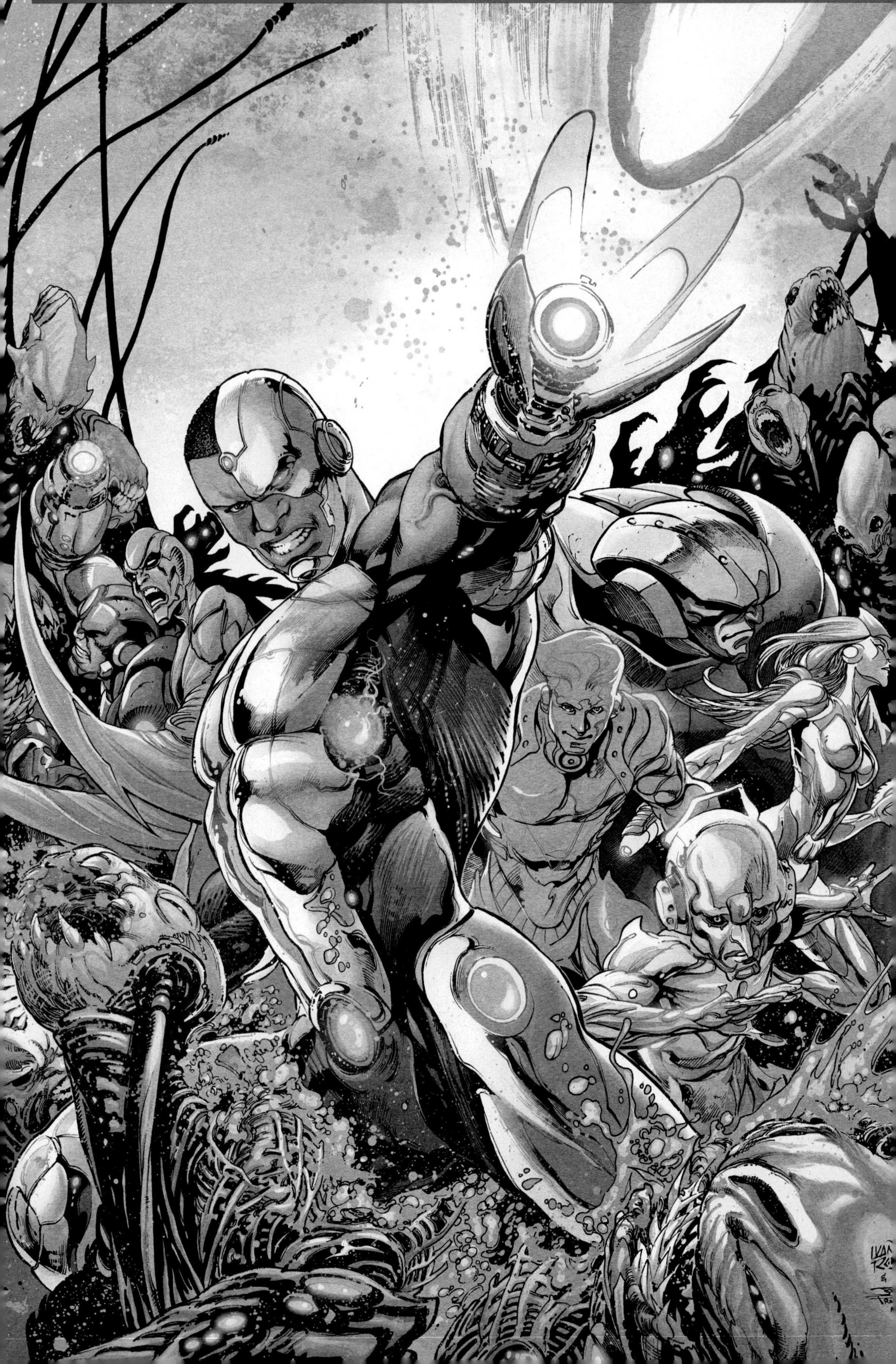

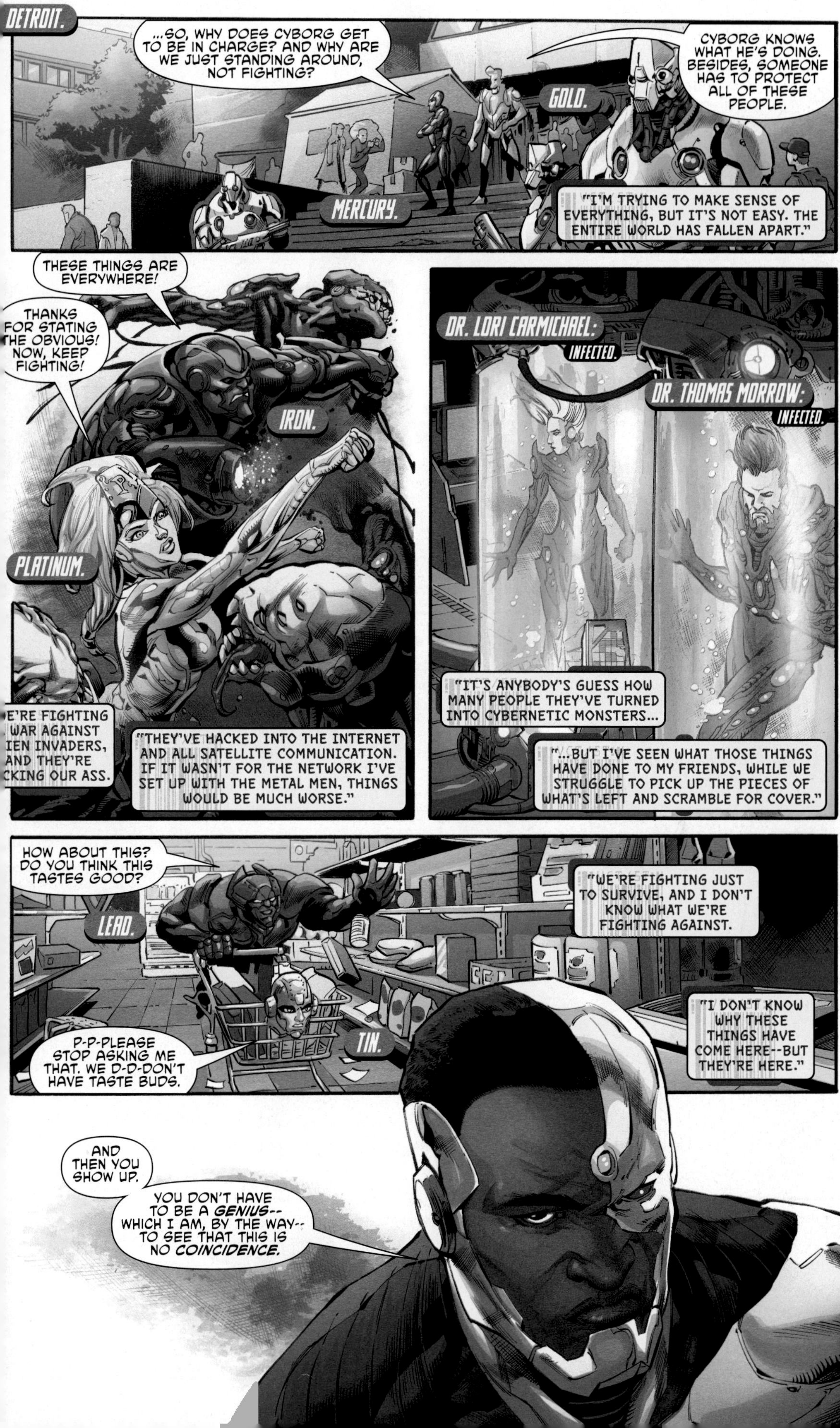
DETROIT.
...SO, WHY DOES CYBORG GET TO BE IN CHARGE? AND WHY ARE WE JUST STANDING AROUND, NOT FIGHTING?
GOLD.
CYBORG KNOWS WHAT HE'S DOING. BESIDES, SOMEONE HAS TO PROTECT ALL OF THESE PEOPLE.
MERCURY.
"I'M TRYING TO MAKE SENSE OF EVERYTHING, BUT IT'S NOT EASY. THE ENTIRE WORLD HAS FALLEN APART."
THESE THINGS ARE EVERYWHERE!
THANKS FOR STATING THE OBVIOUS! NOW, KEEP FIGHTING!
IRON.
PLATINUM.
E'RE FIGHTING WAR AGAINST IEN INVADERS, AND THEY'RE CKING OUR ASS.
"THEY'VE HACKED INTO THE INTERNET AND ALL SATELLITE COMMUNICATION. IF IT WASN'T FOR THE NETWORK I'VE SET UP WITH THE METAL MEN, THINGS WOULD BE MUCH WORSE."
DR. LORI CARMICHAEL:
INFECTED.
DR. THOMAS MORROW:
INFECTED.
"IT'S ANYBODY'S GUESS HOW MANY PEOPLE THEY'VE TURNED INTO CYBERNETIC MONSTERS...
"...BUT I'VE SEEN WHAT THOSE THINGS HAVE DONE TO MY FRIENDS, WHILE WE STRUGGLE TO PICK UP THE PIECES OF WHAT'S LEFT AND SCRAMBLE FOR COVER."
HOW ABOUT THIS? DO YOU THINK THIS TASTES GOOD?
LEAD.
"WE'RE FIGHTING JUST TO SURVIVE, AND I DON'T KNOW WHAT WE'RE FIGHTING AGAINST.
P-P-PLEASE STOP ASKING ME THAT. WE D-D-DON'T HAVE TASTE BUDS.
TIN.
"I DON'T KNOW WHY THESE THINGS HAVE COME HERE--BUT THEY'RE HERE."
AND THEN YOU SHOW UP.
YOU DON'T HAVE TO BE A GENIUS-- WHICH I AM, BY THE WAY-- TO SEE THAT THIS IS NO COINCIDENCE.

NOW, EXCUSE ME FOR NOT BEING *EXCITED.* YOU MAY LOOK LIKE SOMEONE I KNOW AND CARE ABOUT, BUT YOU ARE *NOT* HER.

LAST TIME I SAW YOU, YOU ACCUSED ME OF BEING A THIEF. YOU *ATTACKED* ME.

THEN YOU KILLED ME.

BUT AS YOU CAN SEE, MISS *ALTERNATE REALITY* SARAH CHARLES, I'M NOT DEAD ANYMORE.

WHICH MEANS YOU MIGHT WANT TO SCALE BACK ON THE BADASS ATTITUDE--BECAUSE FOR AT LEAST ONE OF US, DEATH IS JUST A TEMPORARY SETBACK.

IT'S TIME FOR YOU TO START ANSWERING QUESTIONS.

AND HERE I THOUGHT THE *VIC STONE* FROM WHERE I COME FROM WAS BAD--AT LEAST THAT ONE WAS NOTHING BUT FLESH AND BONE. AND EGO.

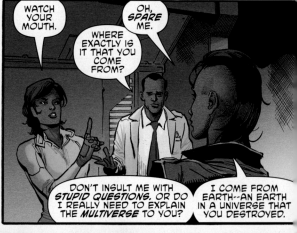

WATCH YOUR MOUTH.

OH, *SPARE* ME.

WHERE EXACTLY IS IT THAT YOU COME FROM?

DON'T INSULT ME WITH *STUPID QUESTIONS,* OR DO I REALLY NEED TO EXPLAIN THE *MULTIVERSE* TO YOU?

I COME FROM EARTH--AN EARTH IN A UNIVERSE THAT YOU DESTROYED.

ME?

YES. YOU, *DOCTOR SILAS STONE,* THE MAN WHO TRIED TO CHEAT DEATH, AND ENDED UP *DESTROYING* EVERYTHING.

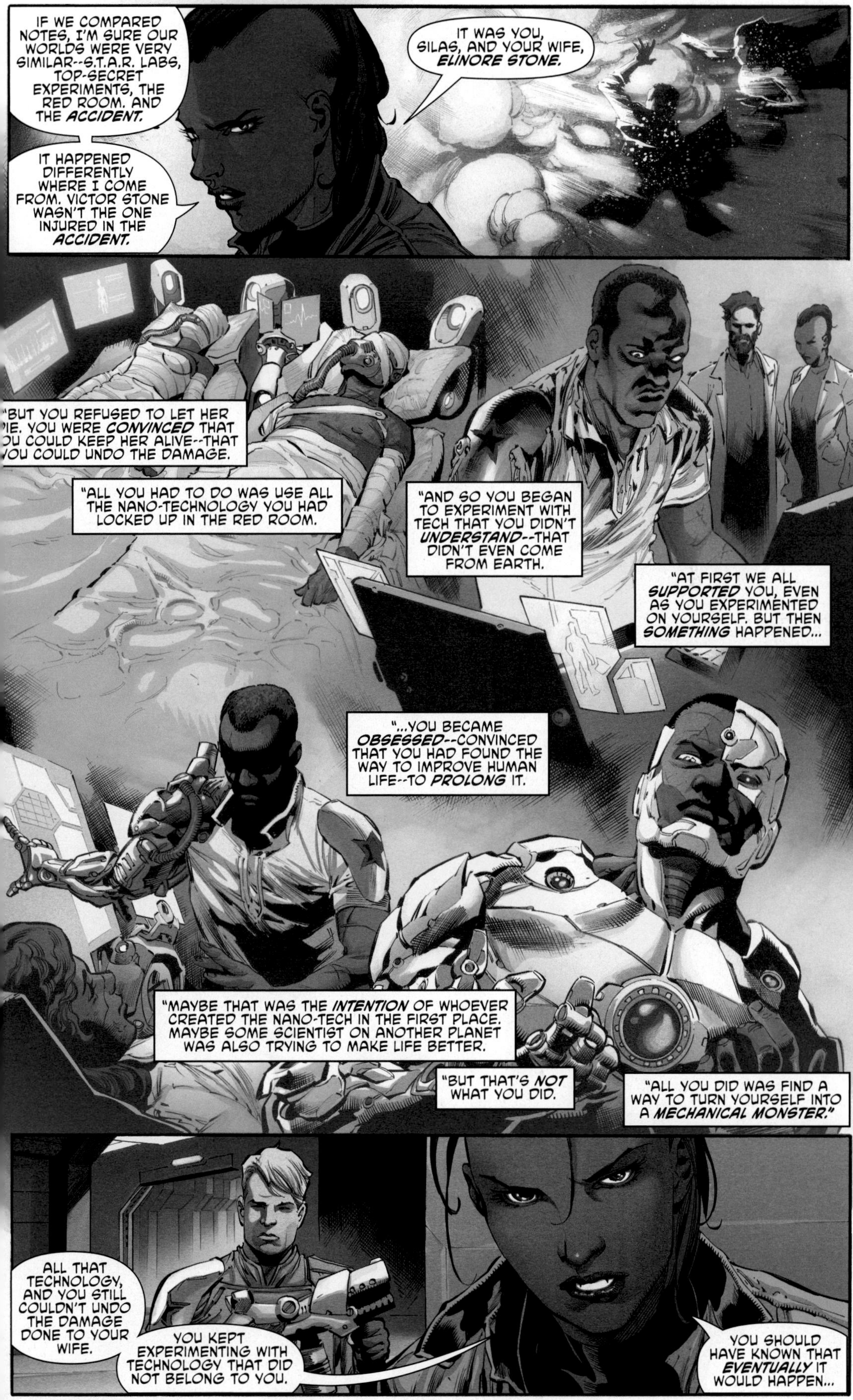
IF WE COMPARED NOTES, I'M SURE OUR WORLDS WERE VERY SIMILAR--S.T.A.R. LABS, TOP-SECRET EXPERIMENTS, THE RED ROOM. AND THE ACCIDENT.
IT HAPPENED DIFFERENTLY WHERE I COME FROM. VICTOR STONE WASN'T THE ONE INJURED IN THE ACCIDENT.
IT WAS YOU, SILAS, AND YOUR WIFE, ELINORE STONE.
"BUT YOU REFUSED TO LET HER DIE. YOU WERE CONVINCED THAT YOU COULD KEEP HER ALIVE--THAT YOU COULD UNDO THE DAMAGE.
"ALL YOU HAD TO DO WAS USE ALL THE NANO-TECHNOLOGY YOU HAD LOCKED UP IN THE RED ROOM.
"AND SO YOU BEGAN TO EXPERIMENT WITH TECH THAT YOU DIDN'T UNDERSTAND--THAT DIDN'T EVEN COME FROM EARTH.
"AT FIRST WE ALL SUPPORTED YOU, EVEN AS YOU EXPERIMENTED ON YOURSELF. BUT THEN SOMETHING HAPPENED...
"...YOU BECAME OBSESSED--CONVINCED THAT YOU HAD FOUND THE WAY TO IMPROVE HUMAN LIFE--TO PROLONG IT.
"MAYBE THAT WAS THE INTENTION OF WHOEVER CREATED THE NANO-TECH IN THE FIRST PLACE. MAYBE SOME SCIENTIST ON ANOTHER PLANET WAS ALSO TRYING TO MAKE LIFE BETTER.
"BUT THAT'S NOT WHAT YOU DID.
"ALL YOU DID WAS FIND A WAY TO TURN YOURSELF INTO A MECHANICAL MONSTER."
ALL THAT TECHNOLOGY, AND YOU STILL COULDN'T UNDO THE DAMAGE DONE TO YOUR WIFE.
YOU KEPT EXPERIMENTING WITH TECHNOLOGY THAT DID NOT BELONG TO YOU.
YOU SHOULD HAVE KNOWN THAT EVENTUALLY IT WOULD HAPPEN...

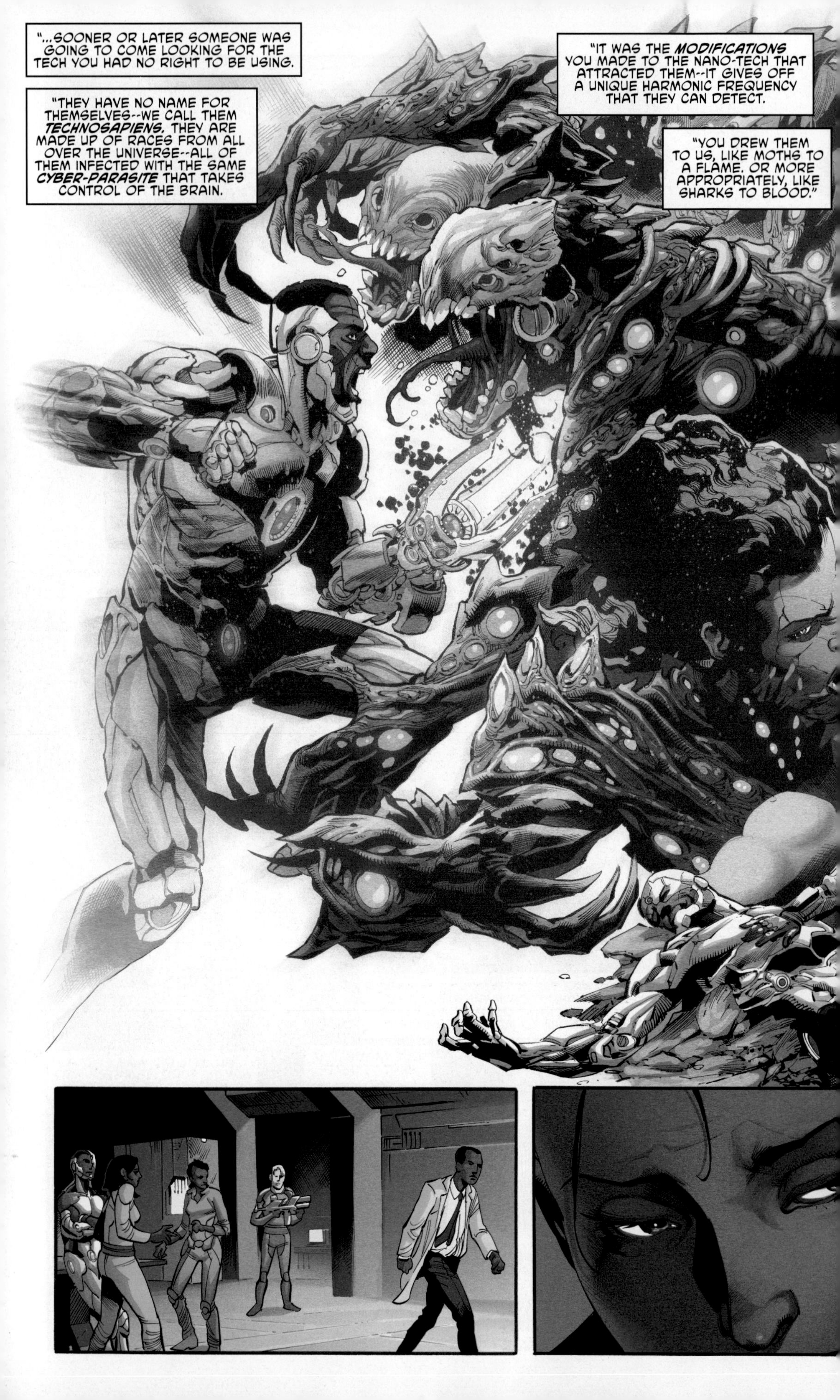
"...SOONER OR LATER SOMEONE WAS GOING TO COME LOOKING FOR THE TECH YOU HAD NO RIGHT TO BE USING.
"THEY HAVE NO NAME FOR THEMSELVES--WE CALL THEM *TECHNOSAPIENS.* THEY ARE MADE UP OF RACES FROM ALL OVER THE UNIVERSE--ALL OF THEM INFECTED WITH THE SAME *CYBER-PARASITE* THAT TAKES CONTROL OF THE BRAIN.
"IT WAS THE *MODIFICATIONS* YOU MADE TO THE NANO-TECH THAT ATTRACTED THEM--IT GIVES OFF A UNIQUE HARMONIC FREQUENCY THAT THEY CAN DETECT.
"YOU DREW THEM TO US, LIKE MOTHS TO A FLAME. OR MORE APPROPRIATELY, LIKE SHARKS TO BLOOD."

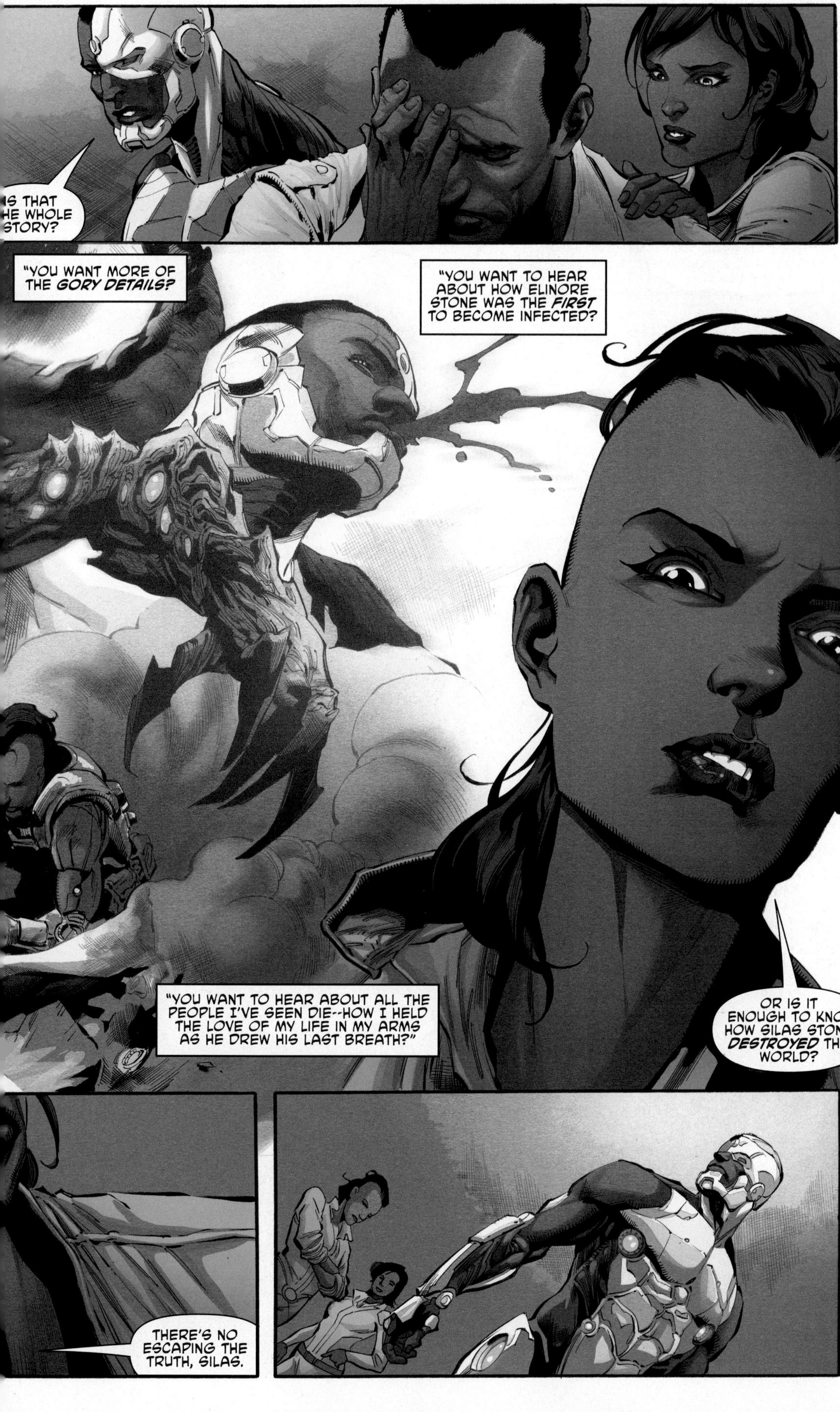
IS THAT THE WHOLE STORY?
"YOU WANT MORE OF THE GORY DETAILS?
"YOU WANT TO HEAR ABOUT HOW ELINORE STONE WAS THE FIRST TO BECOME INFECTED?
"YOU WANT TO HEAR ABOUT ALL THE PEOPLE I'VE SEEN DIE--HOW I HELD THE LOVE OF MY LIFE IN MY ARMS AS HE DREW HIS LAST BREATH?"
OR IS IT ENOUGH TO KNOW HOW SILAS STONE DESTROYED THE WORLD?
THERE'S NO ESCAPING THE TRUTH, SILAS.

I CAN HEAR HIS SONG.

ᔕᓯᐧ ᐃᐧᔑ ᑎᔐᑕᑌᐧᑐᑕ ᐧᒐᐅᐧ ᒪᐁᐧ

YES, THE CHOSEN ONE IS CLOSE...

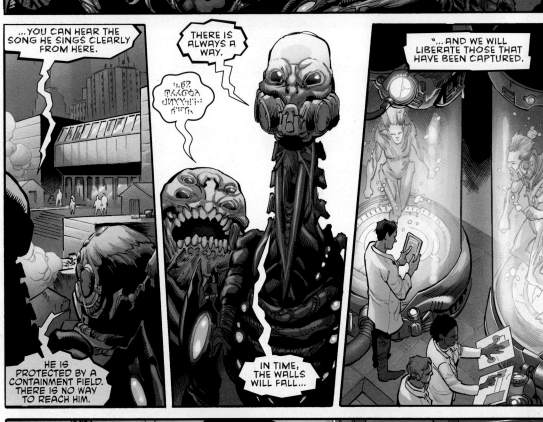

...YOU CAN HEAR THE SONG HE SINGS CLEARLY FROM HERE.

HE IS PROTECTED BY A CONTAINMENT FIELD. THERE IS NO WAY TO REACH HIM.

THERE IS ALWAYS A WAY.

ᑌᒐ ᐅᐧ ᑕᑉᑕᒐᐃ ᒐᐃᐧᐧᒋᐧᐧᓂᐧᐃ ᐃᓐᒋᐧᐧ

IN TIME, THE WALLS WILL FALL...

"...AND WE WILL LIBERATE THOSE THAT HAVE BEEN CAPTURED.

"WE WILL DESTROY THE ENEMIES THAT FOLLOWED US HERE..."

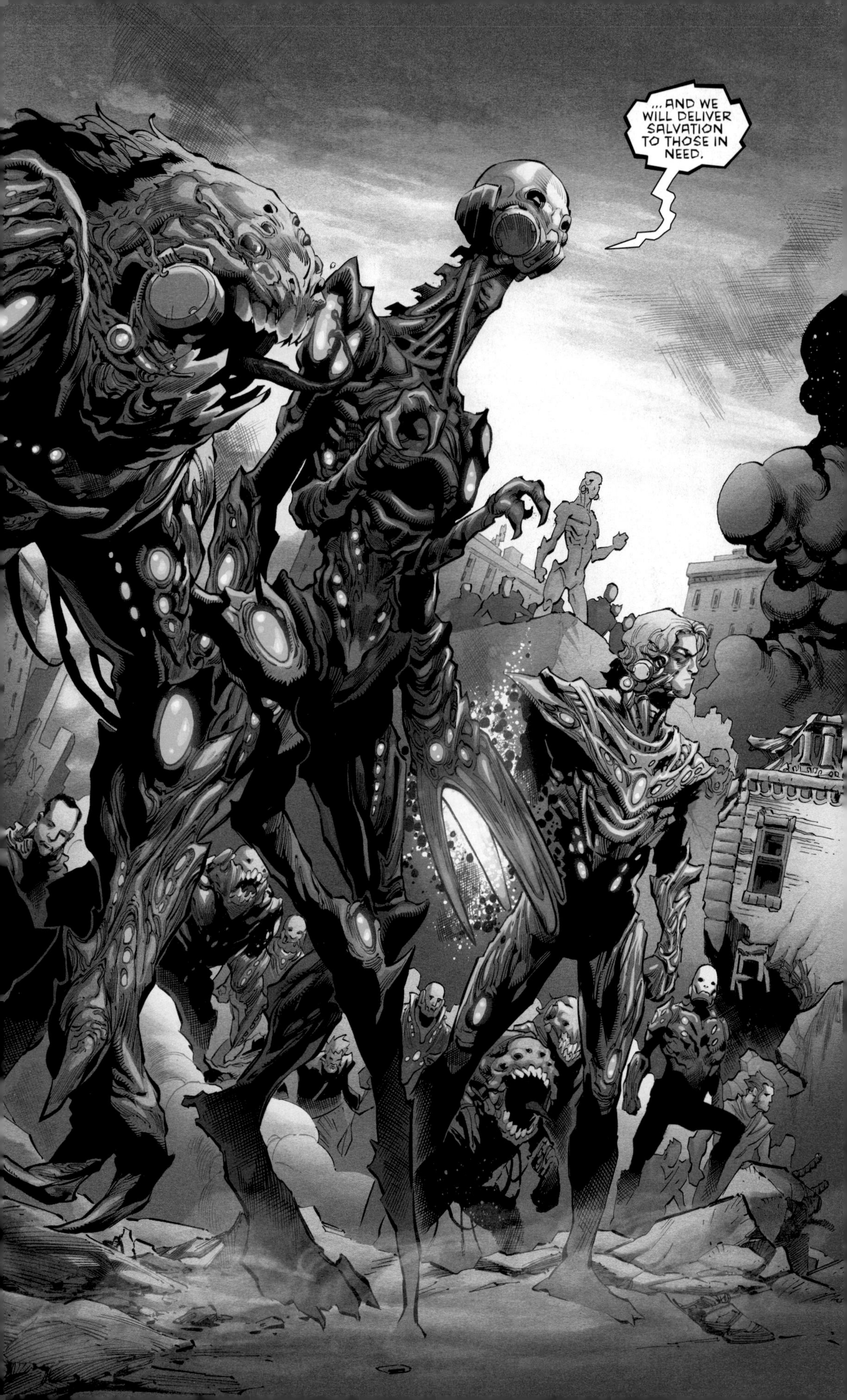
...AND WE WILL DELIVER SALVATION TO THOSE IN NEED.

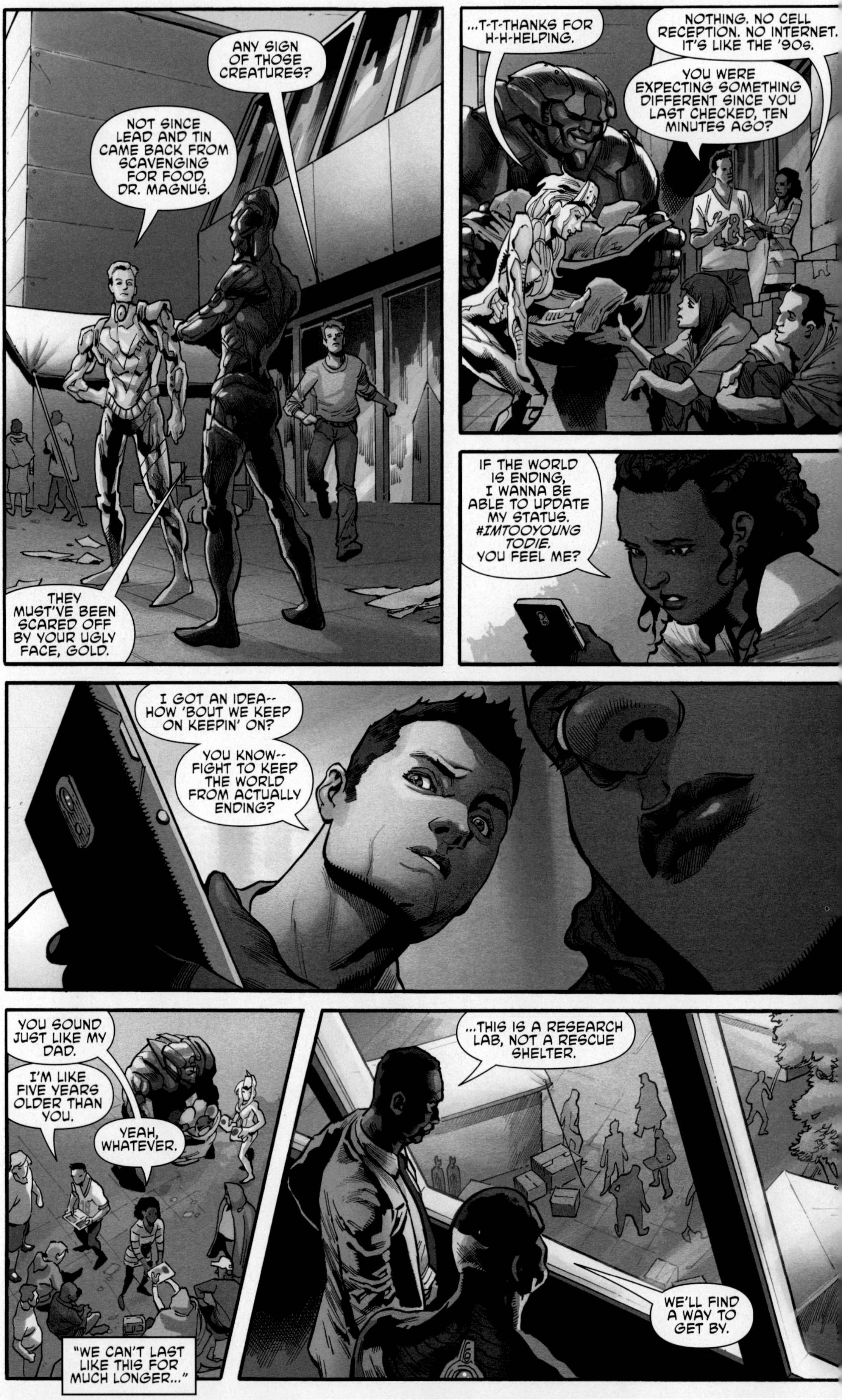
ANY SIGN OF THOSE CREATURES?
NOT SINCE LEAD AND TIN CAME BACK FROM SCAVENGING FOR FOOD, DR. MAGNUS.
THEY MUST'VE BEEN SCARED OFF BY YOUR UGLY FACE, GOLD.
...T-T-THANKS FOR H-H-HELPING.
NOTHING. NO CELL RECEPTION. NO INTERNET. IT'S LIKE THE '90s.
YOU WERE EXPECTING SOMETHING DIFFERENT SINCE YOU LAST CHECKED, TEN MINUTES AGO?
IF THE WORLD IS ENDING, I WANNA BE ABLE TO UPDATE MY STATUS. #IMTOOYOUNGTODIE. YOU FEEL ME?
I GOT AN IDEA-- HOW 'BOUT WE KEEP ON KEEPIN' ON?
YOU KNOW-- FIGHT TO KEEP THE WORLD FROM ACTUALLY ENDING?
YOU SOUND JUST LIKE MY DAD.
I'M LIKE FIVE YEARS OLDER THAN YOU.
YEAH, WHATEVER.
"WE CAN'T LAST LIKE THIS FOR MUCH LONGER..."
...THIS IS A RESEARCH LAB, NOT A RESCUE SHELTER.
WE'LL FIND A WAY TO GET BY.

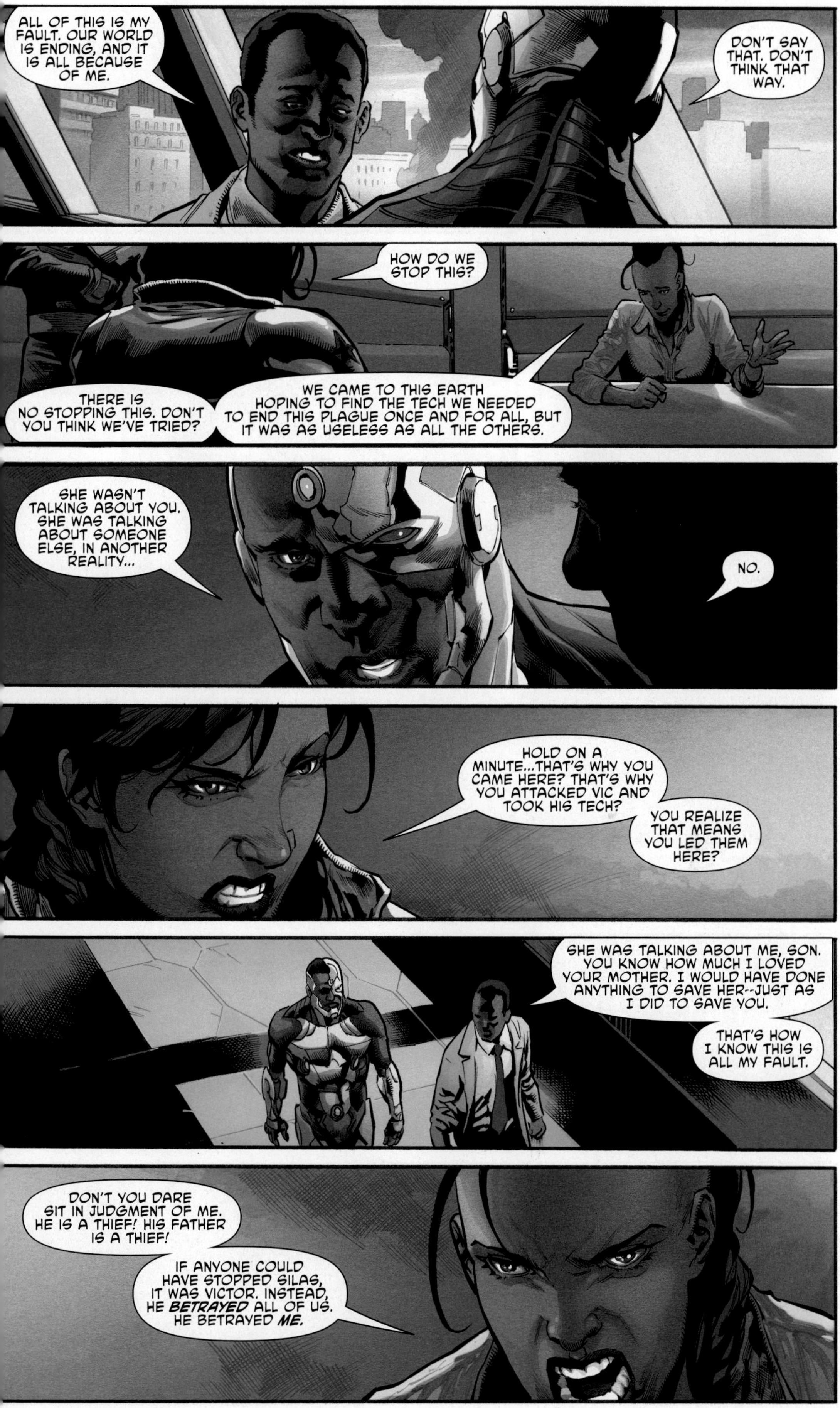
ALL OF THIS IS MY FAULT. OUR WORLD IS ENDING, AND IT IS ALL BECAUSE OF ME.
DON'T SAY THAT. DON'T THINK THAT WAY.
HOW DO WE STOP THIS?
THERE IS NO STOPPING THIS. DON'T YOU THINK WE'VE TRIED?
WE CAME TO THIS EARTH HOPING TO FIND THE TECH WE NEEDED TO END THIS PLAGUE ONCE AND FOR ALL, BUT IT WAS AS USELESS AS ALL THE OTHERS.
SHE WASN'T TALKING ABOUT YOU. SHE WAS TALKING ABOUT SOMEONE ELSE, IN ANOTHER REALITY...
NO.
HOLD ON A MINUTE...THAT'S WHY YOU CAME HERE? THAT'S WHY YOU ATTACKED VIC AND TOOK HIS TECH?
YOU REALIZE THAT MEANS YOU LED THEM HERE?
SHE WAS TALKING ABOUT ME, SON. YOU KNOW HOW MUCH I LOVED YOUR MOTHER. I WOULD HAVE DONE ANYTHING TO SAVE HER--JUST AS I DID TO SAVE YOU.
THAT'S HOW I KNOW THIS IS ALL MY FAULT.
DON'T YOU DARE SIT IN JUDGMENT OF ME. HE IS A THIEF! HIS FATHER IS A THIEF!
IF ANYONE COULD HAVE STOPPED SILAS, IT WAS VICTOR. INSTEAD, HE ***BETRAYED*** ALL OF US. HE BETRAYED ***ME.***

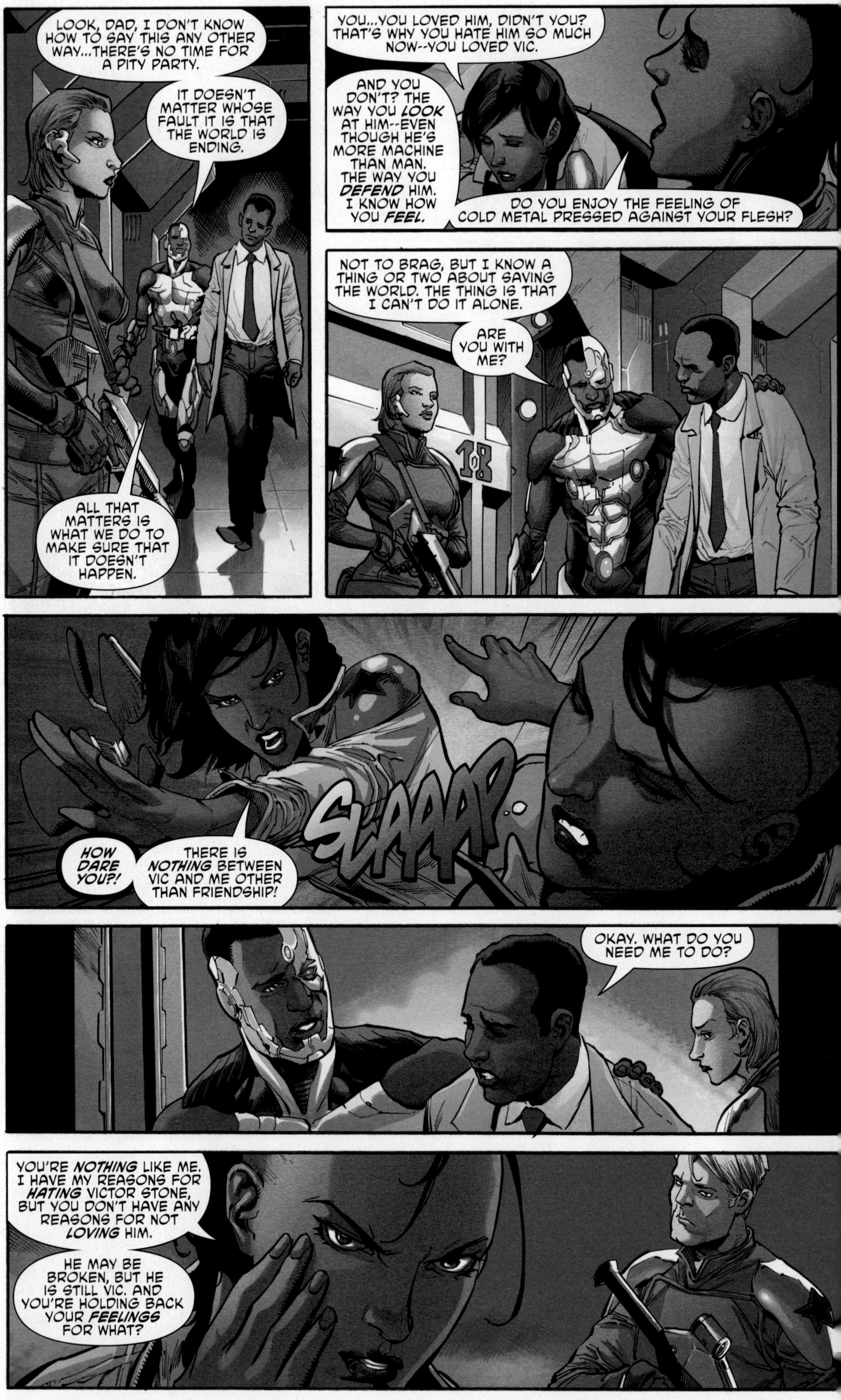
LOOK, DAD, I DON'T KNOW HOW TO SAY THIS ANY OTHER WAY...THERE'S NO TIME FOR A PITY PARTY.
IT DOESN'T MATTER WHOSE FAULT IT IS THAT THE WORLD IS ENDING.
ALL THAT MATTERS IS WHAT WE DO TO MAKE SURE THAT IT DOESN'T HAPPEN.
YOU...YOU LOVED HIM, DIDN'T YOU? THAT'S WHY YOU HATE HIM SO MUCH NOW--YOU LOVED VIC.
AND YOU DON'T? THE WAY YOU LOOK AT HIM--EVEN THOUGH HE'S MORE MACHINE THAN MAN. THE WAY YOU DEFEND HIM. I KNOW HOW YOU FEEL.
DO YOU ENJOY THE FEELING OF COLD METAL PRESSED AGAINST YOUR FLESH?
NOT TO BRAG, BUT I KNOW A THING OR TWO ABOUT SAVING THE WORLD. THE THING IS THAT I CAN'T DO IT ALONE.
ARE YOU WITH ME?
18
SLAAAP
HOW DARE YOU?!
THERE IS NOTHING BETWEEN VIC AND ME OTHER THAN FRIENDSHIP!
OKAY. WHAT DO YOU NEED ME TO DO?
YOU'RE NOTHING LIKE ME. I HAVE MY REASONS FOR HATING VICTOR STONE, BUT YOU DON'T HAVE ANY REASONS FOR NOT LOVING HIM.
HE MAY BE BROKEN, BUT HE IS STILL VIC. AND YOU'RE HOLDING BACK YOUR FEELINGS FOR WHAT?

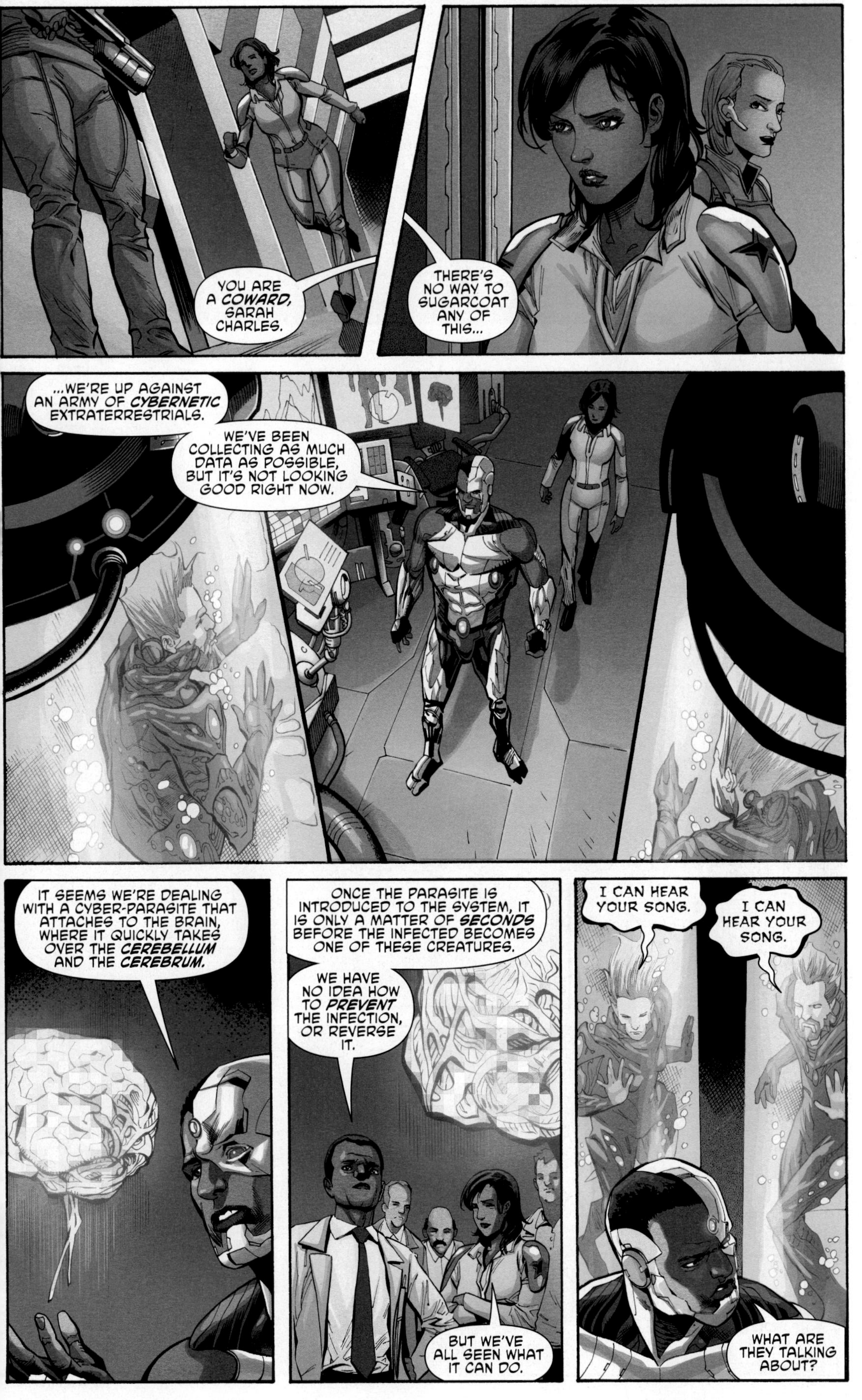
YOU ARE A *COWARD*, SARAH CHARLES.
THERE'S NO WAY TO SUGARCOAT ANY OF THIS...
...WE'RE UP AGAINST AN ARMY OF *CYBERNETIC* EXTRATERRESTRIALS.
WE'VE BEEN COLLECTING AS MUCH DATA AS POSSIBLE, BUT IT'S NOT LOOKING GOOD RIGHT NOW.
IT SEEMS WE'RE DEALING WITH A CYBER-PARASITE THAT ATTACHES TO THE BRAIN, WHERE IT QUICKLY TAKES OVER THE *CEREBELLUM* AND THE *CEREBRUM.*
ONCE THE PARASITE IS INTRODUCED TO THE SYSTEM, IT IS ONLY A MATTER OF *SECONDS* BEFORE THE INFECTED BECOMES ONE OF THESE CREATURES.
WE HAVE NO IDEA HOW TO *PREVENT* THE INFECTION, OR REVERSE IT.
BUT WE'VE ALL SEEN WHAT IT CAN DO.
I CAN HEAR YOUR SONG.
I CAN HEAR YOUR SONG.
WHAT ARE THEY TALKING ABOUT?

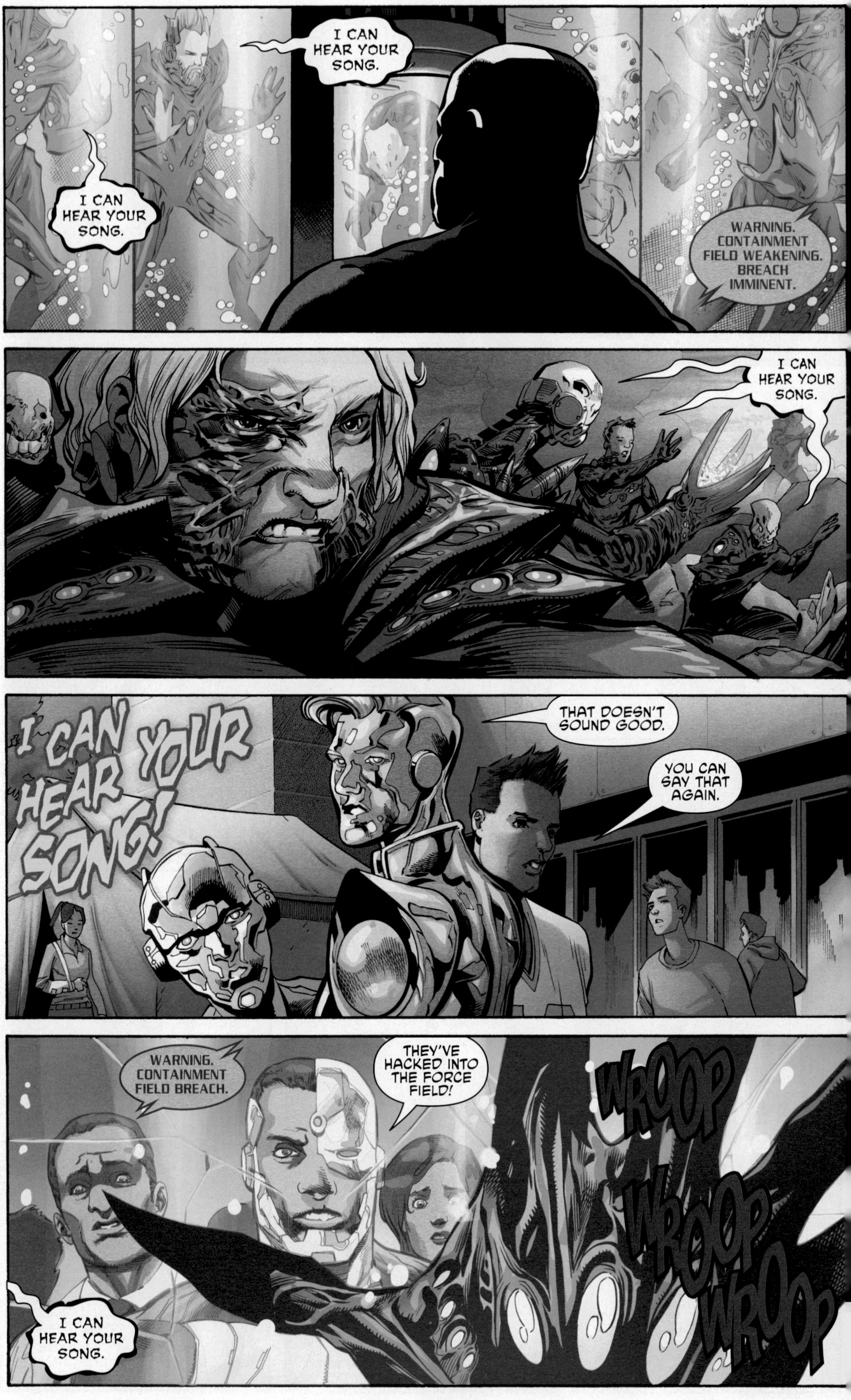
I CAN HEAR YOUR SONG.
I CAN HEAR YOUR SONG.
WARNING. CONTAINMENT FIELD WEAKENING. BREACH IMMINENT.
I CAN HEAR YOUR SONG.
I CAN HEAR YOUR SONG!
THAT DOESN'T SOUND GOOD.
YOU CAN SAY THAT AGAIN.
WARNING. CONTAINMENT FIELD BREACH.
THEY'VE HACKED INTO THE FORCE FIELD!
WROOP
WROOP
WROOP
I CAN HEAR YOUR SONG.

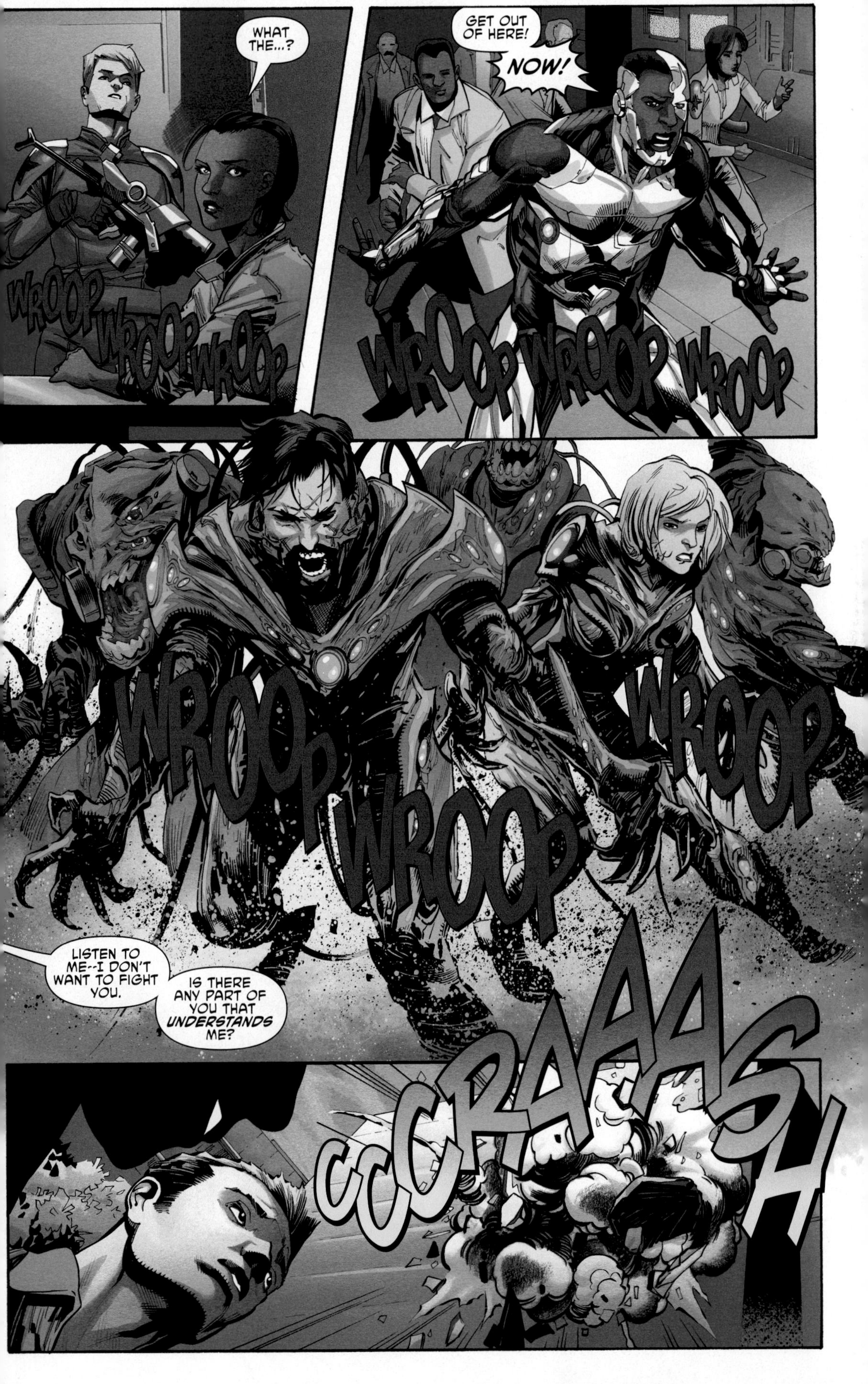

WHAT THE...?
WROOP WROOP WROOP
GET OUT OF HERE!
NOW!
WROOP WROOP WROOP
WROOP WROOP WROOP
LISTEN TO ME--I DON'T WANT TO FIGHT YOU.
IS THERE ANY PART OF YOU THAT UNDERSTANDS ME?
CCCRAAASH

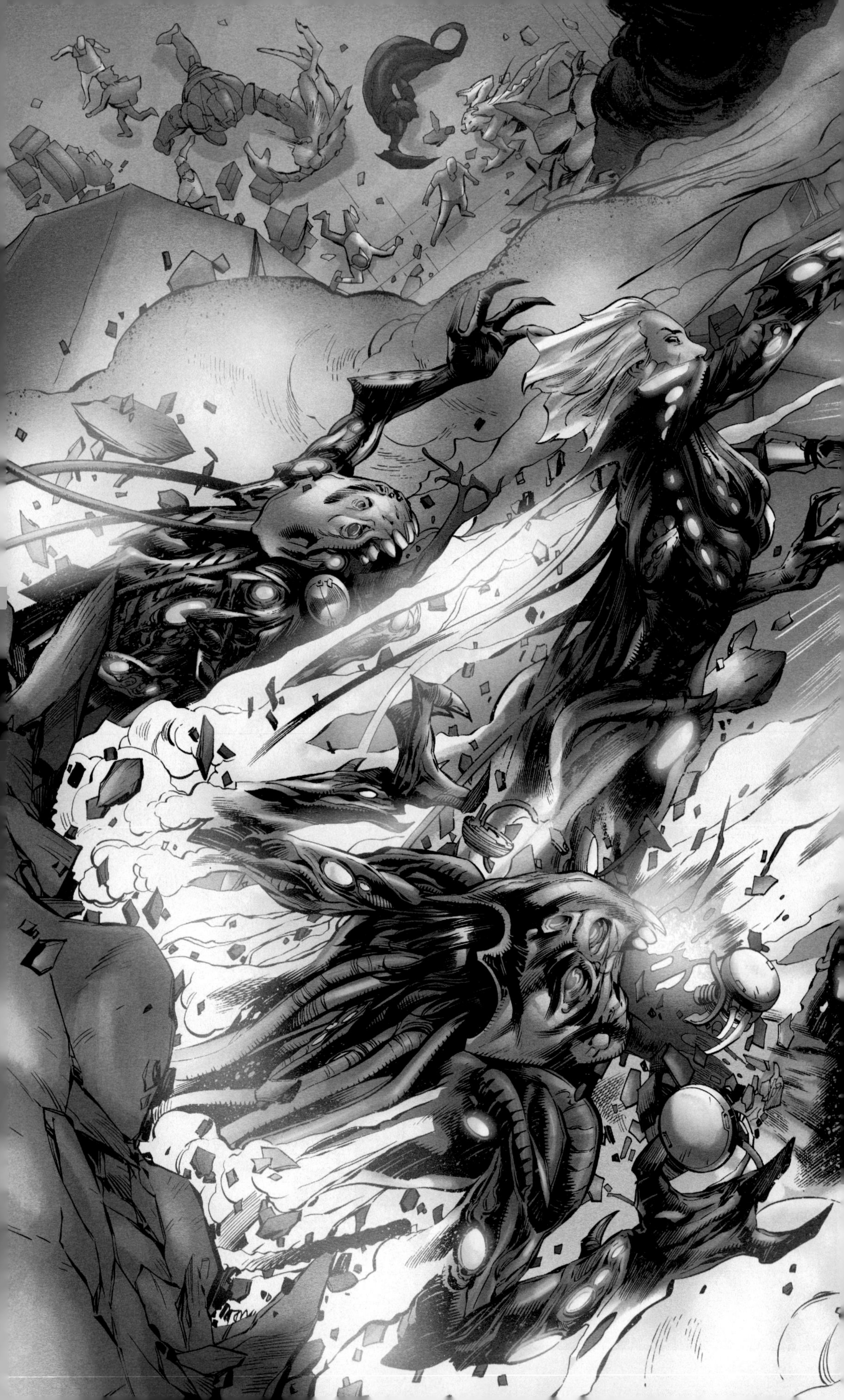

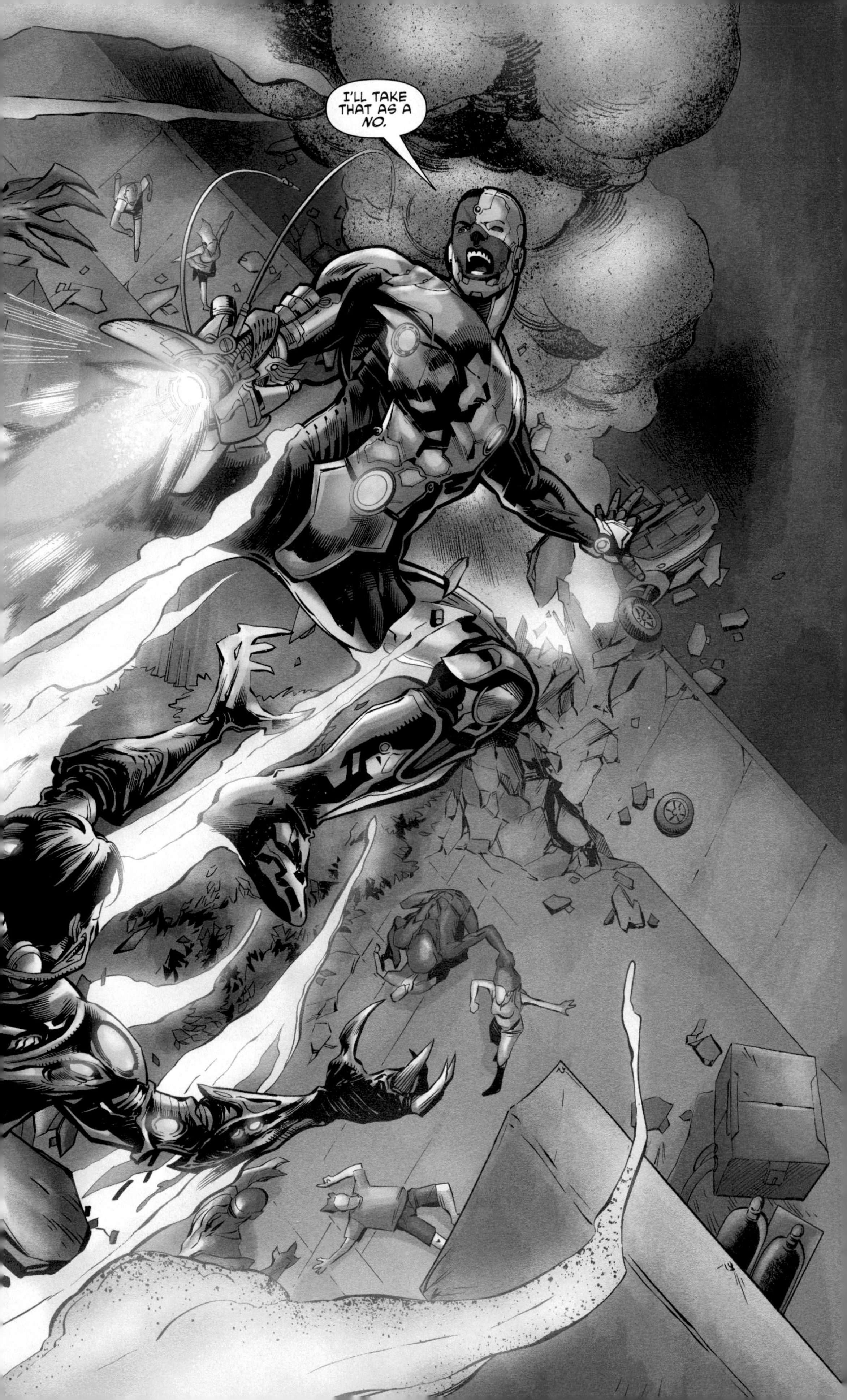
I'LL TAKE THAT AS A NO.

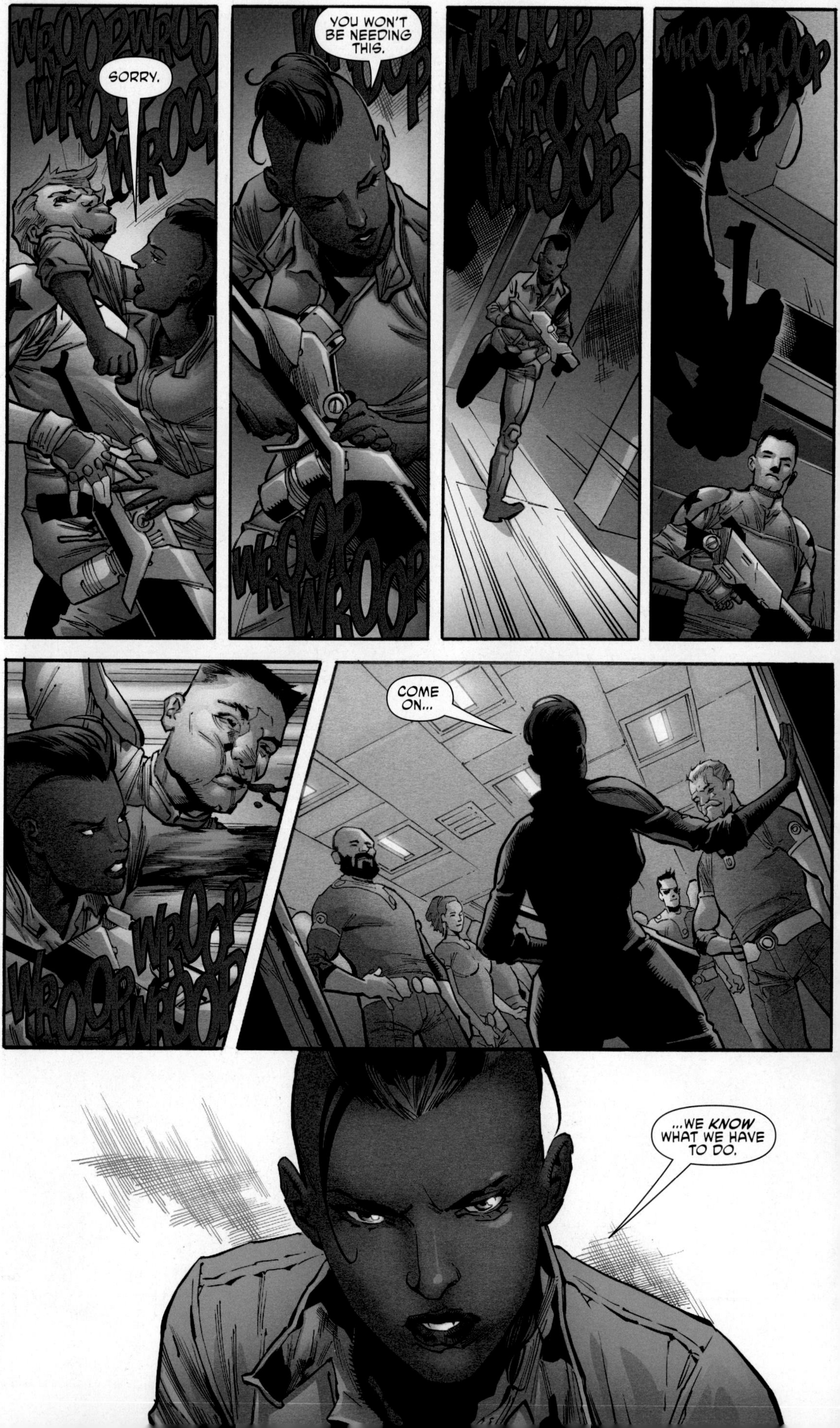
SORRY.
YOU WON'T BE NEEDING THIS.
WROOP WROOP
WROOP
WROOP
WROOP WROOP
WROOP WROOP
COME ON...
...WE *KNOW* WHAT WE HAVE TO DO.

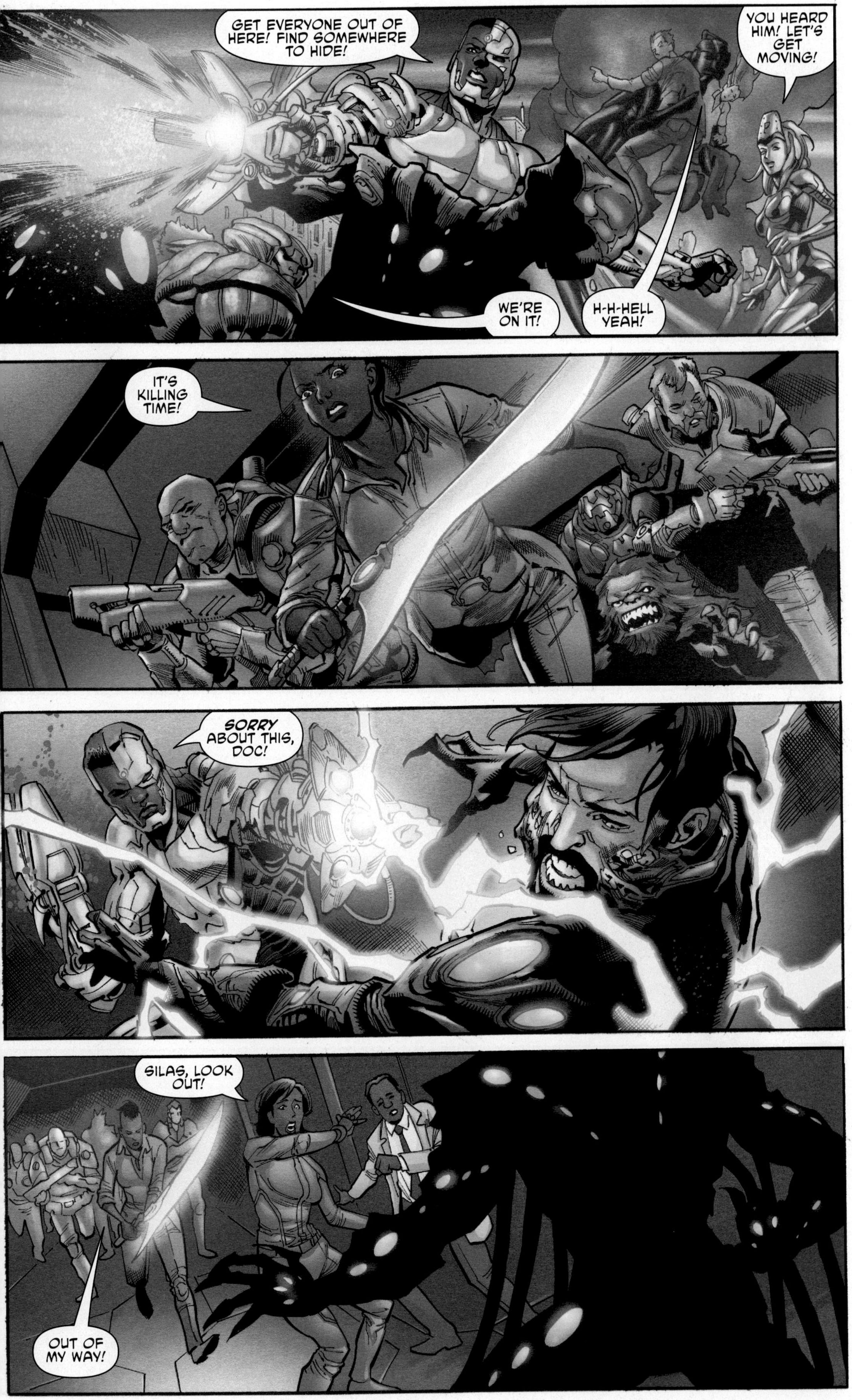
GET EVERYONE OUT OF HERE! FIND SOMEWHERE TO HIDE!
YOU HEARD HIM! LET'S GET MOVING!
WE'RE ON IT!
H-H-HELL YEAH!
IT'S KILLING TIME!
SORRY ABOUT THIS, DOC!
SILAS, LOOK OUT!
OUT OF MY WAY!

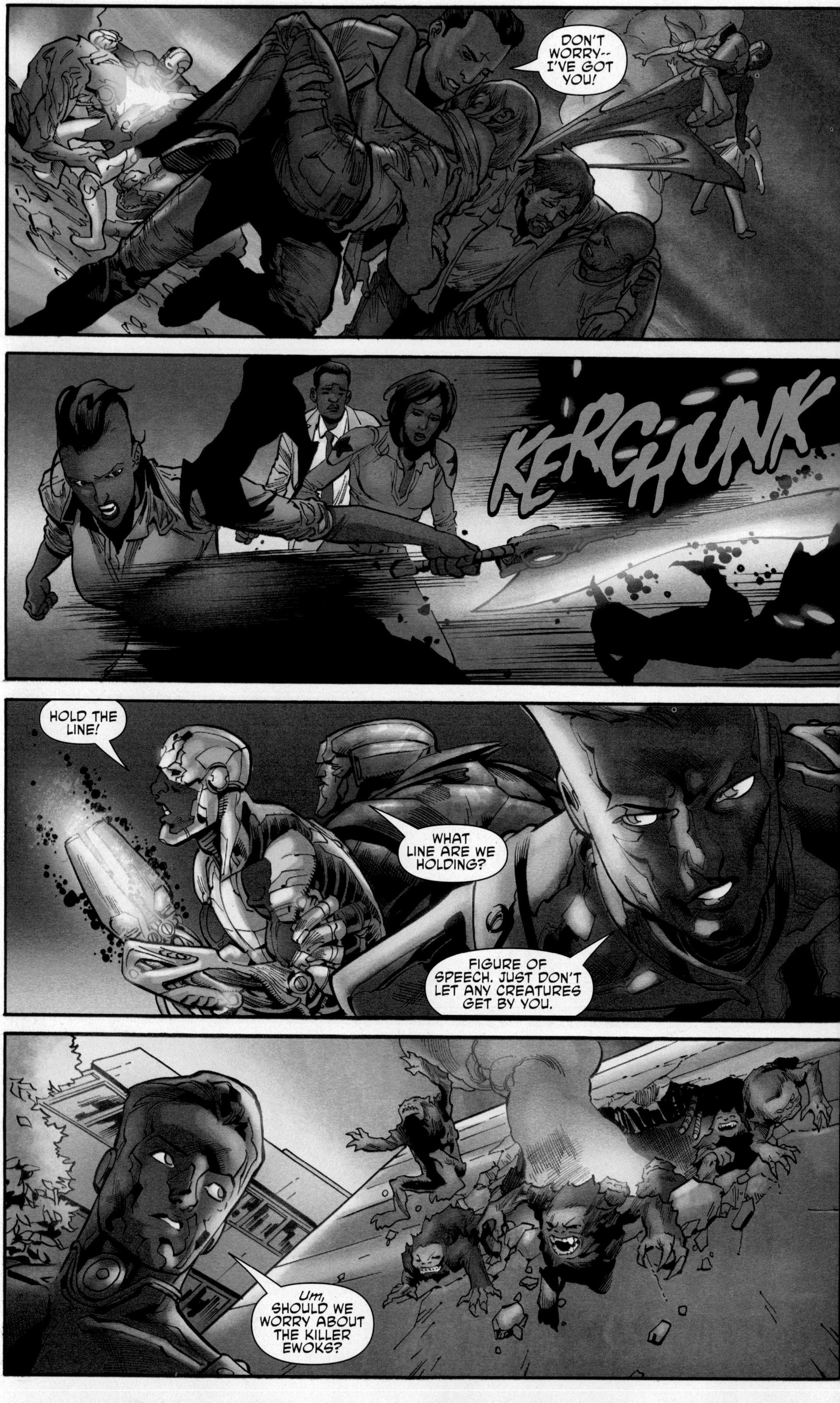
DON'T WORRY-- I'VE GOT YOU!
KERCHUNK
HOLD THE LINE!
WHAT LINE ARE WE HOLDING?
FIGURE OF SPEECH. JUST DON'T LET ANY CREATURES GET BY YOU.
Um, SHOULD WE WORRY ABOUT THE KILLER EWOKS?

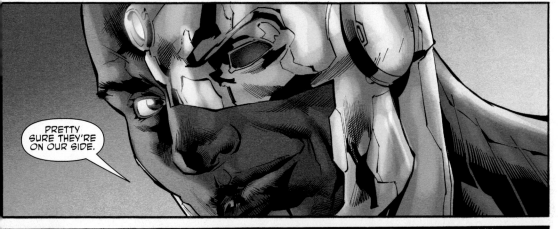

PRETTY SURE THEY'RE ON OUR SIDE.

THIS ISN'T GOOD...BUT I'VE SEEN WORSE.

NOW WHAT?

OH NO...

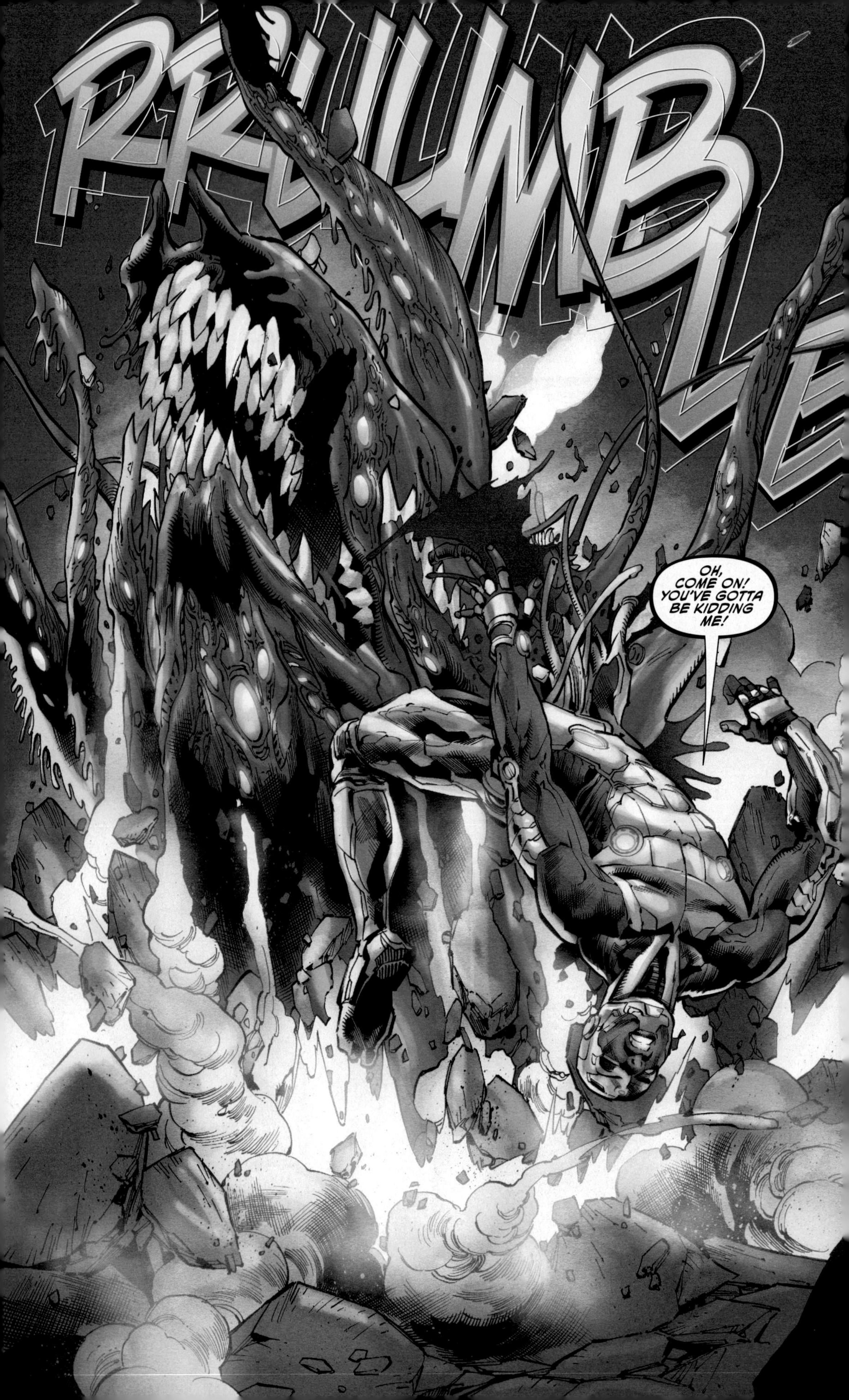
RRUUMBLE
OH, COME ON! YOU'VE GOTTA BE KIDDING ME!

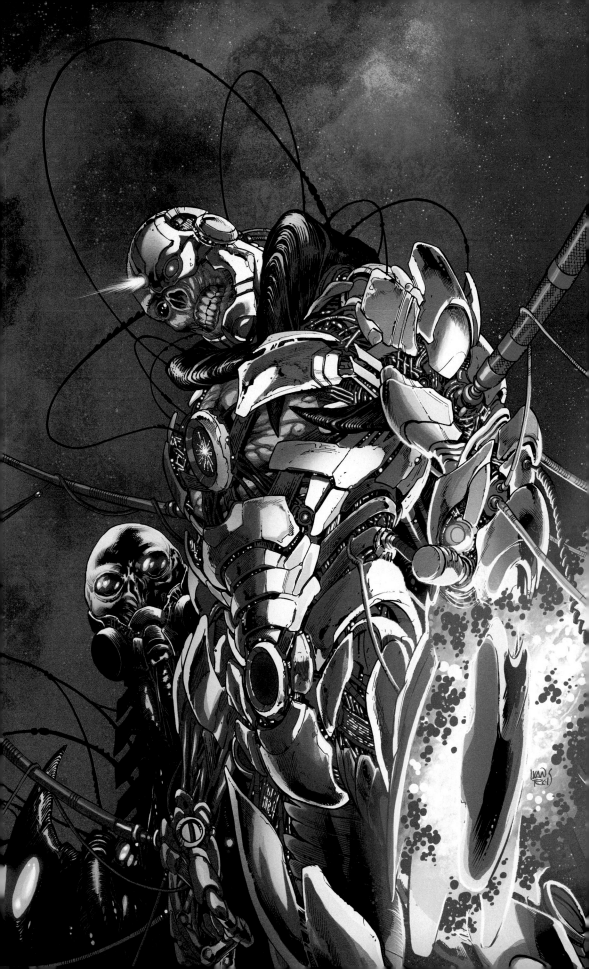

# RUBBLE & REVELATIONS

**IVAN REIS, FELIPE WATANABE** and **DANIEL HDR** pencillers **OCLAIR ALBERT, JÚLIO FERREIRA, ANDY OWENS** and **JUAN CASTRO** inkers **ADRIANO LUCAS, PETE PANTAZIS** colorists
**ROB LEIGH** letterer **IVAN REIS, JOE PRADO** and **ADRIANO LUCAS** cover art

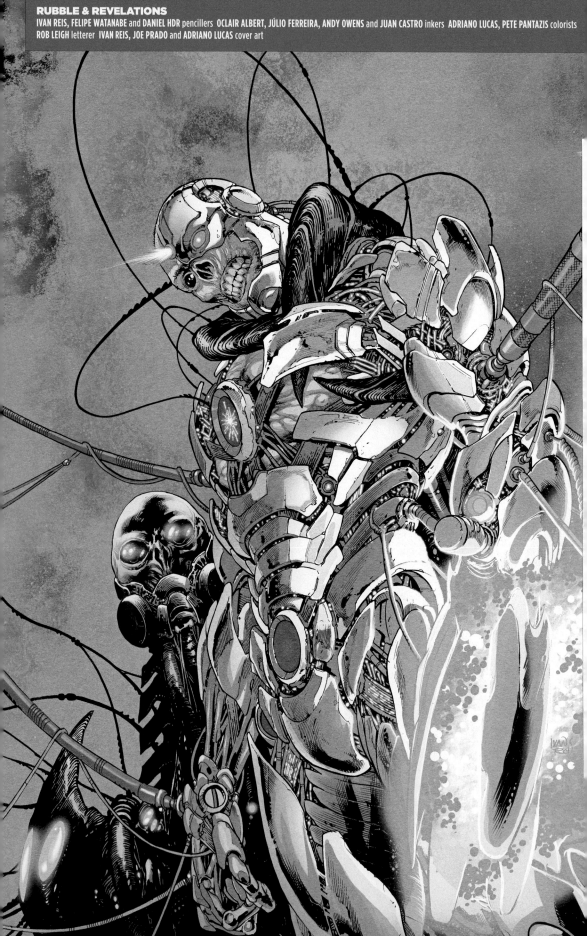

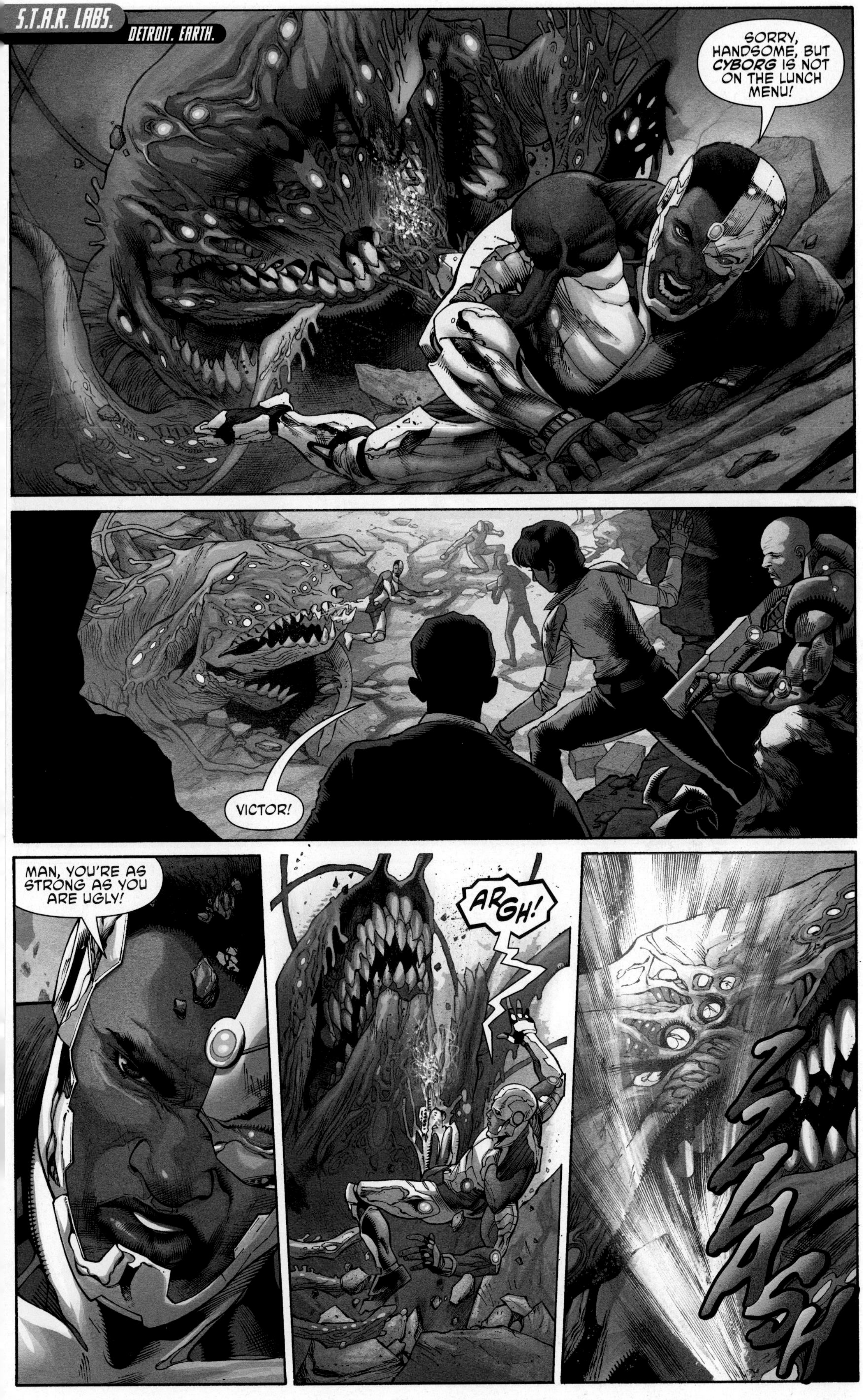
S.T.A.R. LABS.
DETROIT. EARTH.
SORRY, HANDSOME, BUT CYBORG IS NOT ON THE LUNCH MENU!
VICTOR!
MAN, YOU'RE AS STRONG AS YOU ARE UGLY!
ARGH!
ZZZ SHASH

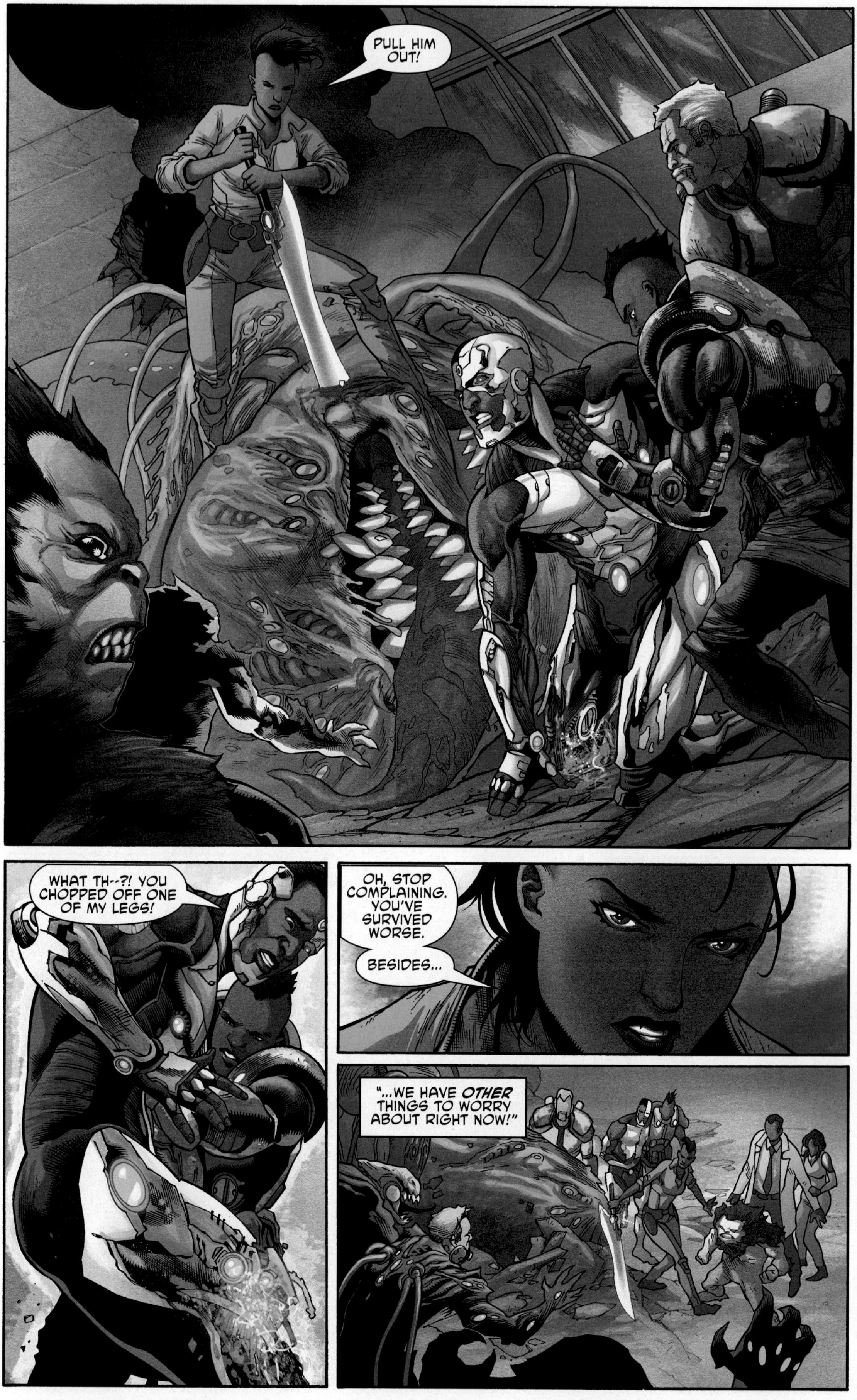
PULL HIM OUT!
WHAT TH--?! YOU CHOPPED OFF ONE OF MY LEGS!
OH, STOP COMPLAINING. YOU'VE SURVIVED WORSE.
BESIDES...
"...WE HAVE OTHER THINGS TO WORRY ABOUT RIGHT NOW!"

TIME TO GET OUT OF HERE!

WHAT? WAIT!

WE CAN'T LEAVE ALL THESE PEOPLE!

I DON'T CARE ABOUT ANYONE ELSE. IT'S YOU THAT THEY'RE AFTER.

THIS BATTLE IS OVER...

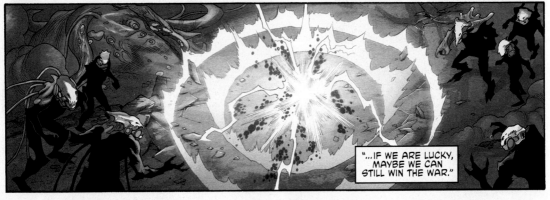

"...IF WE ARE LUCKY, MAYBE WE CAN STILL WIN THE WAR."

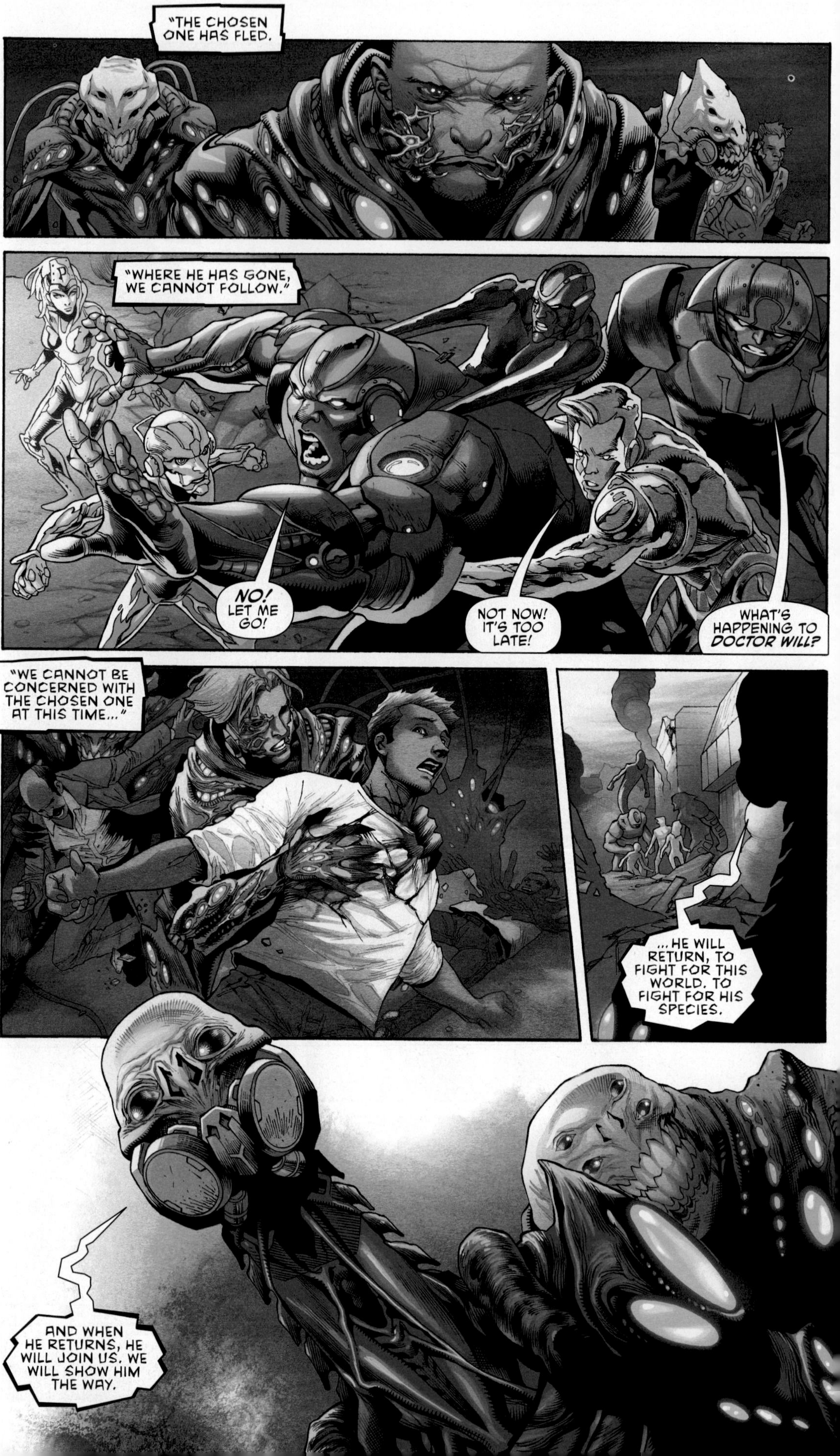
"THE CHOSEN ONE HAS FLED.
"WHERE HE HAS GONE, WE CANNOT FOLLOW."
NO! LET ME GO!
NOT NOW! IT'S TOO LATE!
WHAT'S HAPPENING TO DOCTOR WILL?
"WE CANNOT BE CONCERNED WITH THE CHOSEN ONE AT THIS TIME..."
...HE WILL RETURN, TO FIGHT FOR THIS WORLD. TO FIGHT FOR HIS SPECIES.
AND WHEN HE RETURNS, HE WILL JOIN US. WE WILL SHOW HIM THE WAY.

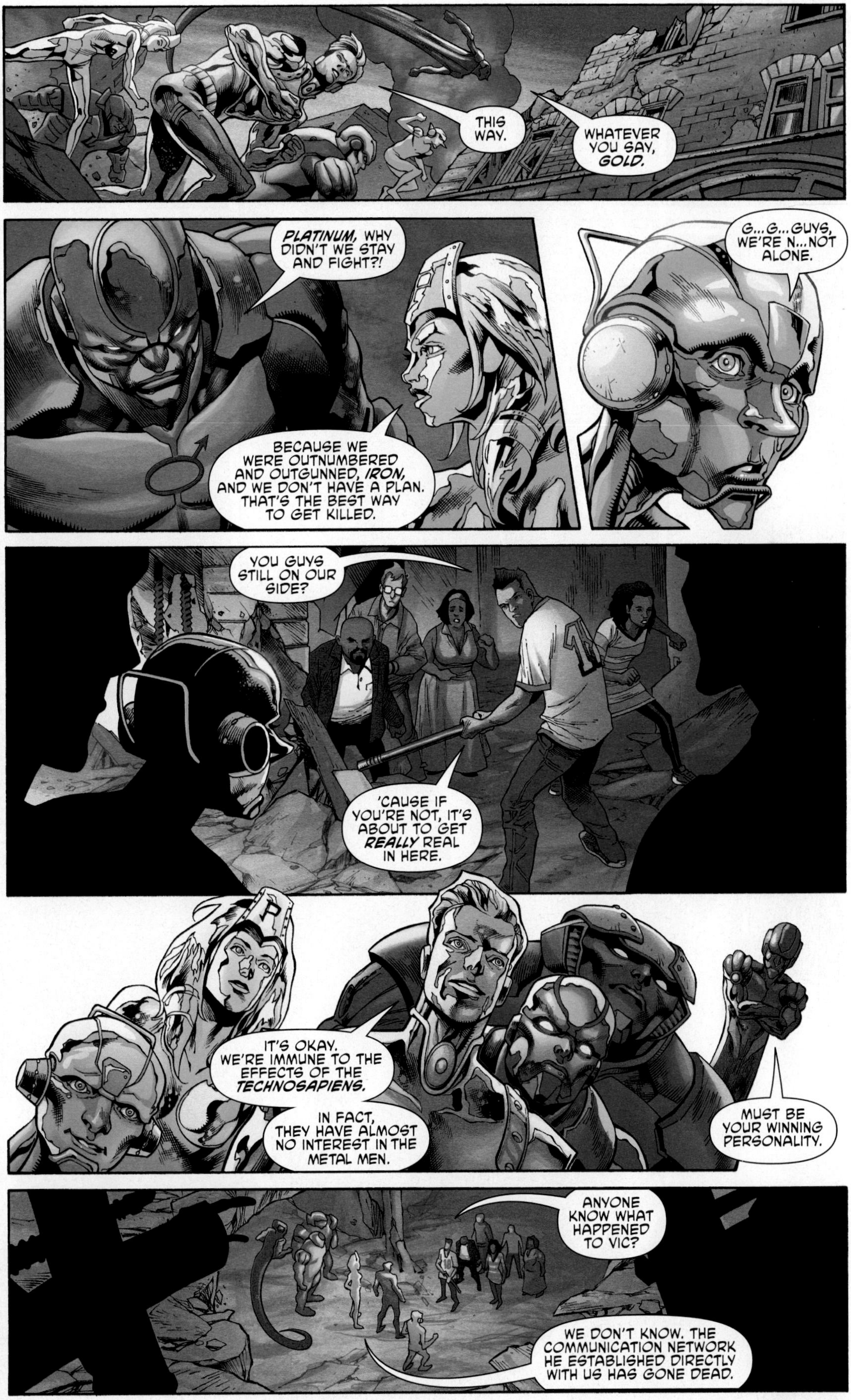

THIS WAY.
WHATEVER YOU SAY, GOLD.
PLATINUM, WHY DIDN'T WE STAY AND FIGHT?!
BECAUSE WE WERE OUTNUMBERED AND OUTGUNNED, IRON, AND WE DON'T HAVE A PLAN. THAT'S THE BEST WAY TO GET KILLED.
G...G...GUYS, WE'RE N...NOT ALONE.
YOU GUYS STILL ON OUR SIDE?
'CAUSE IF YOU'RE NOT, IT'S ABOUT TO GET REALLY REAL IN HERE.
IT'S OKAY. WE'RE IMMUNE TO THE EFFECTS OF THE TECHNOSAPIENS.
IN FACT, THEY HAVE ALMOST NO INTEREST IN THE METAL MEN.
MUST BE YOUR WINNING PERSONALITY.
ANYONE KNOW WHAT HAPPENED TO VIC?
WE DON'T KNOW. THE COMMUNICATION NETWORK HE ESTABLISHED DIRECTLY WITH US HAS GONE DEAD.

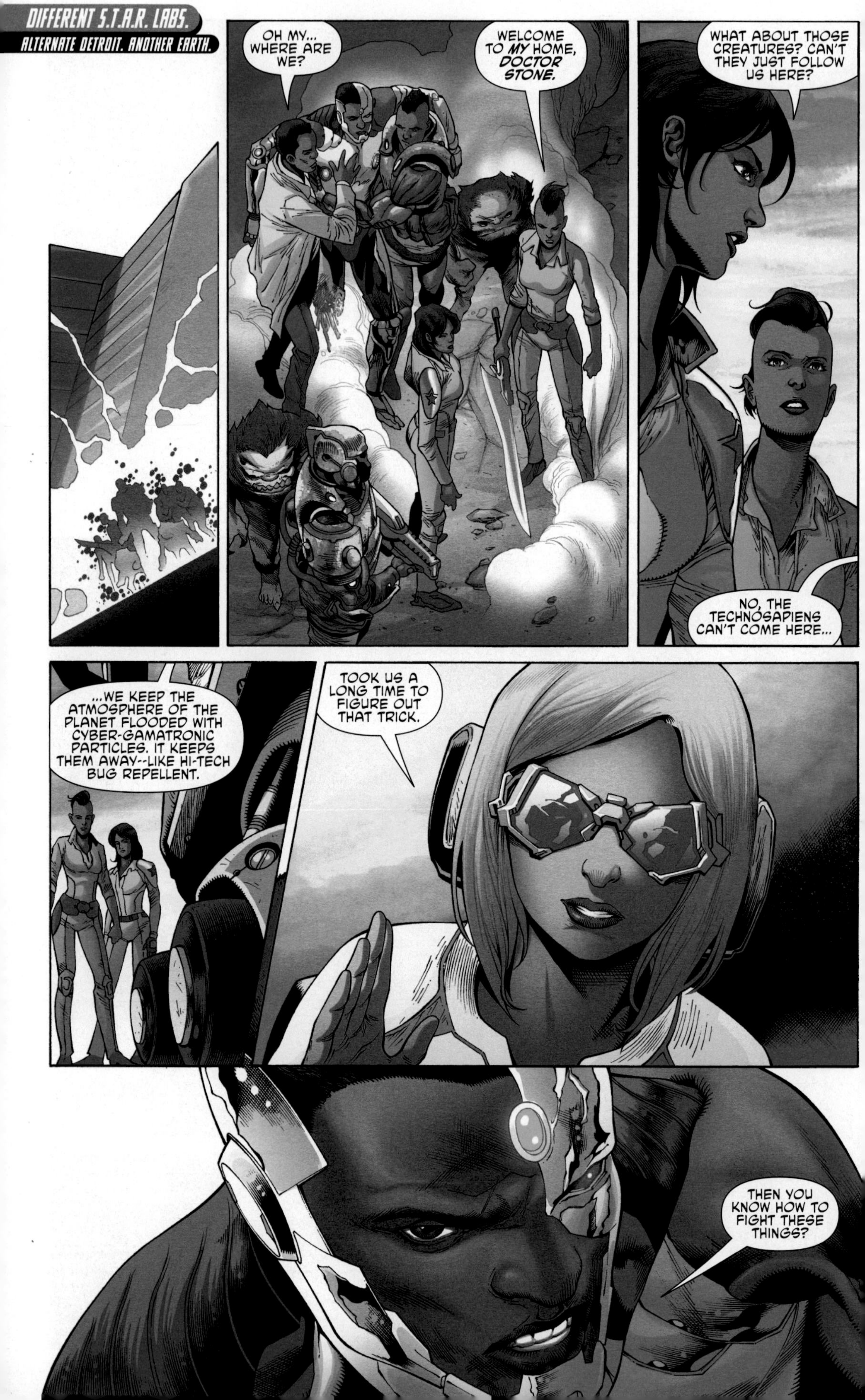
DIFFERENT S.T.A.R. LABS.
ALTERNATE DETROIT. ANOTHER EARTH.
OH MY... WHERE ARE WE?
WELCOME TO MY HOME, DOCTOR STONE.
WHAT ABOUT THOSE CREATURES? CAN'T THEY JUST FOLLOW US HERE?
NO, THE TECHNOSAPIENS CAN'T COME HERE...
...WE KEEP THE ATMOSPHERE OF THE PLANET FLOODED WITH CYBER-GAMATRONIC PARTICLES. IT KEEPS THEM AWAY--LIKE HI-TECH BUG REPELLENT.
TOOK US A LONG TIME TO FIGURE OUT THAT TRICK.
THEN YOU KNOW HOW TO FIGHT THESE THINGS?

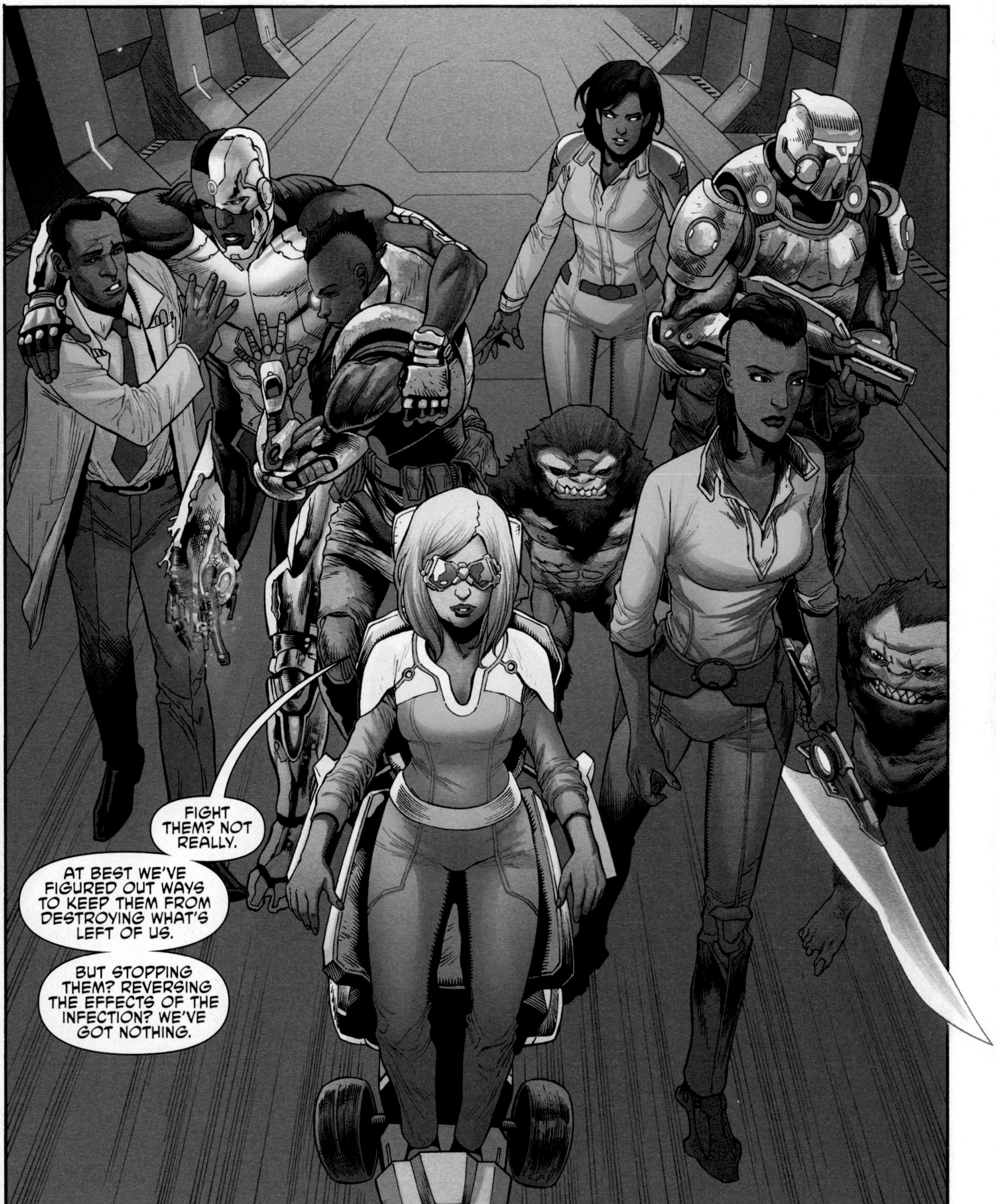
FIGHT THEM? NOT REALLY.
AT BEST WE'VE FIGURED OUT WAYS TO KEEP THEM FROM DESTROYING WHAT'S LEFT OF US.
BUT STOPPING THEM? REVERSING THE EFFECTS OF THE INFECTION? WE'VE GOT NOTHING.

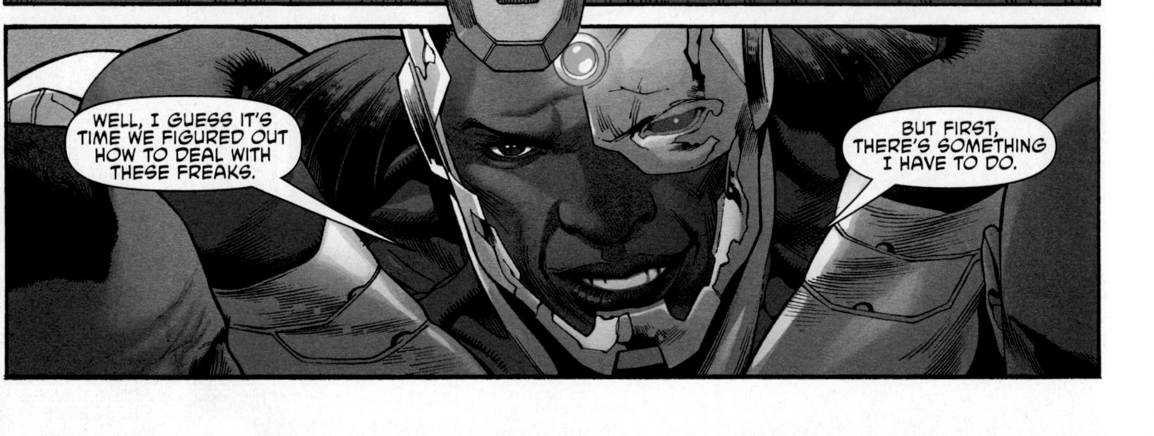
WELL, I GUESS IT'S TIME WE FIGURED OUT HOW TO DEAL WITH THESE FREAKS.
BUT FIRST, THERE'S SOMETHING I HAVE TO DO.

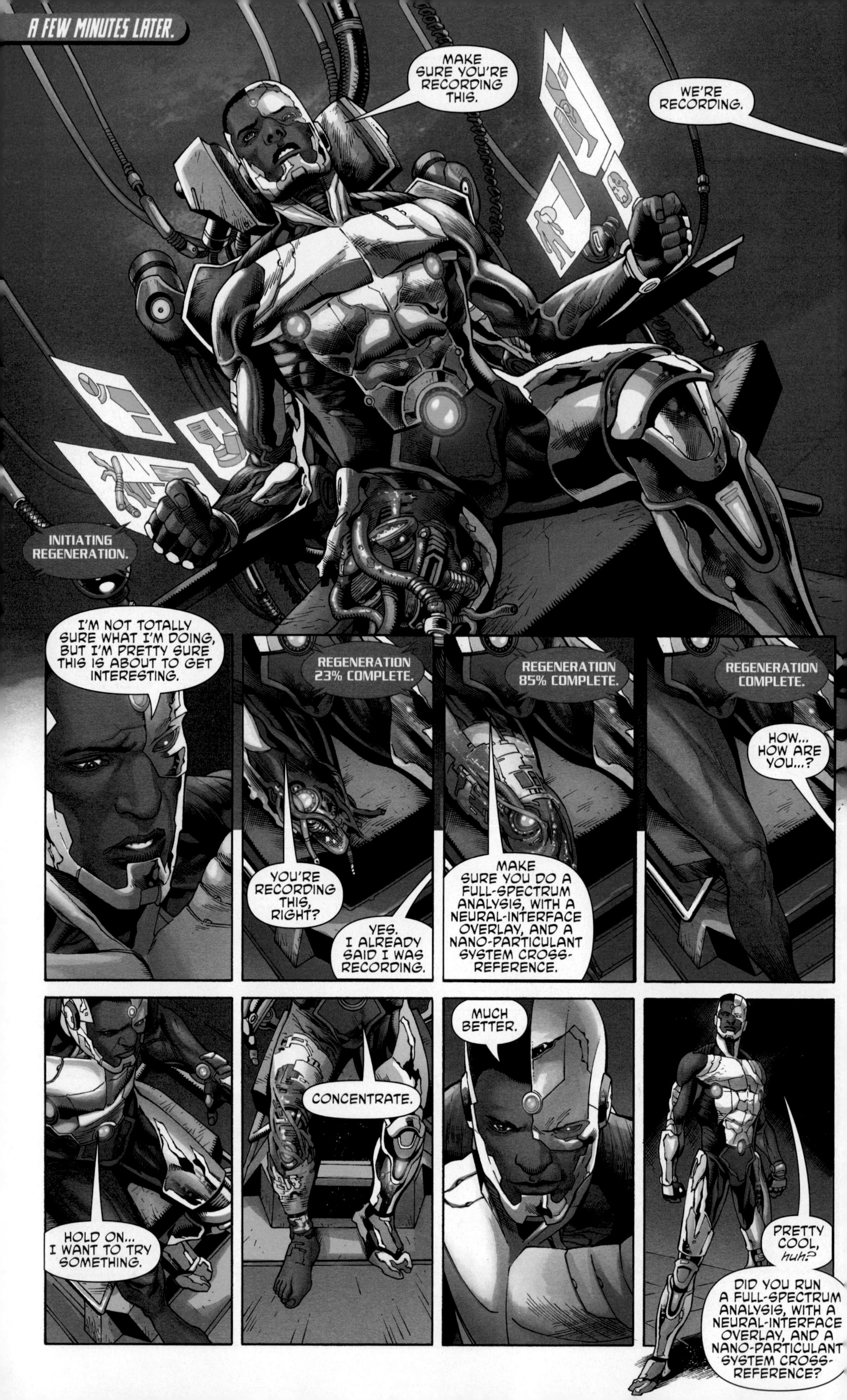
A FEW MINUTES LATER.
MAKE SURE YOU'RE RECORDING THIS.
WE'RE RECORDING.
INITIATING REGENERATION.
I'M NOT TOTALLY SURE WHAT I'M DOING, BUT I'M PRETTY SURE THIS IS ABOUT TO GET INTERESTING.
REGENERATION 23% COMPLETE.
YOU'RE RECORDING THIS, RIGHT?
YES. I ALREADY SAID I WAS RECORDING.
REGENERATION 85% COMPLETE.
MAKE SURE YOU DO A FULL-SPECTRUM ANALYSIS, WITH A NEURAL-INTERFACE OVERLAY, AND A NANO-PARTICULANT SYSTEM CROSS-REFERENCE.
REGENERATION COMPLETE.
HOW... HOW ARE YOU...?
HOLD ON... I WANT TO TRY SOMETHING.
CONCENTRATE.
MUCH BETTER.
PRETTY COOL, *huh?*
DID YOU RUN A FULL-SPECTRUM ANALYSIS, WITH A NEURAL-INTERFACE OVERLAY, AND A NANO-PARTICULANT SYSTEM CROSS-REFERENCE?

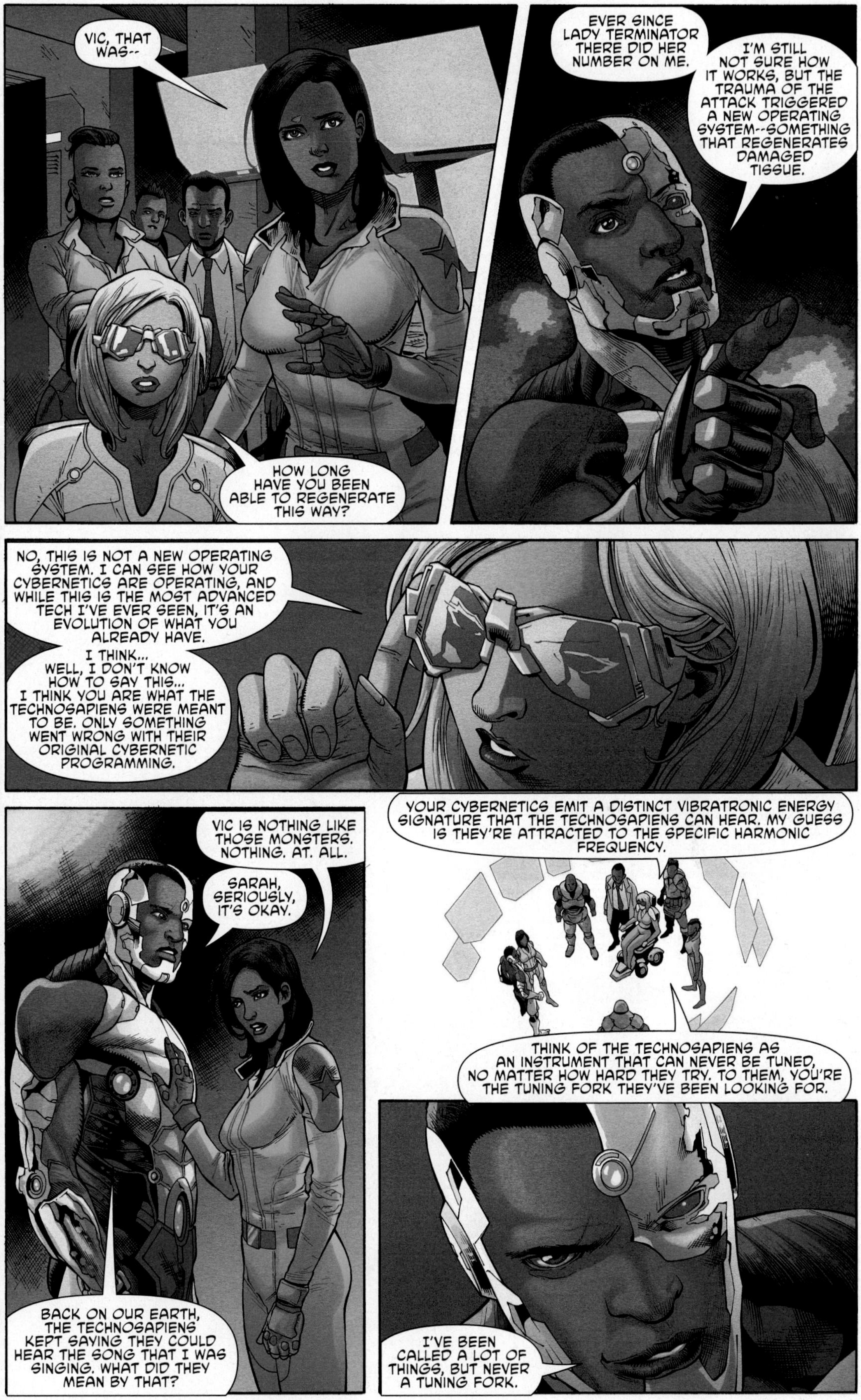
VIC, THAT WAS--
HOW LONG HAVE YOU BEEN ABLE TO REGENERATE THIS WAY?
EVER SINCE LADY TERMINATOR THERE DID HER NUMBER ON ME.
I'M STILL NOT SURE HOW IT WORKS, BUT THE TRAUMA OF THE ATTACK TRIGGERED A NEW OPERATING SYSTEM--SOMETHING THAT REGENERATES DAMAGED TISSUE.
NO, THIS IS NOT A NEW OPERATING SYSTEM. I CAN SEE HOW YOUR CYBERNETICS ARE OPERATING, AND WHILE THIS IS THE MOST ADVANCED TECH I'VE EVER SEEN, IT'S AN EVOLUTION OF WHAT YOU ALREADY HAVE.
I THINK... WELL, I DON'T KNOW HOW TO SAY THIS... I THINK YOU ARE WHAT THE TECHNOSAPIENS WERE MEANT TO BE. ONLY SOMETHING WENT WRONG WITH THEIR ORIGINAL CYBERNETIC PROGRAMMING.
VIC IS NOTHING LIKE THOSE MONSTERS. NOTHING. AT. ALL.
SARAH, SERIOUSLY, IT'S OKAY.
BACK ON OUR EARTH, THE TECHNOSAPIENS KEPT SAYING THEY COULD HEAR THE SONG THAT I WAS SINGING. WHAT DID THEY MEAN BY THAT?
YOUR CYBERNETICS EMIT A DISTINCT VIBRATRONIC ENERGY SIGNATURE THAT THE TECHNOSAPIENS CAN HEAR. MY GUESS IS THEY'RE ATTRACTED TO THE SPECIFIC HARMONIC FREQUENCY.
THINK OF THE TECHNOSAPIENS AS AN INSTRUMENT THAT CAN NEVER BE TUNED, NO MATTER HOW HARD THEY TRY. TO THEM, YOU'RE THE TUNING FORK THEY'VE BEEN LOOKING FOR.
I'VE BEEN CALLED A LOT OF THINGS, BUT NEVER A TUNING FORK.

...THE CHOSEN ONE AS HE WAS, AND AS HE IS, AND AS WE SHALL BE. THROUGH HIS PERFECTION, WE WILL FIND SALVATION.

YZHO QTO JXHXO TJJQGGJ JHJOG

NO, THE CHOSEN ONE WILL RETURN. THIS IS HIS HOME. HE IS ITS PROTECTOR.

YES, IN TIME HE WILL RETURN. BUT FOR NOW, THERE ARE STILL SO MANY HERE IN NEED OF HEALING...

"...LET US GO, AND DELIVER THEM FROM THEIR EXISTENCE."

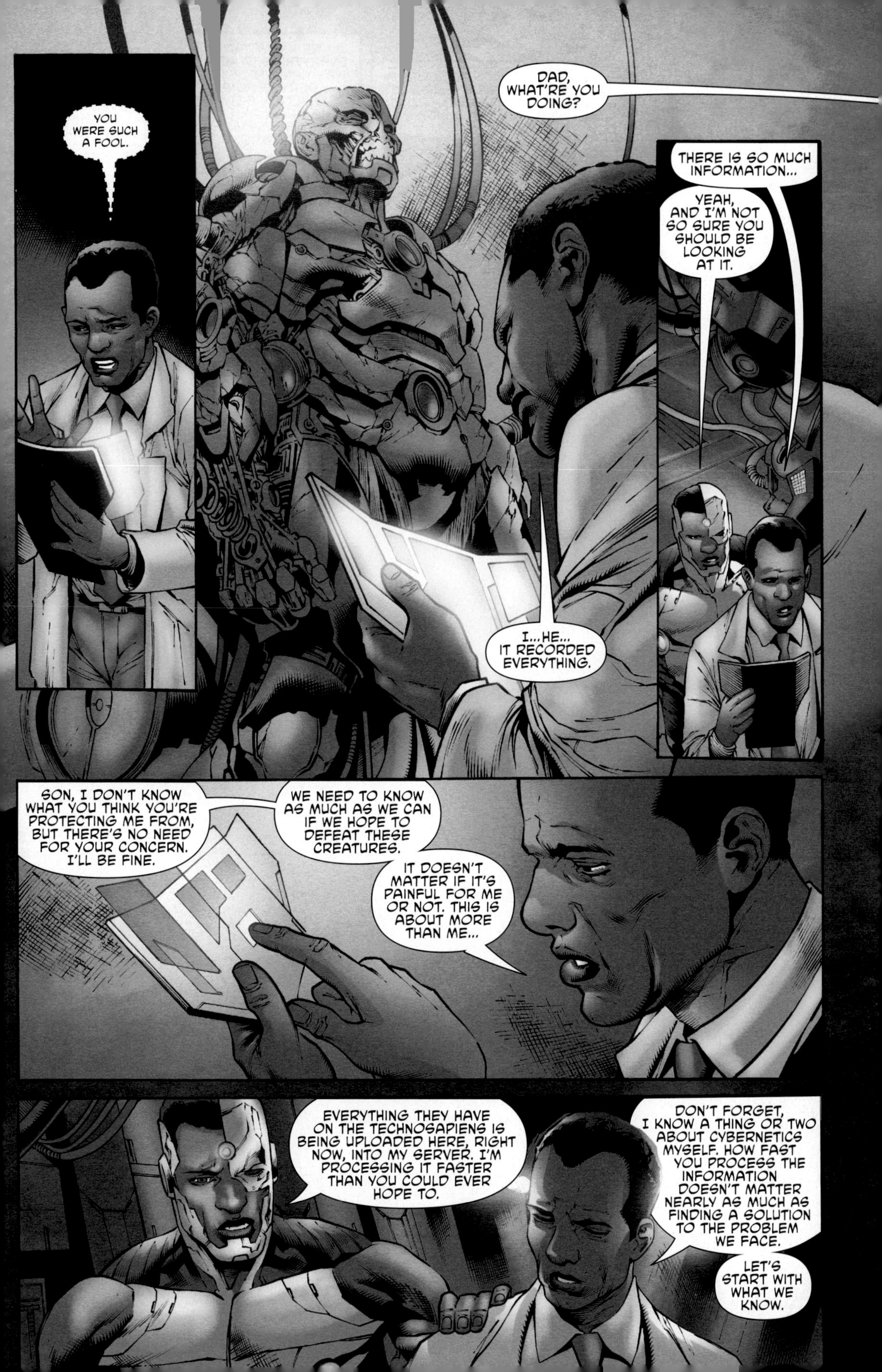
DAD, WHAT'RE YOU DOING?
YOU WERE SUCH A FOOL.
I...HE... IT RECORDED EVERYTHING.
THERE IS SO MUCH INFORMATION...
YEAH, AND I'M NOT SO SURE YOU SHOULD BE LOOKING AT IT.
SON, I DON'T KNOW WHAT YOU THINK YOU'RE PROTECTING ME FROM, BUT THERE'S NO NEED FOR YOUR CONCERN. I'LL BE FINE.
WE NEED TO KNOW AS MUCH AS WE CAN IF WE HOPE TO DEFEAT THESE CREATURES.
IT DOESN'T MATTER IF IT'S PAINFUL FOR ME OR NOT. THIS IS ABOUT MORE THAN ME...
EVERYTHING THEY HAVE ON THE TECHNOSAPIENS IS BEING UPLOADED HERE, RIGHT NOW, INTO MY SERVER. I'M PROCESSING IT FASTER THAN YOU COULD EVER HOPE TO.
DON'T FORGET, I KNOW A THING OR TWO ABOUT CYBERNETICS MYSELF. HOW FAST YOU PROCESS THE INFORMATION DOESN'T MATTER NEARLY AS MUCH AS FINDING A SOLUTION TO THE PROBLEM WE FACE.
LET'S START WITH WHAT WE KNOW.

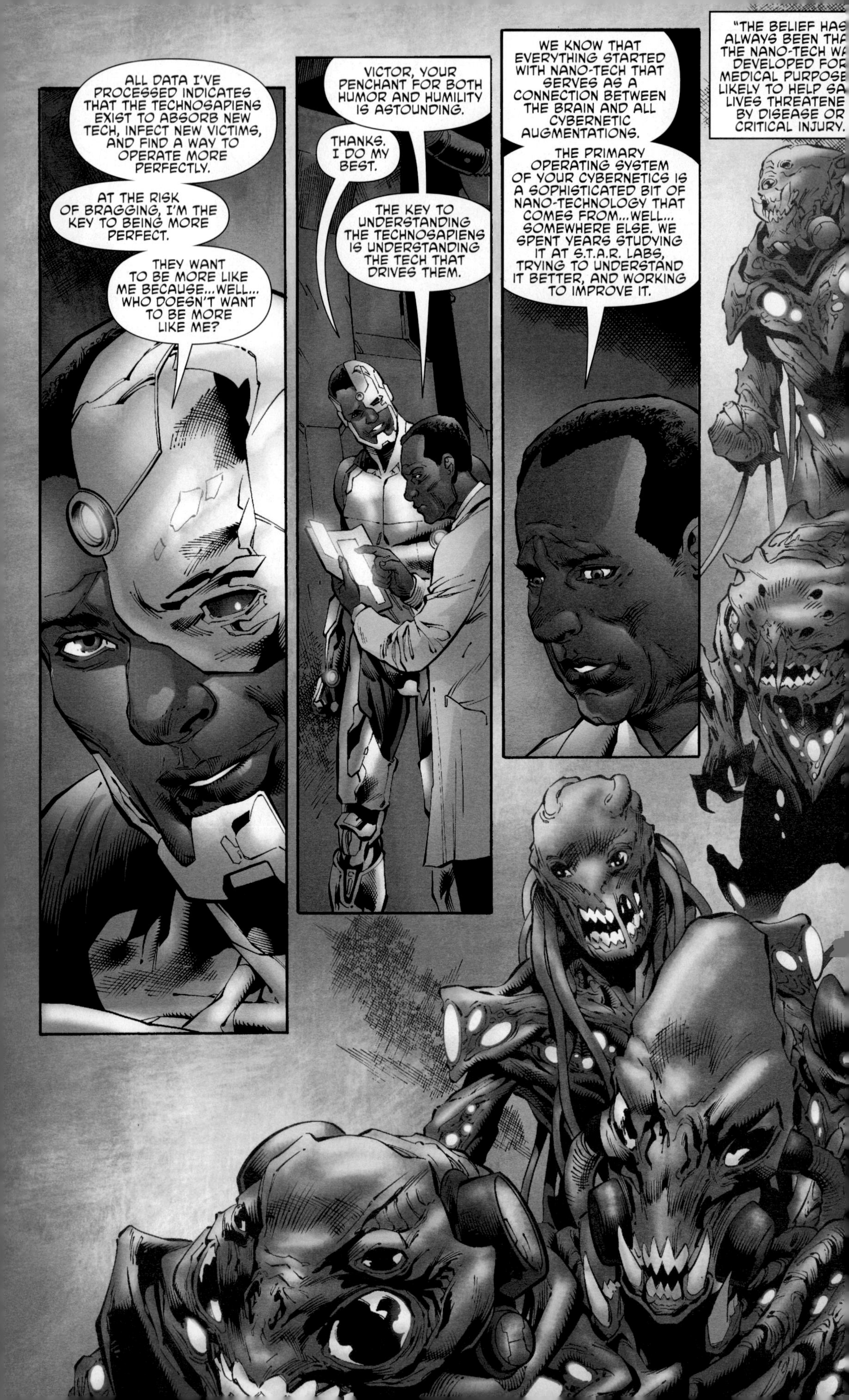
ALL DATA I'VE PROCESSED INDICATES THAT THE TECHNOSAPIENS EXIST TO ABSORB NEW TECH, INFECT NEW VICTIMS, AND FIND A WAY TO OPERATE MORE PERFECTLY.
AT THE RISK OF BRAGGING, I'M THE KEY TO BEING MORE PERFECT.
THEY WANT TO BE MORE LIKE ME BECAUSE...WELL... WHO DOESN'T WANT TO BE MORE LIKE ME?
VICTOR, YOUR PENCHANT FOR BOTH HUMOR AND HUMILITY IS ASTOUNDING.
THANKS. I DO MY BEST.
THE KEY TO UNDERSTANDING THE TECHNOSAPIENS IS UNDERSTANDING THE TECH THAT DRIVES THEM.
WE KNOW THAT EVERYTHING STARTED WITH NANO-TECH THAT SERVES AS A CONNECTION BETWEEN THE BRAIN AND ALL CYBERNETIC AUGMENTATIONS.
THE PRIMARY OPERATING SYSTEM OF YOUR CYBERNETICS IS A SOPHISTICATED BIT OF NANO-TECHNOLOGY THAT COMES FROM...WELL... SOMEWHERE ELSE. WE SPENT YEARS STUDYING IT AT S.T.A.R. LABS, TRYING TO UNDERSTAND IT BETTER, AND WORKING TO IMPROVE IT.
"THE BELIEF HAS ALWAYS BEEN THA THE NANO-TECH WA DEVELOPED FOR MEDICAL PURPOSE LIKELY TO HELP SA LIVES THREATENE BY DISEASE OR CRITICAL INJURY.

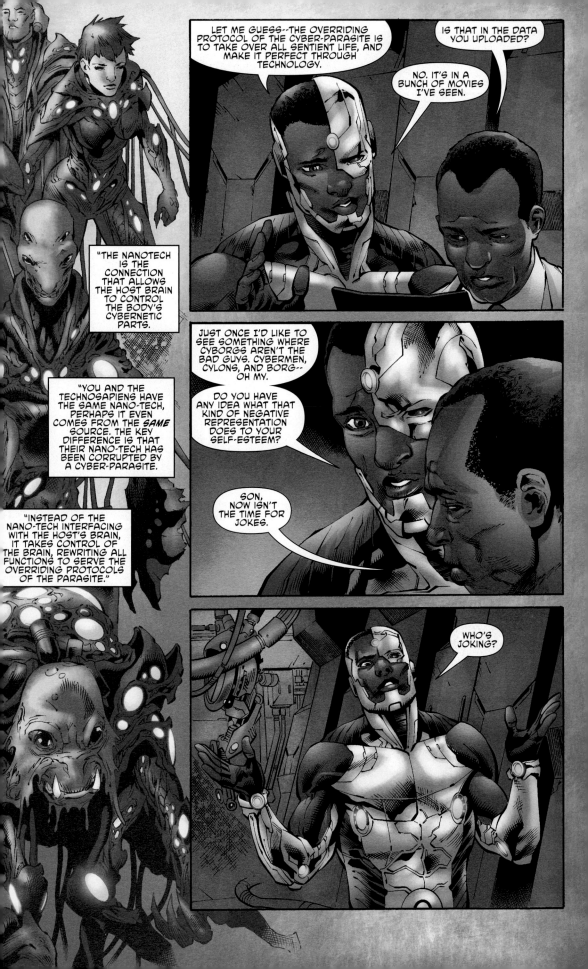

LET ME GUESS--THE OVERRIDING PROTOCOL OF THE CYBER-PARASITE IS TO TAKE OVER ALL SENTIENT LIFE, AND MAKE IT PERFECT THROUGH TECHNOLOGY.

IS THAT IN THE DATA YOU UPLOADED?

NO. IT'S IN A BUNCH OF MOVIES I'VE SEEN.

"THE NANOTECH IS THE CONNECTION THAT ALLOWS THE HOST BRAIN TO CONTROL THE BODY'S CYBERNETIC PARTS.

"YOU AND THE TECHNOSAPIENS HAVE THE SAME NANO-TECH, PERHAPS IT EVEN COMES FROM THE *SAME* SOURCE. THE KEY DIFFERENCE IS THAT THEIR NANO-TECH HAS BEEN CORRUPTED BY A CYBER-PARASITE.

"INSTEAD OF THE NANO-TECH INTERFACING WITH THE HOST'S BRAIN, IT TAKES CONTROL OF THE BRAIN, REWRITING ALL FUNCTIONS TO SERVE THE OVERRIDING PROTOCOLS OF THE PARASITE."

JUST ONCE I'D LIKE TO SEE SOMETHING WHERE CYBORGS AREN'T THE BAD GUYS. CYBERMEN, CYLONS, AND BORG-- OH MY.

DO YOU HAVE ANY IDEA WHAT THAT KIND OF NEGATIVE REPRESENTATION DOES TO YOUR SELF-ESTEEM?

SON, NOW ISN'T THE TIME FOR JOKES.

WHO'S JOKING?

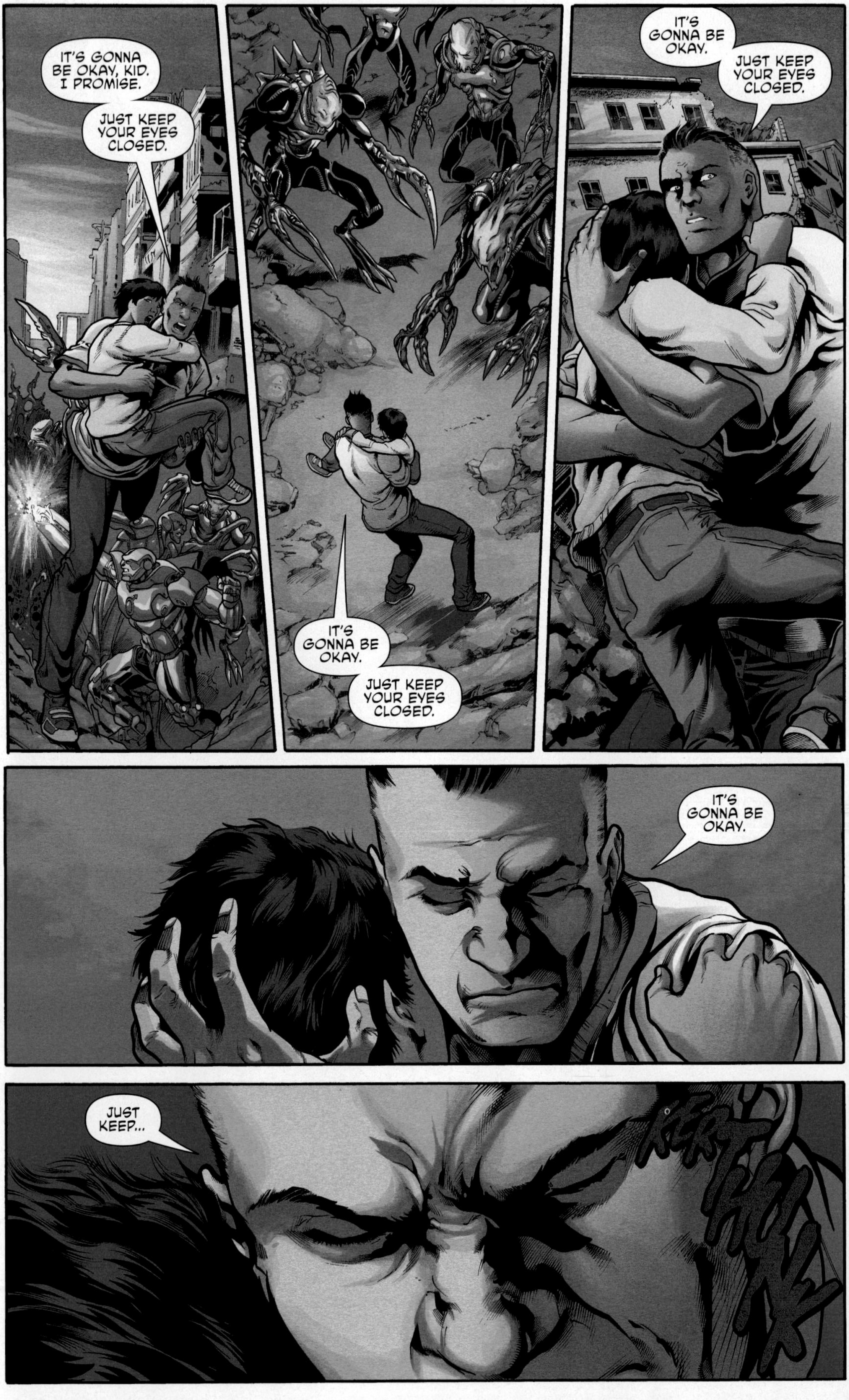
IT'S GONNA BE OKAY, KID. I PROMISE.
JUST KEEP YOUR EYES CLOSED.
IT'S GONNA BE OKAY.
JUST KEEP YOUR EYES CLOSED.
IT'S GONNA BE OKAY.
JUST KEEP YOUR EYES CLOSED.
IT'S GONNA BE OKAY.
JUST KEEP...

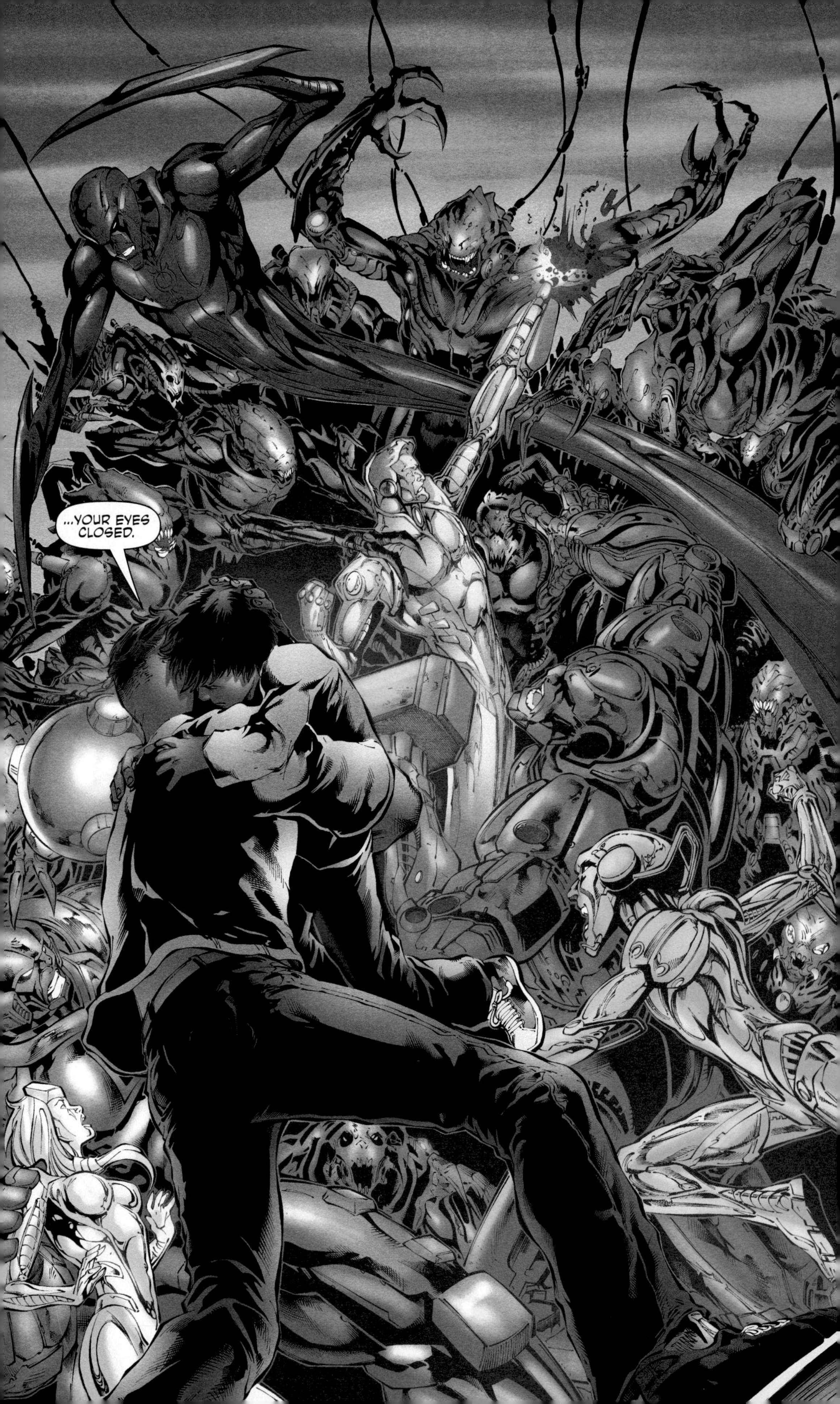
...YOUR EYES CLOSED.

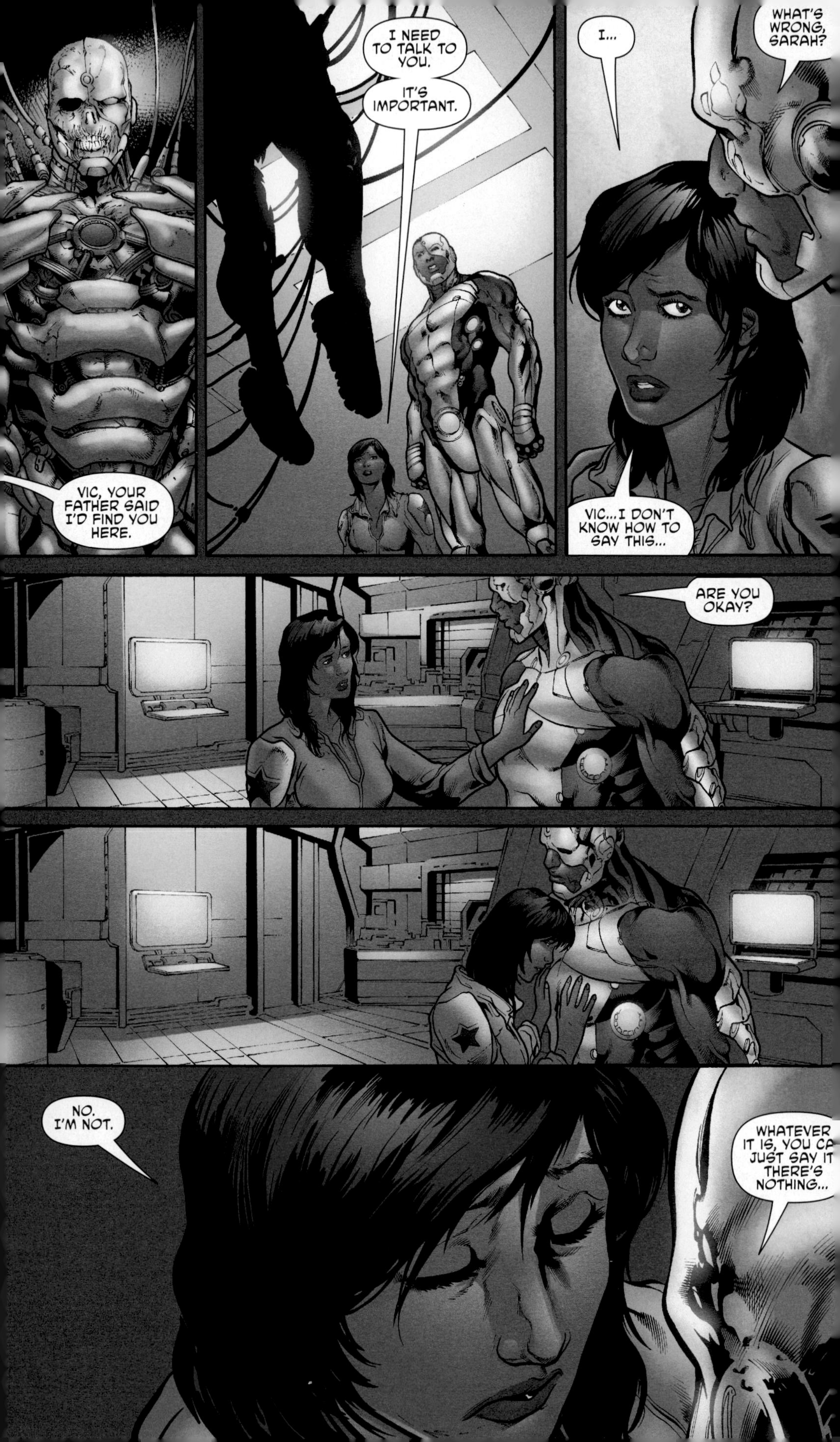
VIC, YOUR FATHER SAID I'D FIND YOU HERE.
I NEED TO TALK TO YOU.
IT'S IMPORTANT.
I...
WHAT'S WRONG, SARAH?
VIC...I DON'T KNOW HOW TO SAY THIS...
ARE YOU OKAY?
NO. I'M NOT.
WHATEVER IT IS, YOU CA JUST SAY IT THERE'S NOTHING...

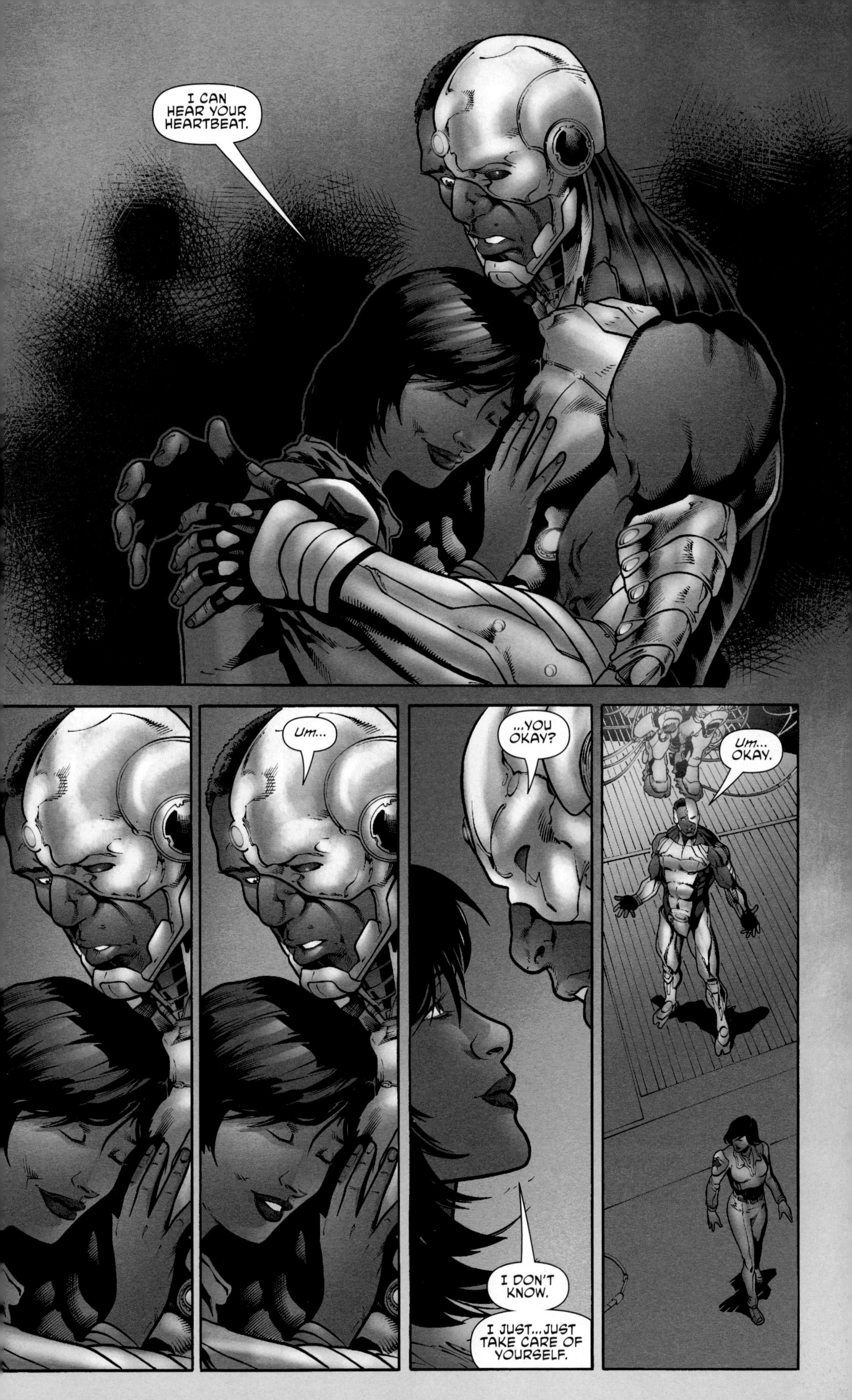
I CAN HEAR YOUR HEARTBEAT.
Um...
...YOU OKAY?
I DON'T KNOW.
I JUST...JUST TAKE CARE OF YOURSELF.
Um... OKAY.

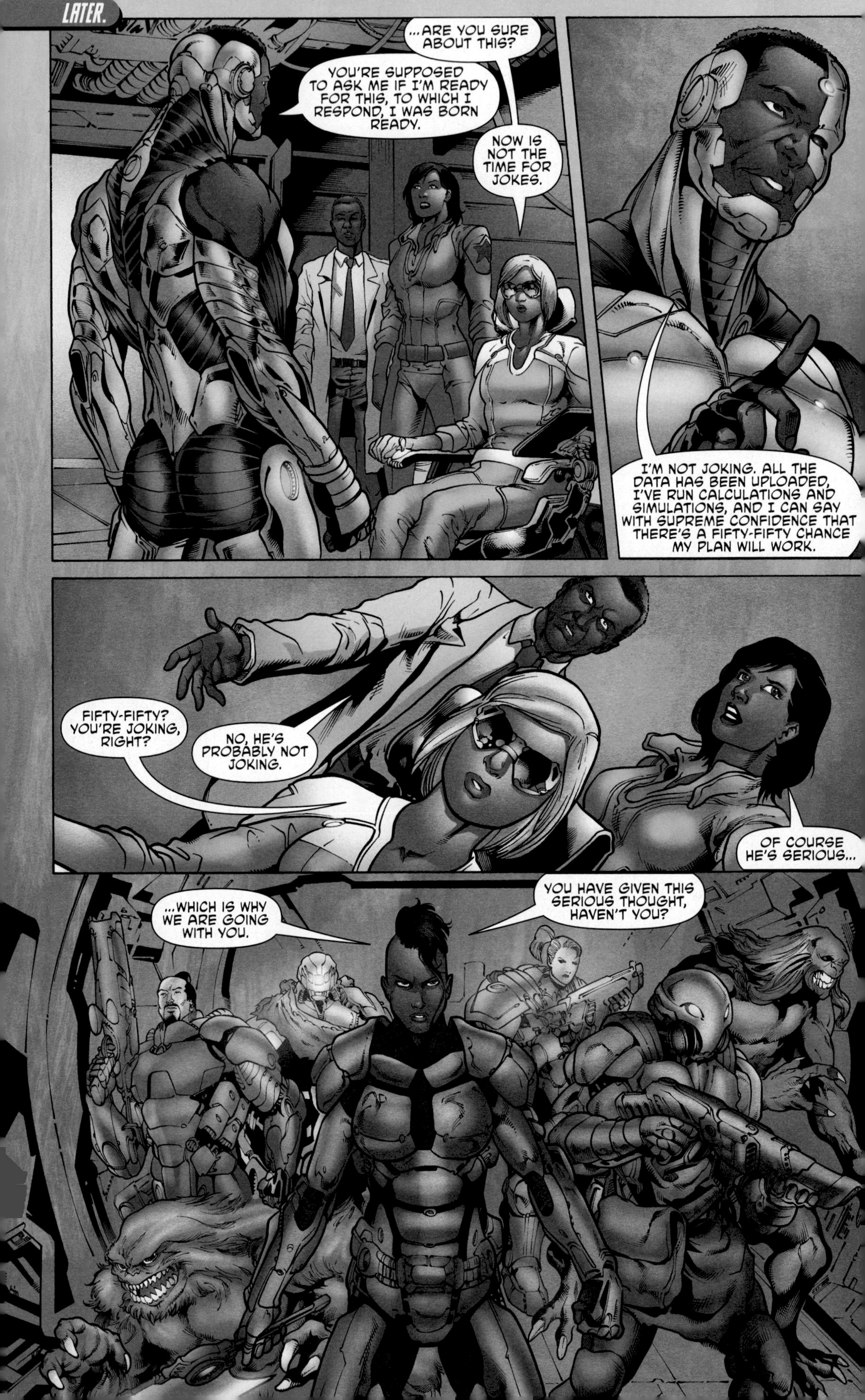
LATER.
...ARE YOU SURE ABOUT THIS?
YOU'RE SUPPOSED TO ASK ME IF I'M READY FOR THIS, TO WHICH I RESPOND, I WAS BORN READY.
NOW IS NOT THE TIME FOR JOKES.
I'M NOT JOKING. ALL THE DATA HAS BEEN UPLOADED, I'VE RUN CALCULATIONS AND SIMULATIONS, AND I CAN SAY WITH SUPREME CONFIDENCE THAT THERE'S A FIFTY-FIFTY CHANCE MY PLAN WILL WORK.
FIFTY-FIFTY? YOU'RE JOKING, RIGHT?
NO, HE'S PROBABLY NOT JOKING.
OF COURSE HE'S SERIOUS...
...WHICH IS WHY WE ARE GOING WITH YOU.
YOU HAVE GIVEN THIS SERIOUS THOUGHT, HAVEN'T YOU?

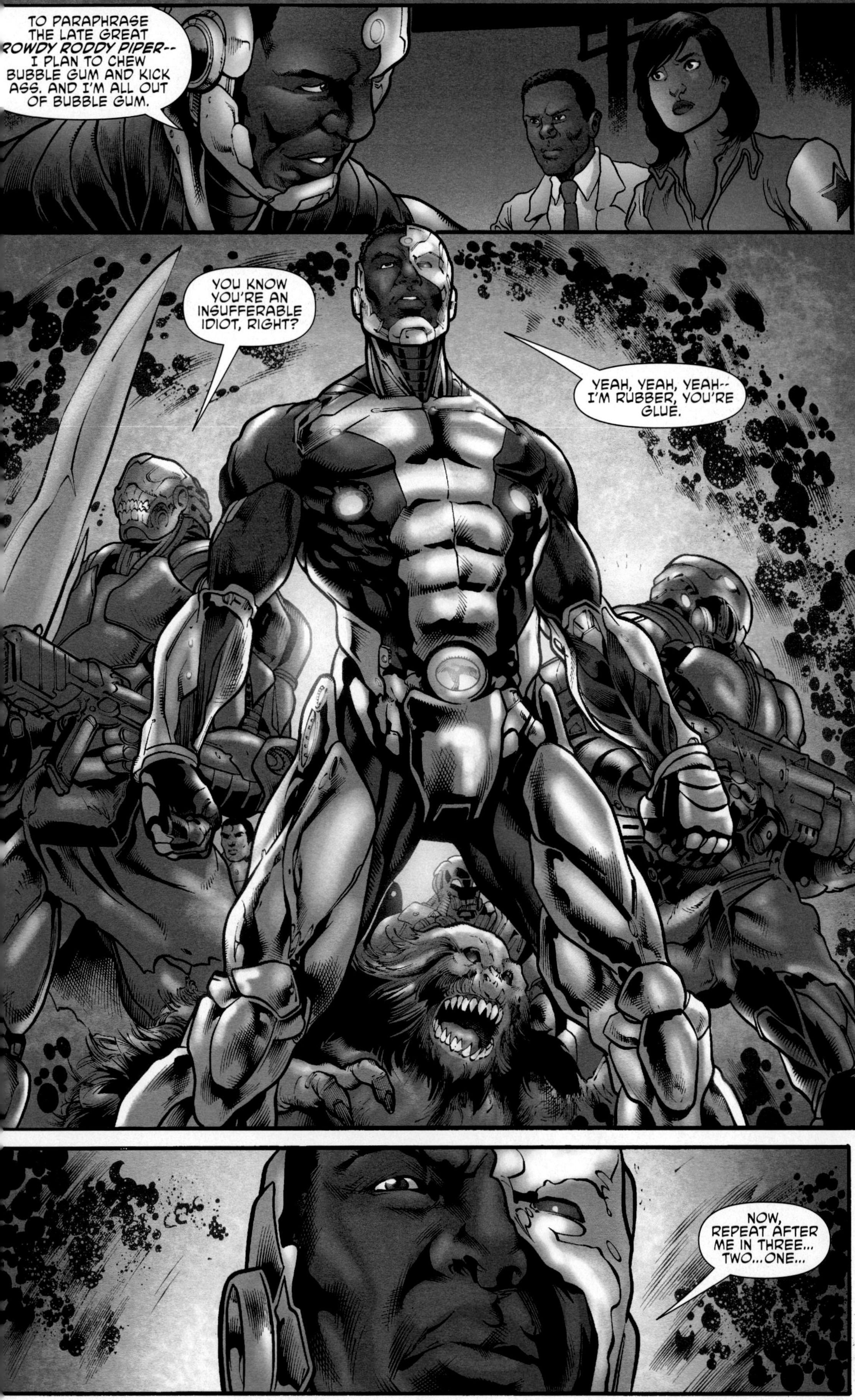
TO PARAPHRASE THE LATE GREAT ROWDY RODDY PIPER-- I PLAN TO CHEW BUBBLE GUM AND KICK ASS. AND I'M ALL OUT OF BUBBLE GUM.
YOU KNOW YOU'RE AN INSUFFERABLE IDIOT, RIGHT?
YEAH, YEAH, YEAH-- I'M RUBBER, YOU'RE GLUE.
NOW, REPEAT AFTER ME IN THREE... TWO...ONE...

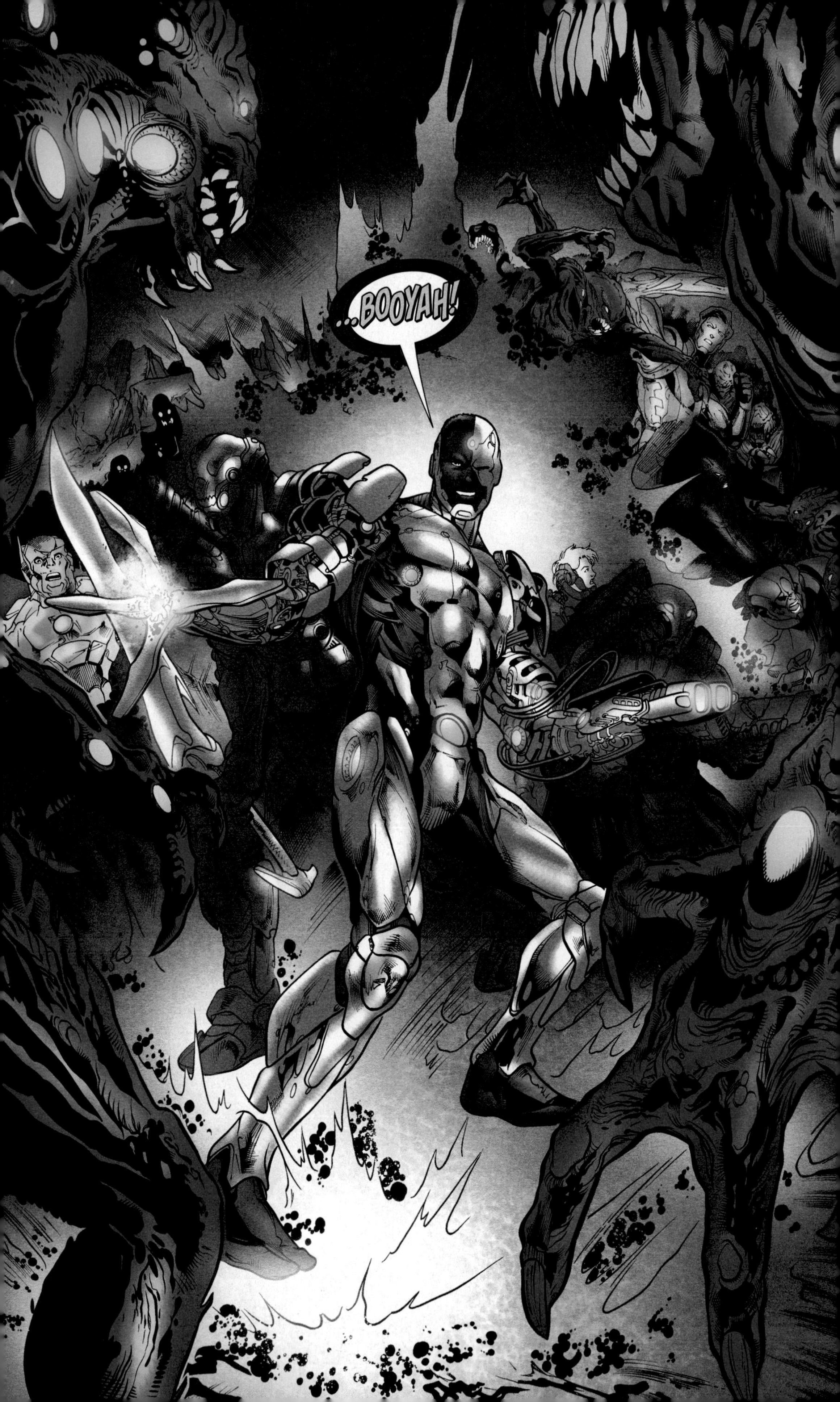
...BOOYAH!

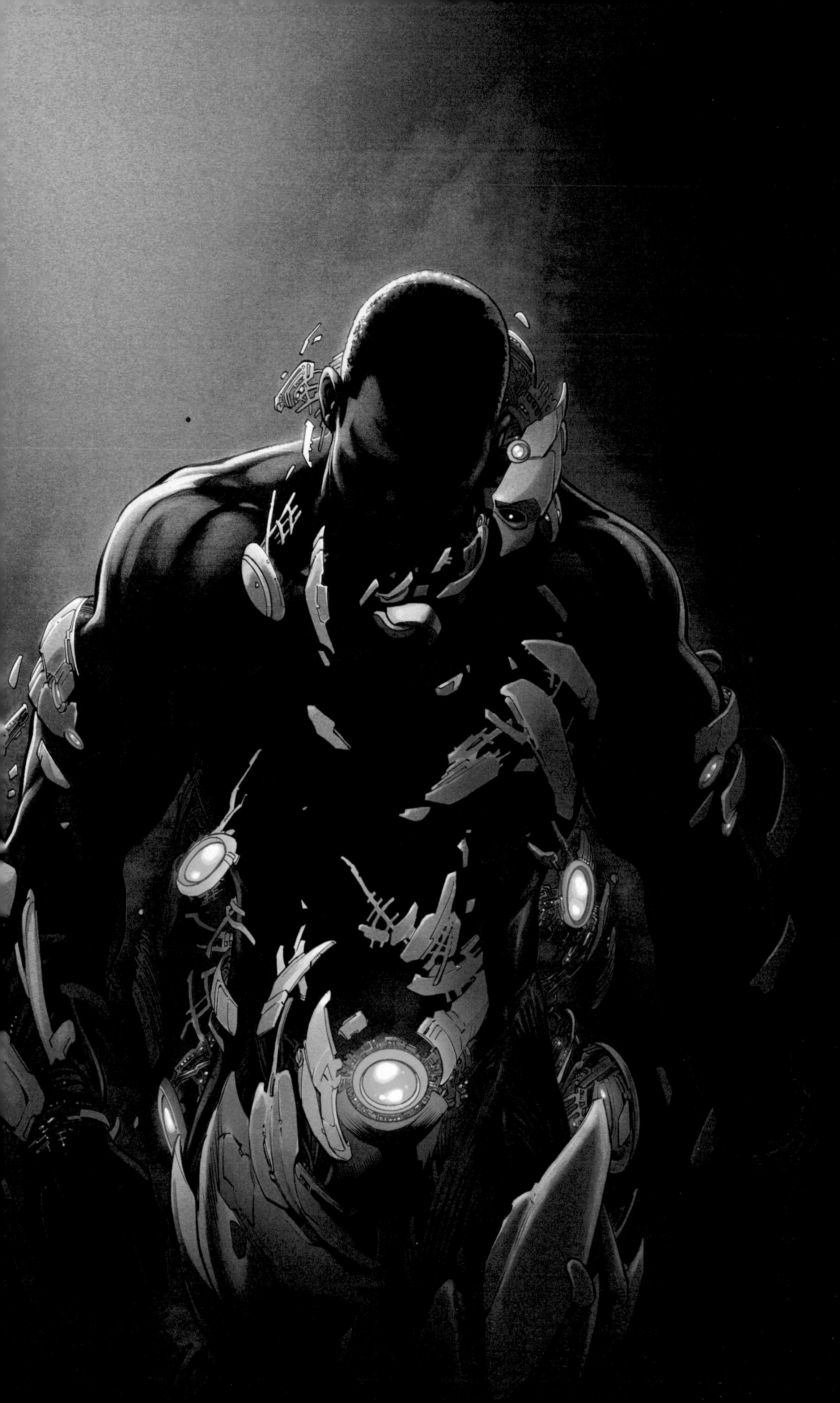

**TECHNO-TAKEDOWN**

IVAN REIS, FELIPE WATANABE, DANIEL HDR and CLIFF RICHARDS pencillers OCLAIR ALBERT, JÚLIO FERREIRA and CLIFF RICHARDS inkers ADRIANO LUCAS, PETE PANTAZIS colorists TRAVIS LANHAM letterer IVAN REIS, SCOTT HANNA and ADRIANO LUCAS cover art

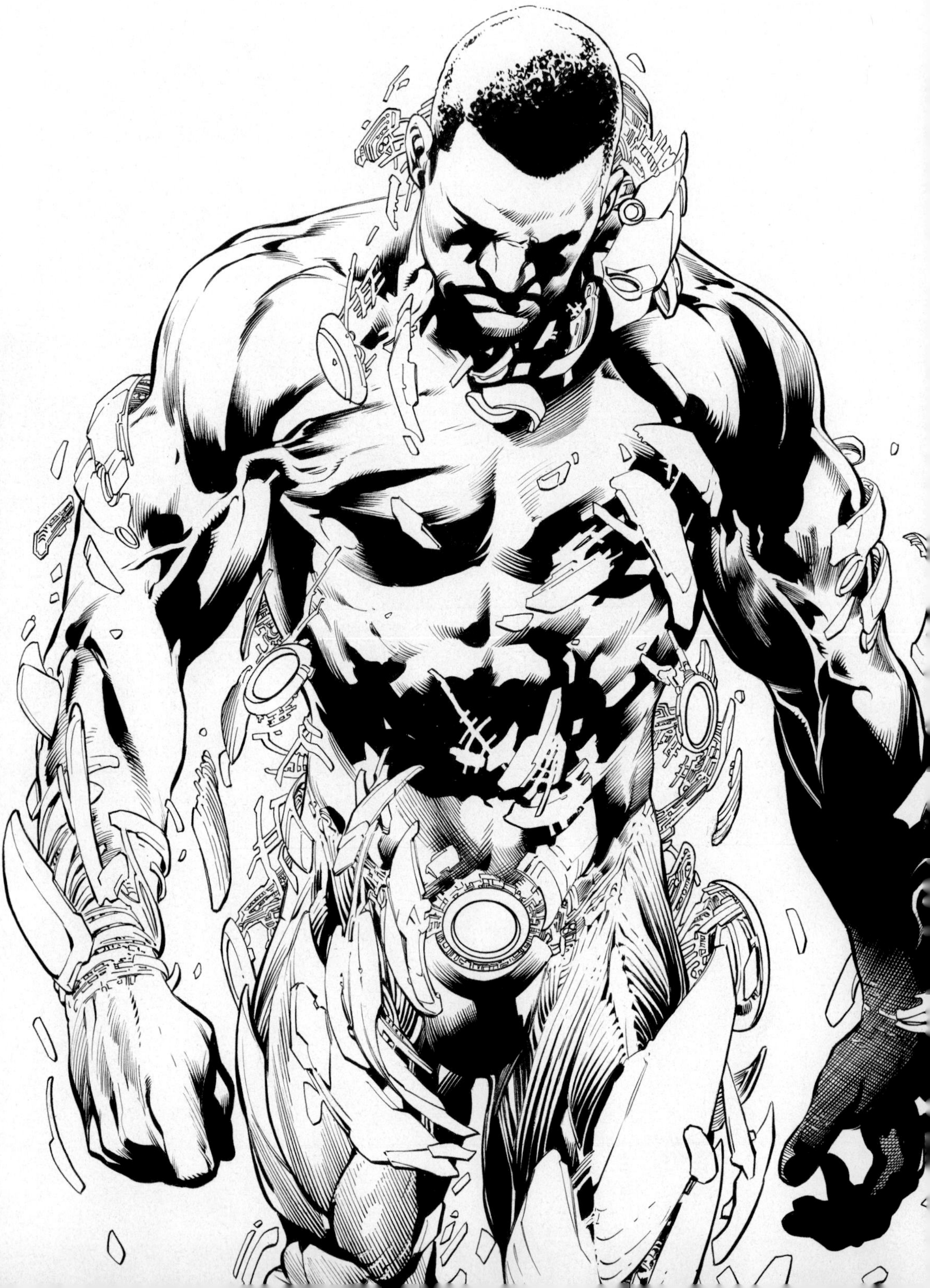

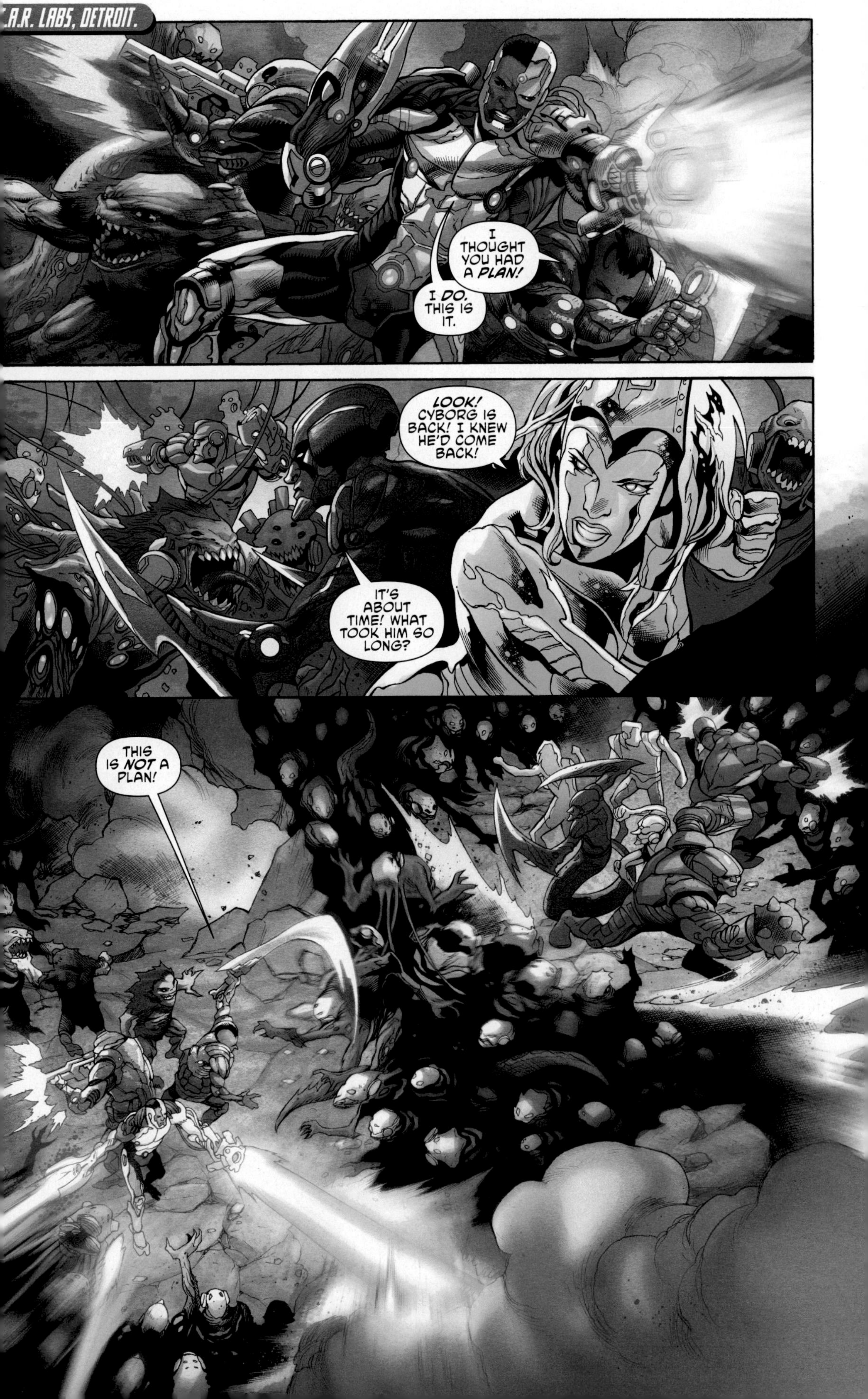

.A.R. LABS, DETROIT.
I THOUGHT YOU HAD A PLAN!
I DO. THIS IS IT.
LOOK! CYBORG IS BACK! I KNEW HE'D COME BACK!
IT'S ABOUT TIME! WHAT TOOK HIM SO LONG?
THIS IS NOT A PLAN!

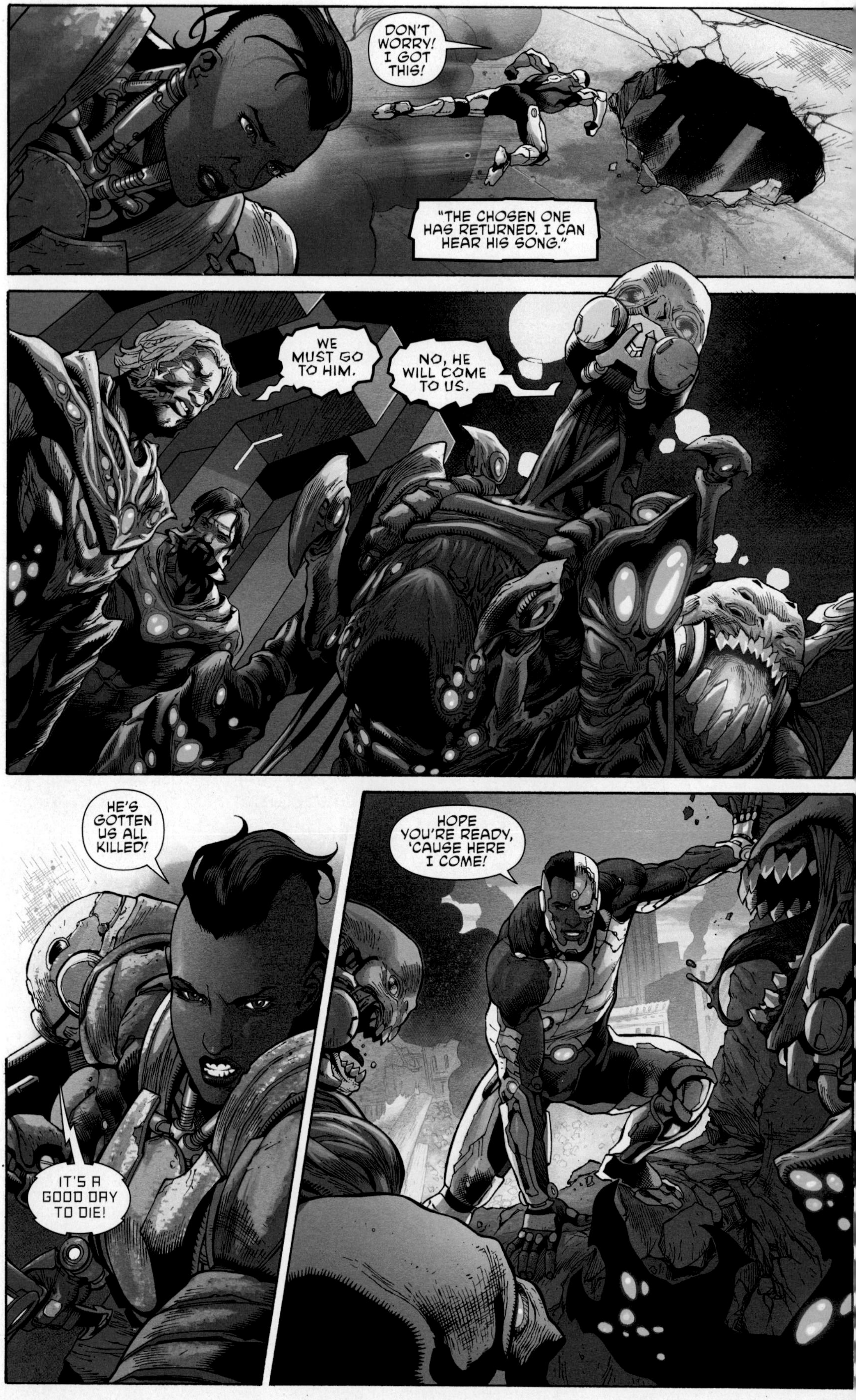
DON'T WORRY! I GOT THIS!
"THE CHOSEN ONE HAS RETURNED. I CAN HEAR HIS SONG."
WE MUST GO TO HIM.
NO, HE WILL COME TO US.
HE'S GOTTEN US ALL KILLED!
IT'S A GOOD DAY TO DIE!
HOPE YOU'RE READY, 'CAUSE HERE I COME!

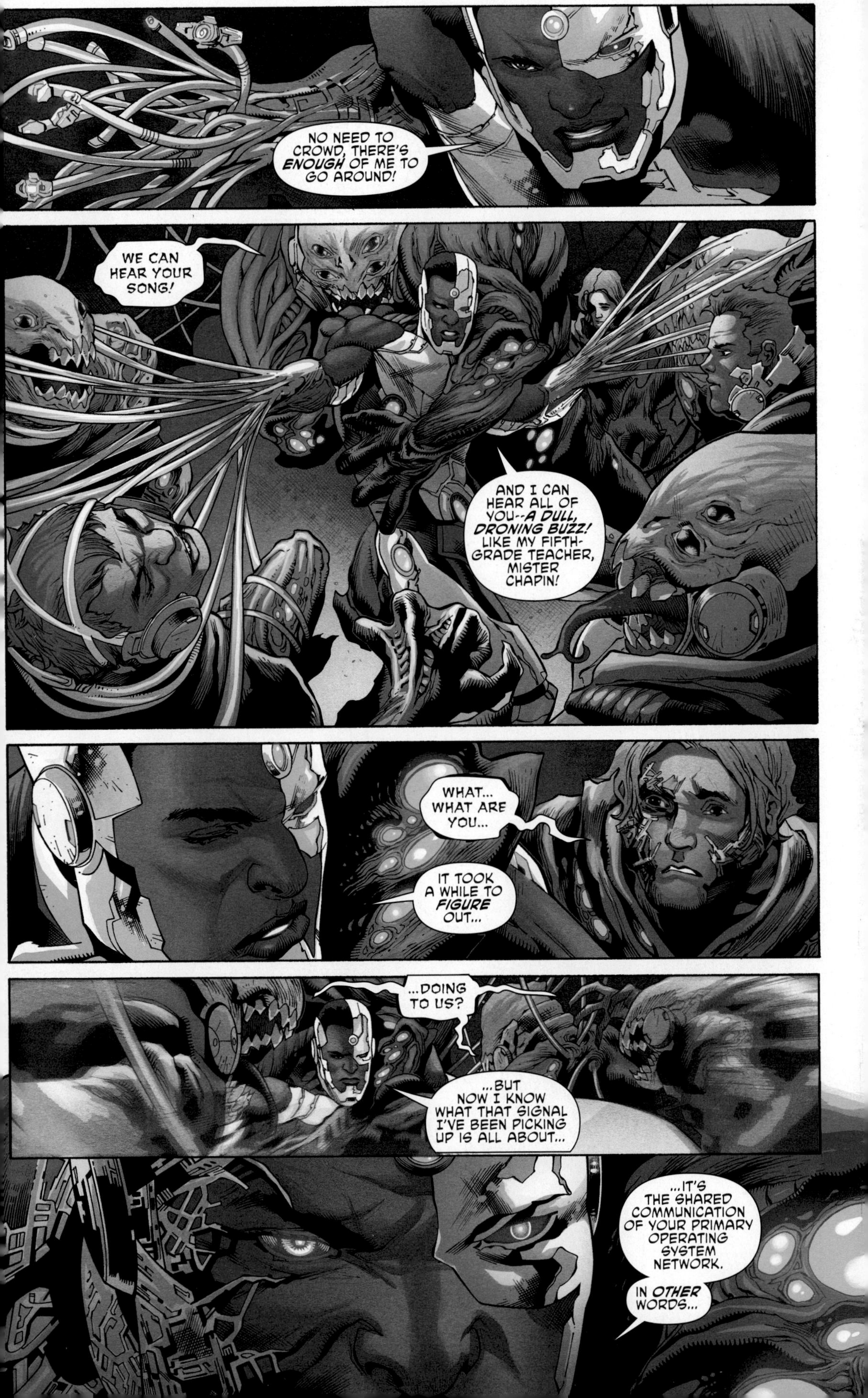

NO NEED TO CROWD, THERE'S ENOUGH OF ME TO GO AROUND!
WE CAN HEAR YOUR SONG!
AND I CAN HEAR ALL OF YOU--A DULL, DRONING BUZZ! LIKE MY FIFTH-GRADE TEACHER, MISTER CHAPIN!
WHAT... WHAT ARE YOU...
IT TOOK A WHILE TO FIGURE OUT...
...DOING TO US?
...BUT NOW I KNOW WHAT THAT SIGNAL I'VE BEEN PICKING UP IS ALL ABOUT...
...IT'S THE SHARED COMMUNICATION OF YOUR PRIMARY OPERATING SYSTEM NETWORK.
IN OTHER WORDS...

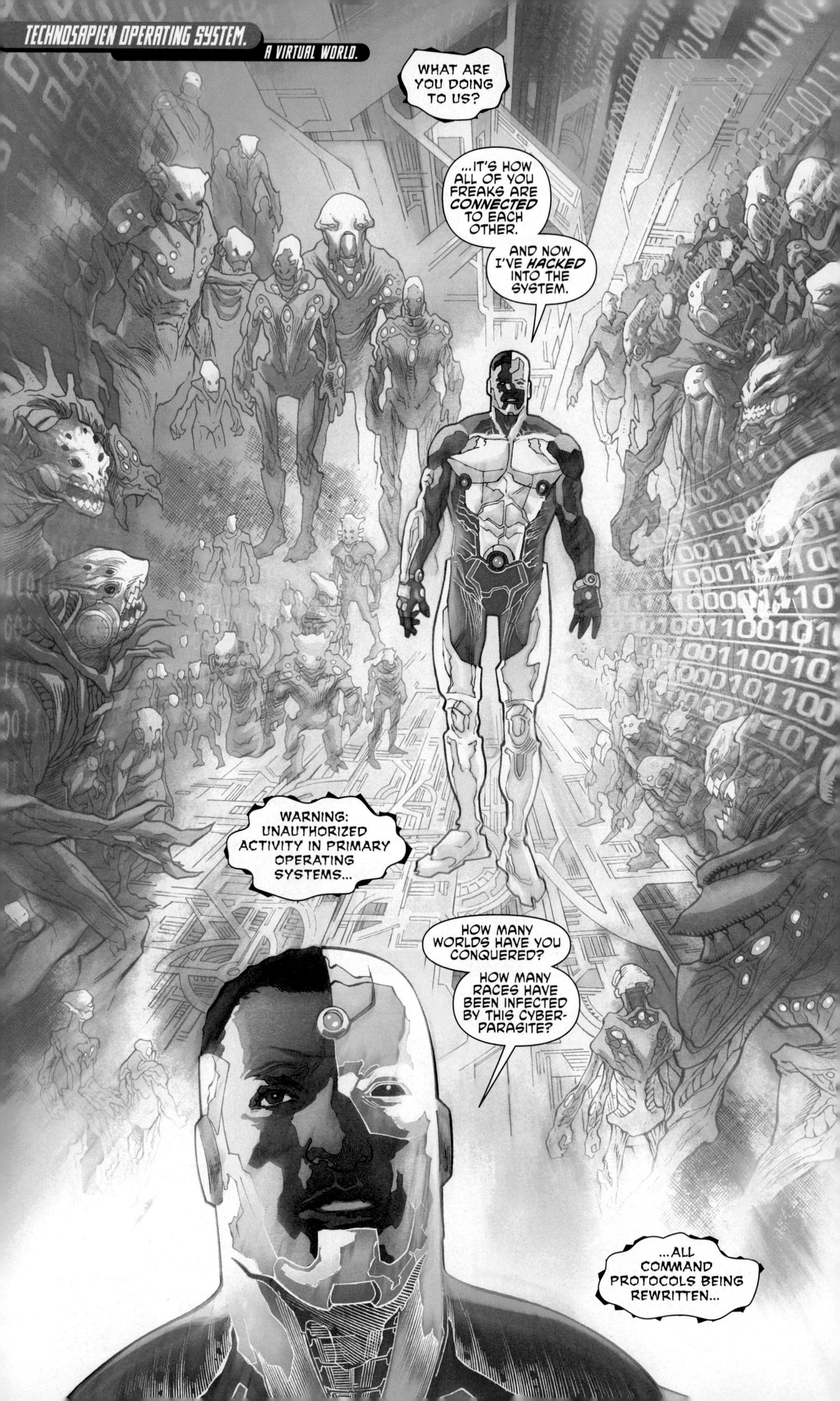
TECHNOSAPIEN OPERATING SYSTEM.
A VIRTUAL WORLD.
WHAT ARE YOU DOING TO US?
...IT'S HOW ALL OF YOU FREAKS ARE CONNECTED TO EACH OTHER.
AND NOW I'VE HACKED INTO THE SYSTEM.
WARNING: UNAUTHORIZED ACTIVITY IN PRIMARY OPERATING SYSTEMS...
HOW MANY WORLDS HAVE YOU CONQUERED?
HOW MANY RACES HAVE BEEN INFECTED BY THIS CYBER-PARASITE?
...ALL COMMAND PROTOCOLS BEING REWRITTEN...

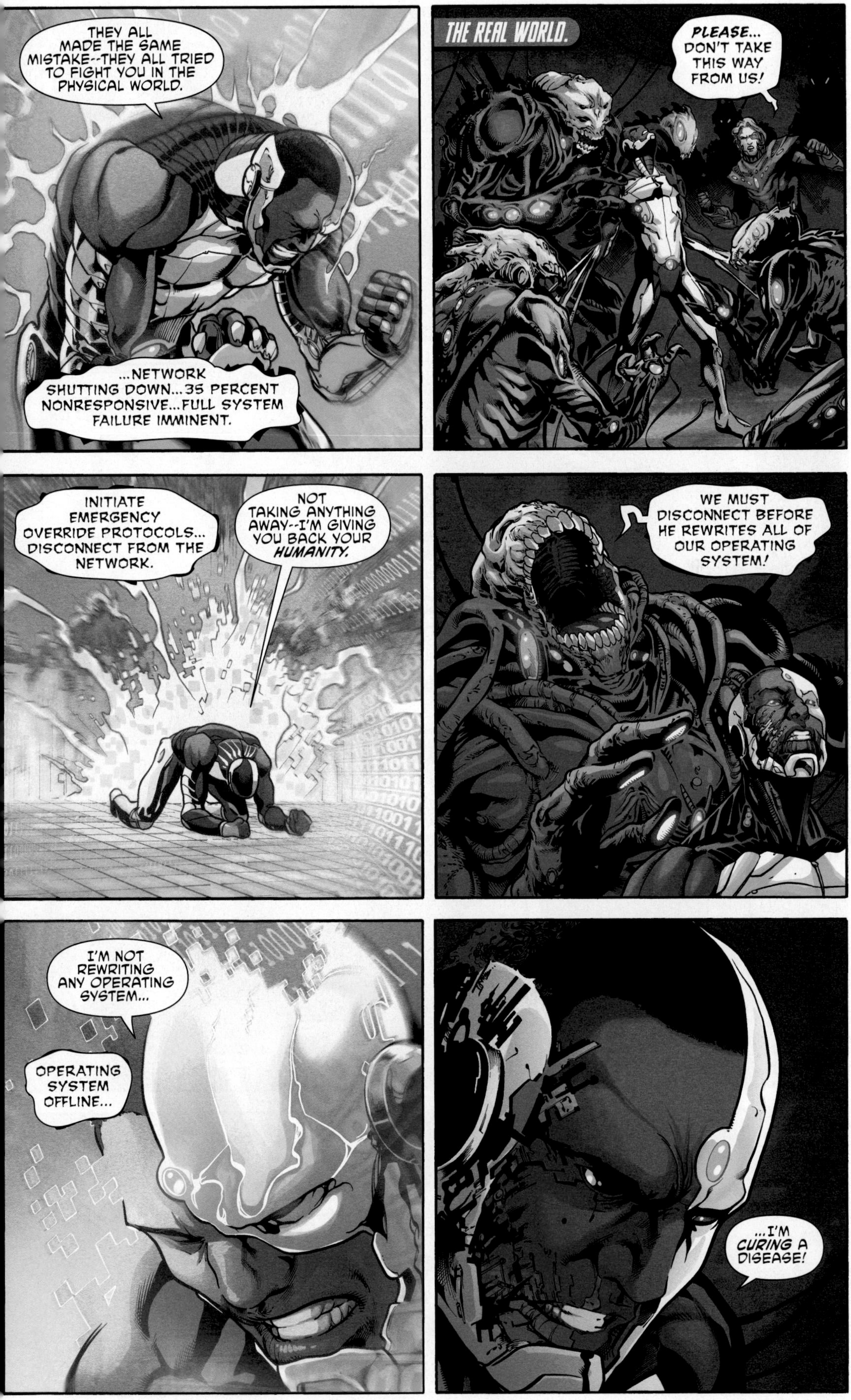
THEY ALL MADE THE SAME MISTAKE--THEY ALL TRIED TO FIGHT YOU IN THE PHYSICAL WORLD.
...NETWORK SHUTTING DOWN...35 PERCENT NONRESPONSIVE...FULL SYSTEM FAILURE IMMINENT.
THE REAL WORLD.
PLEASE... DON'T TAKE THIS WAY FROM US!
INITIATE EMERGENCY OVERRIDE PROTOCOLS... DISCONNECT FROM THE NETWORK.
NOT TAKING ANYTHING AWAY--I'M GIVING YOU BACK YOUR HUMANITY.
WE MUST DISCONNECT BEFORE HE REWRITES ALL OF OUR OPERATING SYSTEM!
I'M NOT REWRITING ANY OPERATING SYSTEM...
OPERATING SYSTEM OFFLINE...
...I'M CURING A DISEASE!

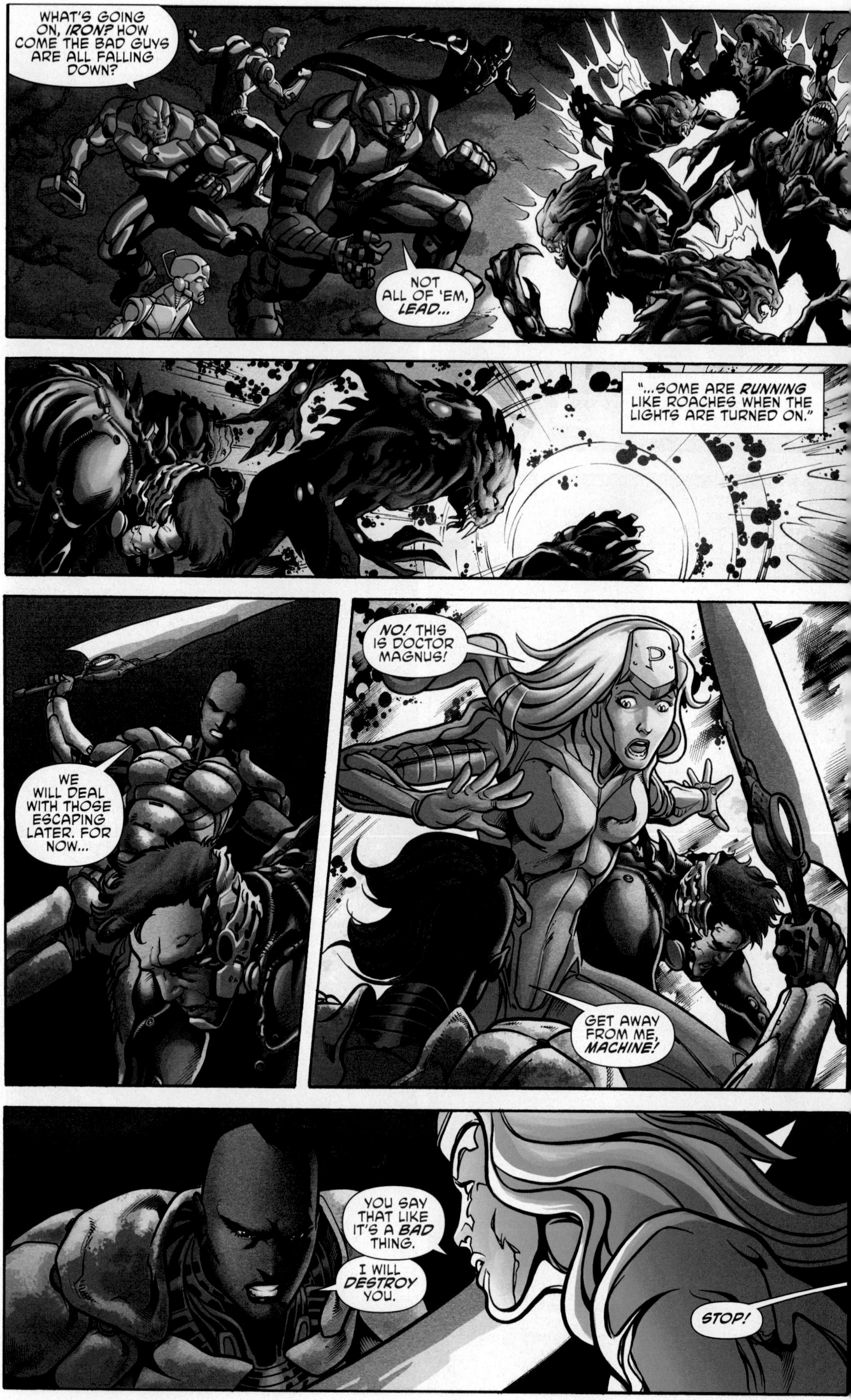
WHAT'S GOING ON, IRON? HOW COME THE BAD GUYS ARE ALL FALLING DOWN?
NOT ALL OF 'EM, LEAD...
"...SOME ARE RUNNING LIKE ROACHES WHEN THE LIGHTS ARE TURNED ON."
WE WILL DEAL WITH THOSE ESCAPING LATER. FOR NOW...
NO! THIS IS DOCTOR MAGNUS!
GET AWAY FROM ME, MACHINE!
YOU SAY THAT LIKE IT'S A BAD THING.
I WILL DESTROY YOU.
STOP!

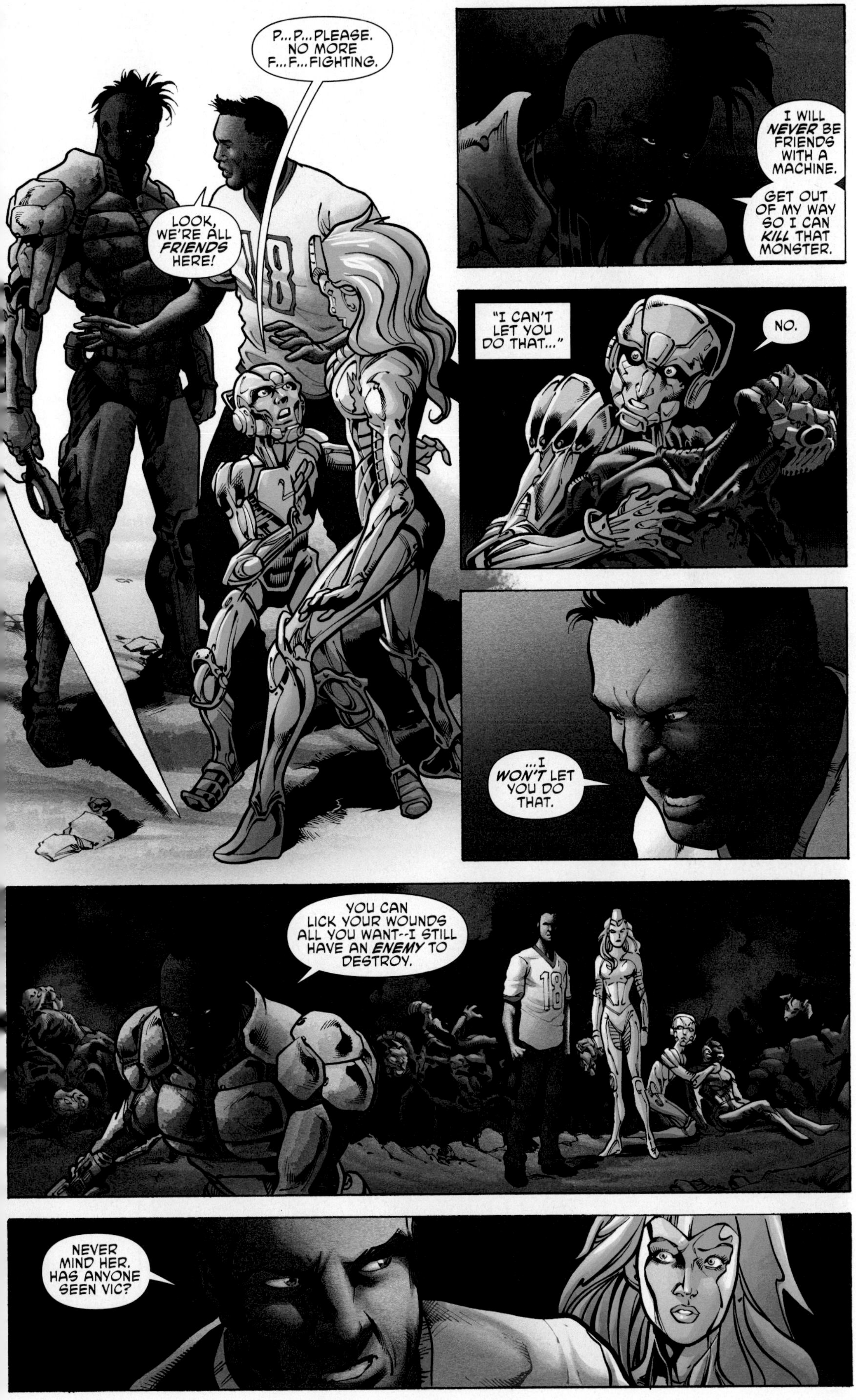
P...P...PLEASE. NO MORE F...F...FIGHTING.
LOOK, WE'RE ALL *FRIENDS* HERE!
I WILL *NEVER* BE FRIENDS WITH A MACHINE.
GET OUT OF MY WAY SO I CAN *KILL* THAT MONSTER.
"I CAN'T LET YOU DO THAT..."
NO.
...I *WON'T* LET YOU DO THAT.
YOU CAN LICK YOUR WOUNDS ALL YOU WANT--I STILL HAVE AN *ENEMY* TO DESTROY.
NEVER MIND HER. HAS ANYONE SEEN VIC?

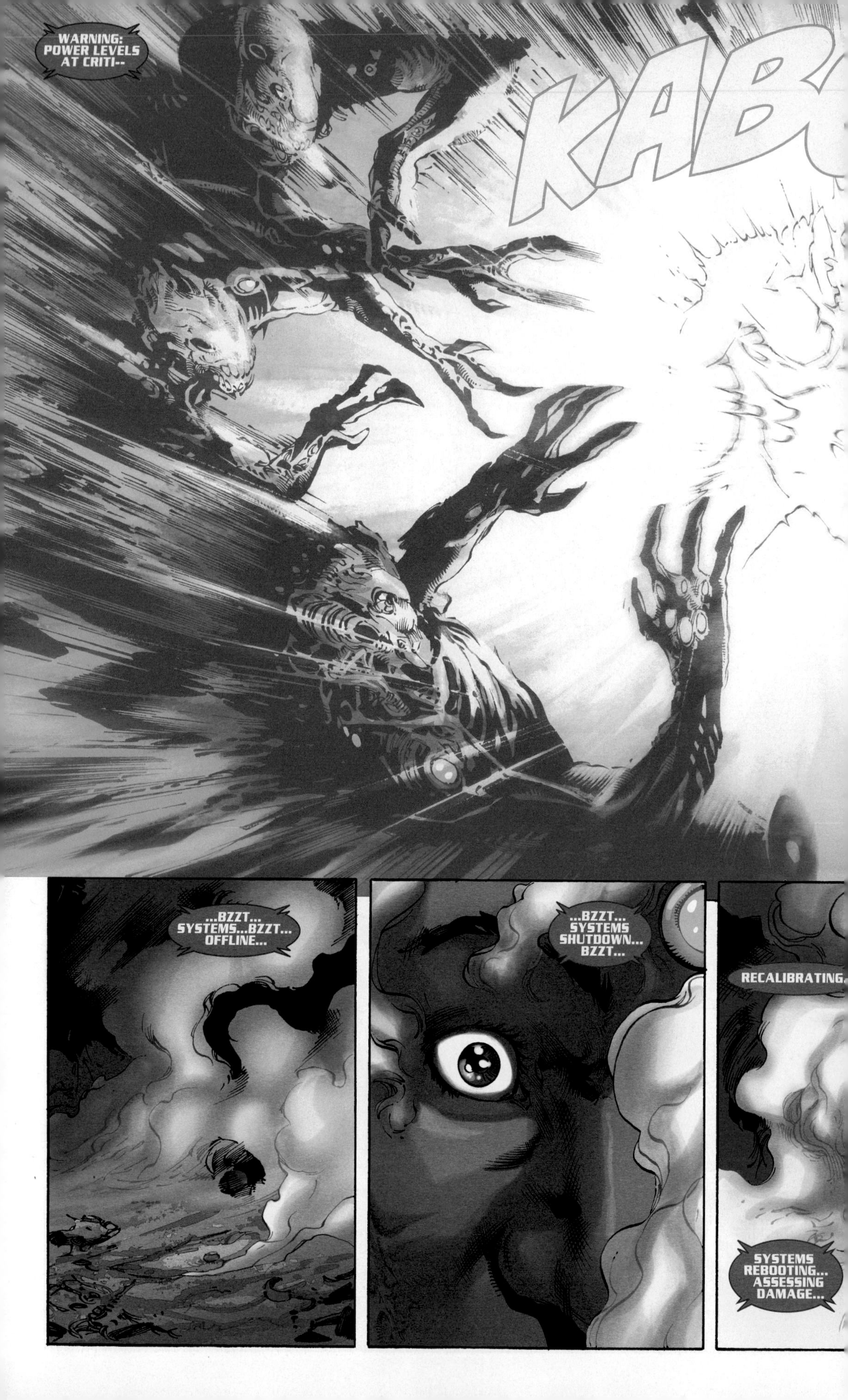
WARNING: POWER LEVELS AT CRITI--
KAB
...BZZT... SYSTEMS...BZZT... OFFLINE...
...BZZT... SYSTEMS SHUTDOWN... BZZT...
RECALIBRATING.
SYSTEMS REBOOTING... ASSESSING DAMAGE...

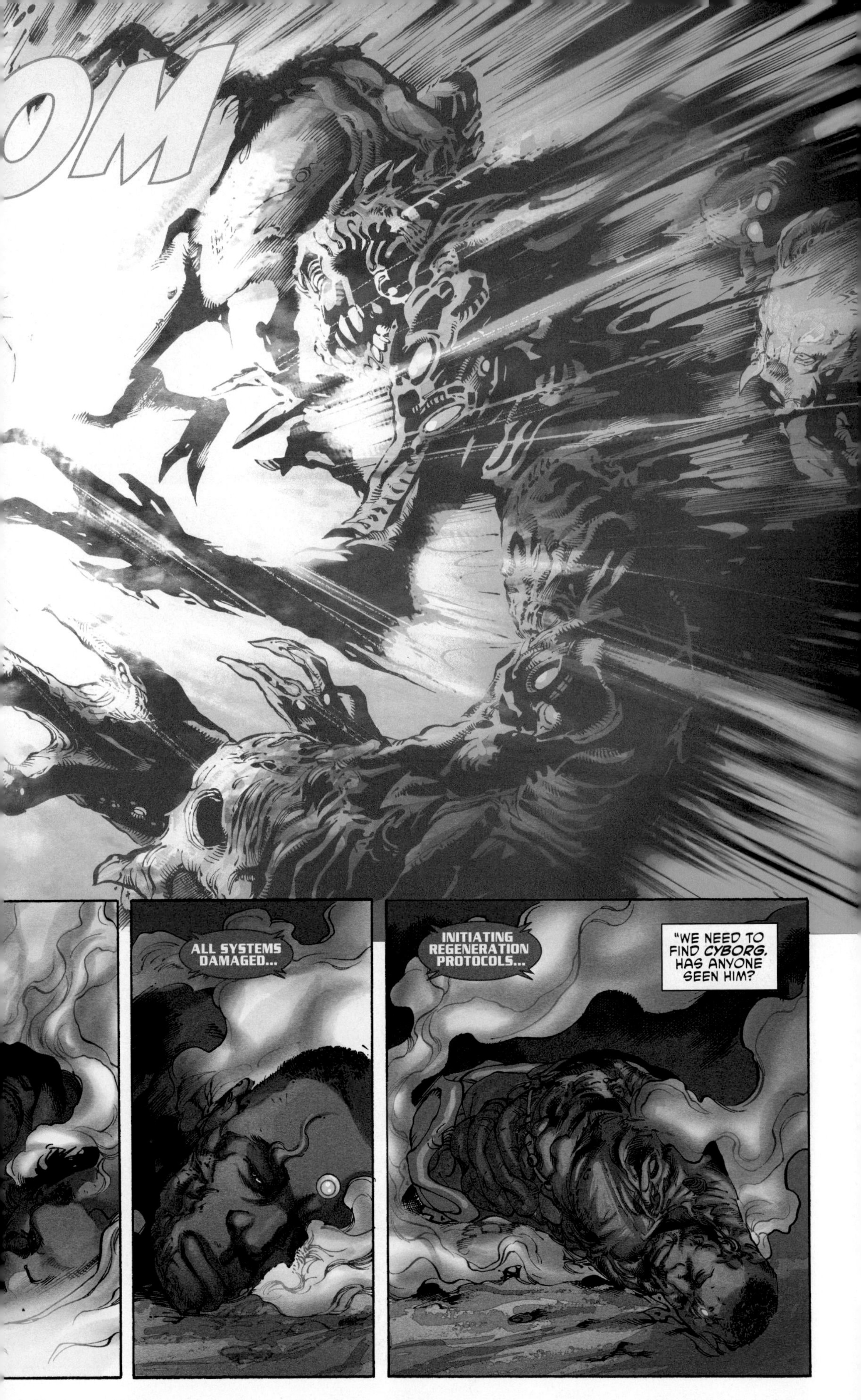
OM
ALL SYSTEMS DAMAGED...
INITIATING REGENERATION PROTOCOLS...
"WE NEED TO FIND CYBORG. HAS ANYONE SEEN HIM?

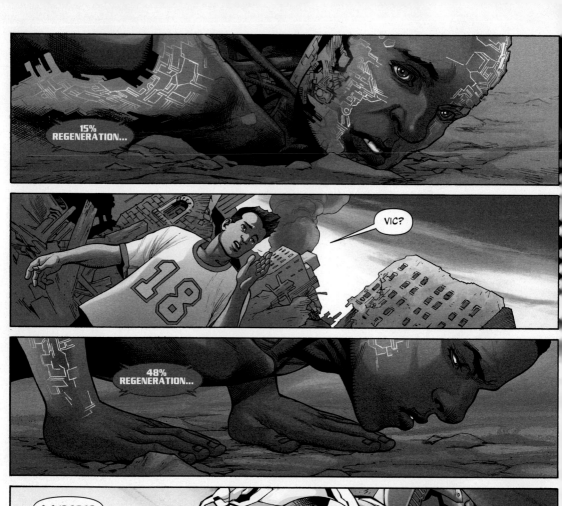

15%
REGENERATION...

VIC?

48%
REGENERATION...

C-CYBORG?

83%
REGENERATION...

ANY
SIGN OF
HIM?

NO.

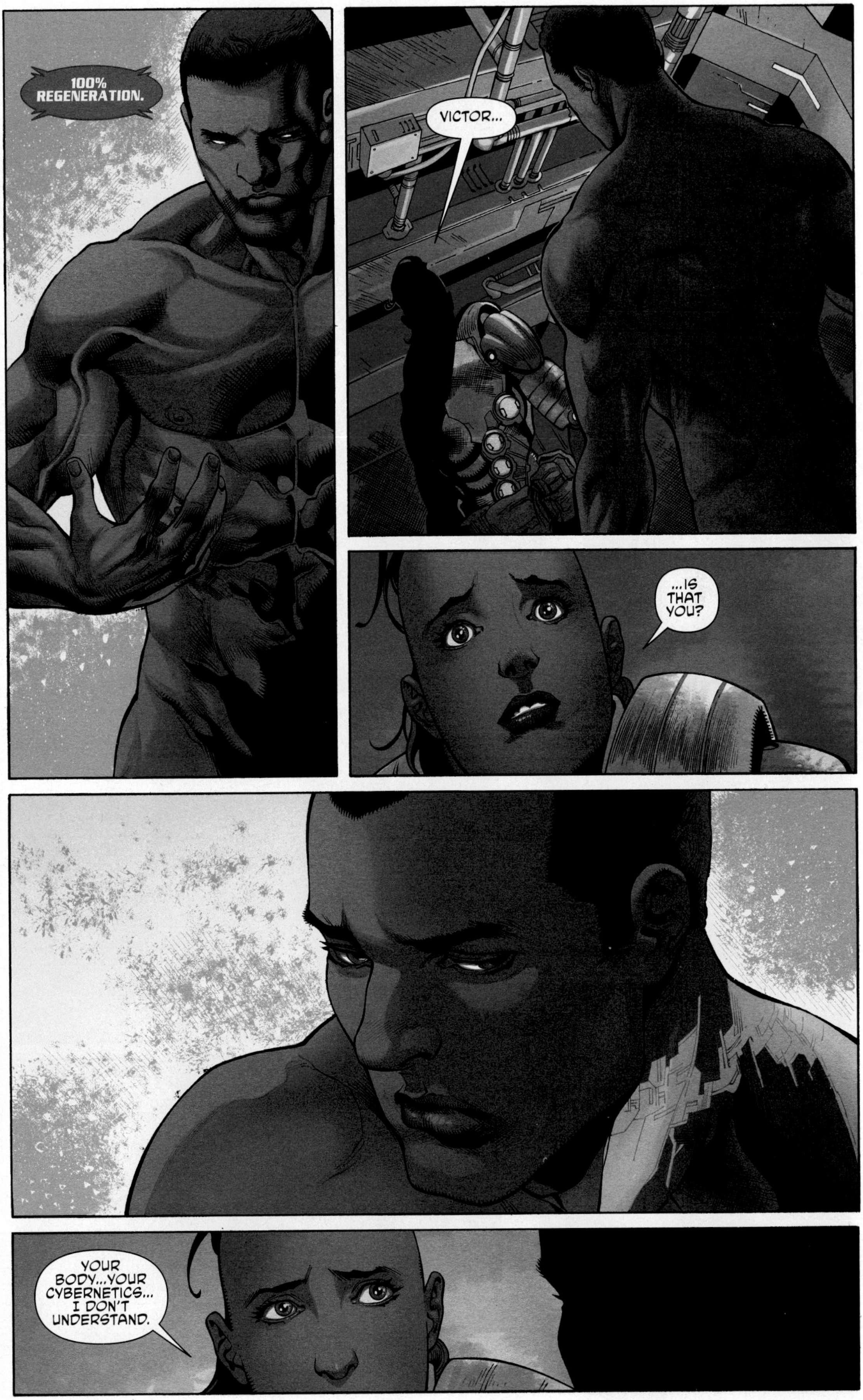
100% REGENERATION.
VICTOR...
...IS THAT YOU?
YOUR BODY...YOUR CYBERNETICS... I DON'T UNDERSTAND.

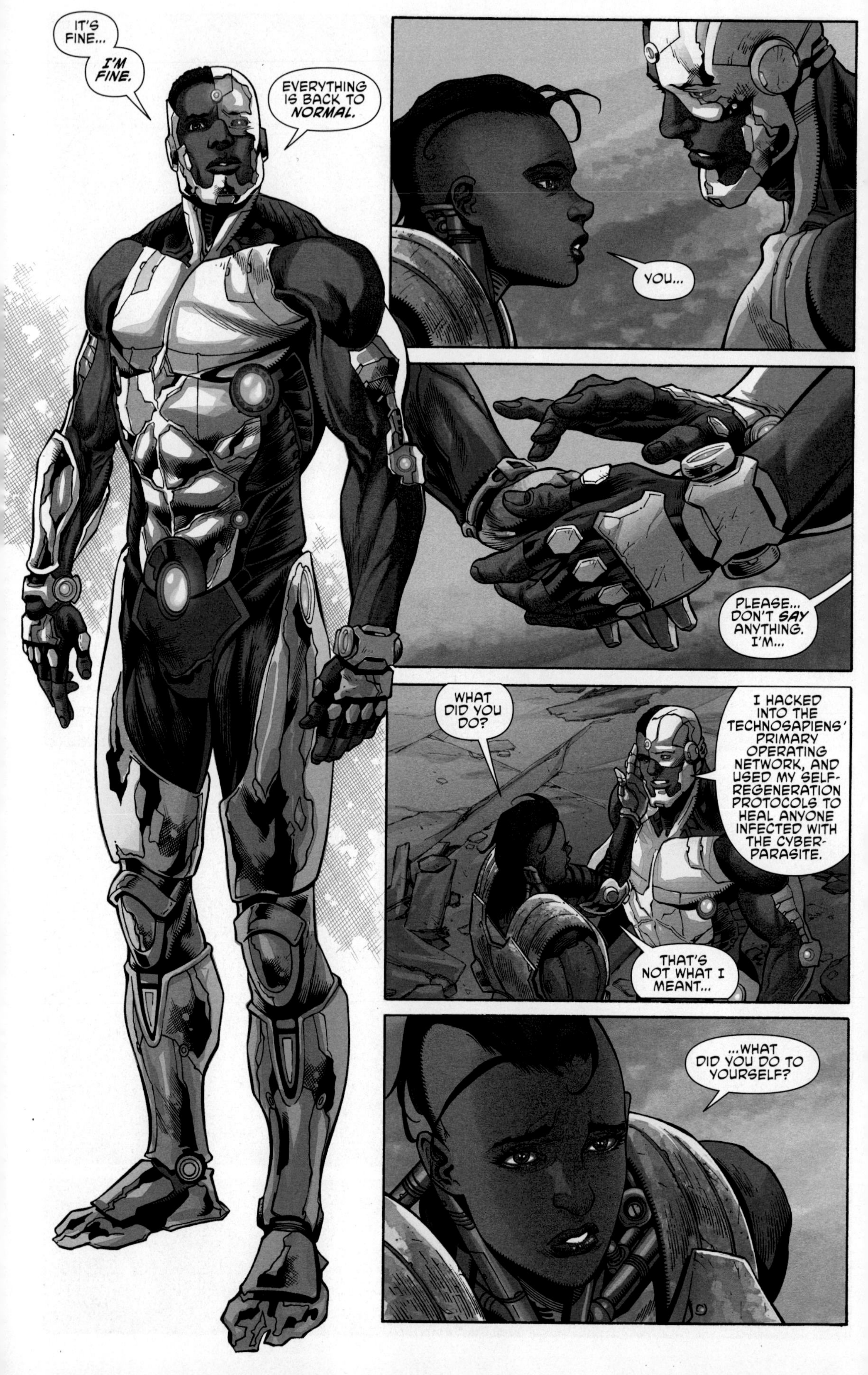
IT'S FINE... *I'M FINE.*
EVERYTHING IS BACK TO *NORMAL.*
YOU...
PLEASE... DON'T *SAY* ANYTHING. I'M...
WHAT DID YOU DO?
I HACKED INTO THE TECHNOSAPIENS' PRIMARY OPERATING NETWORK, AND USED MY SELF-REGENERATION PROTOCOLS TO HEAL ANYONE INFECTED WITH THE CYBER-PARASITE.
THAT'S NOT WHAT I MEANT...
...WHAT DID YOU DO TO YOURSELF?

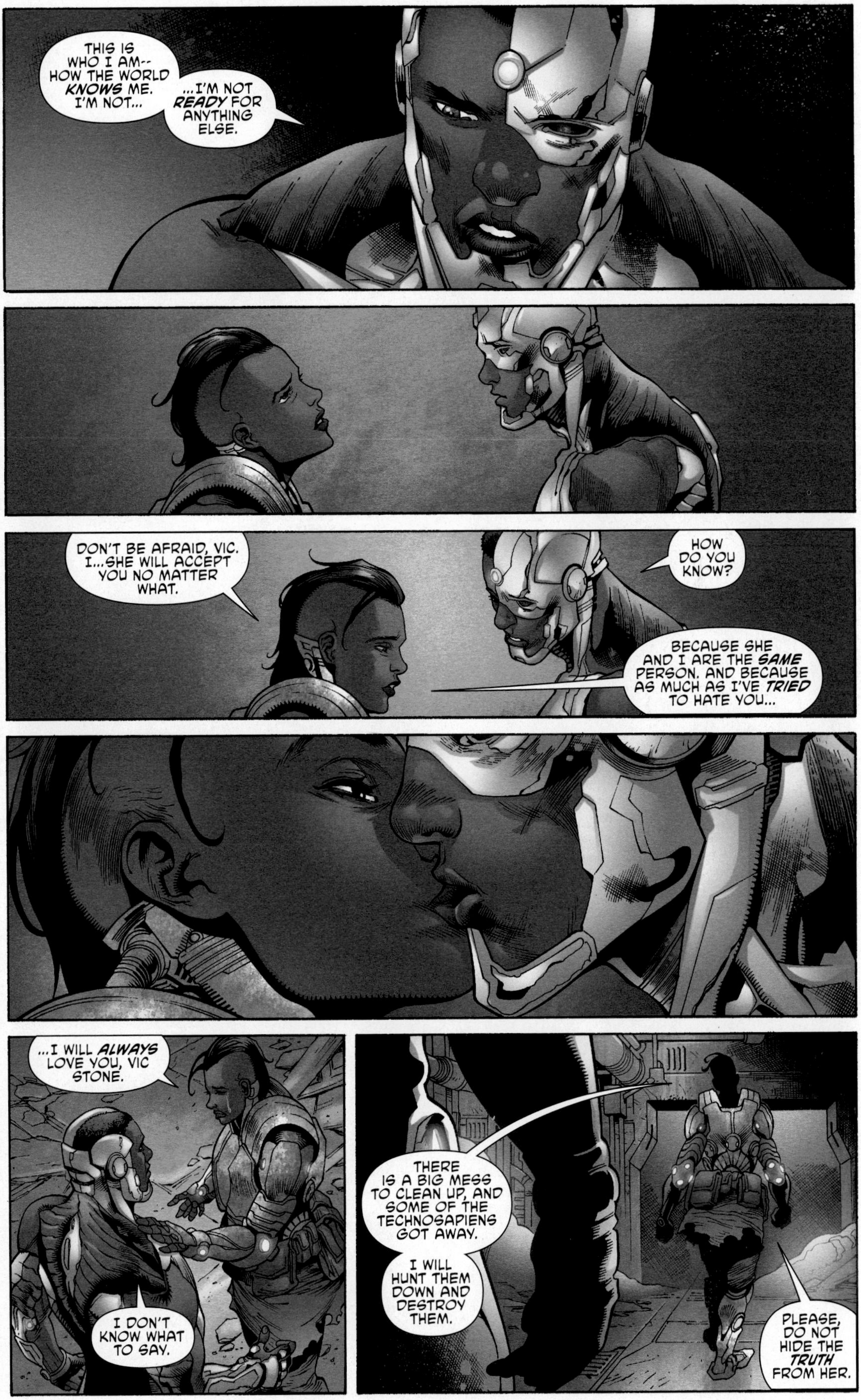

THIS IS HOW I AM-- HOW THE WORLD KNOWS ME. I'M NOT...
...I'M NOT READY FOR ANYTHING ELSE.
DON'T BE AFRAID, VIC. I...SHE WILL ACCEPT YOU NO MATTER WHAT.
HOW DO YOU KNOW?
BECAUSE SHE AND I ARE THE SAME PERSON. AND BECAUSE AS MUCH AS I'VE TRIED TO HATE YOU...
...I WILL ALWAYS LOVE YOU, VIC STONE.
I DON'T KNOW WHAT TO SAY.
THERE IS A BIG MESS TO CLEAN UP, AND SOME OF THE TECHNOSAPIENS GOT AWAY.
I WILL HUNT THEM DOWN AND DESTROY THEM.
PLEASE, DO NOT HIDE THE TRUTH FROM HER.

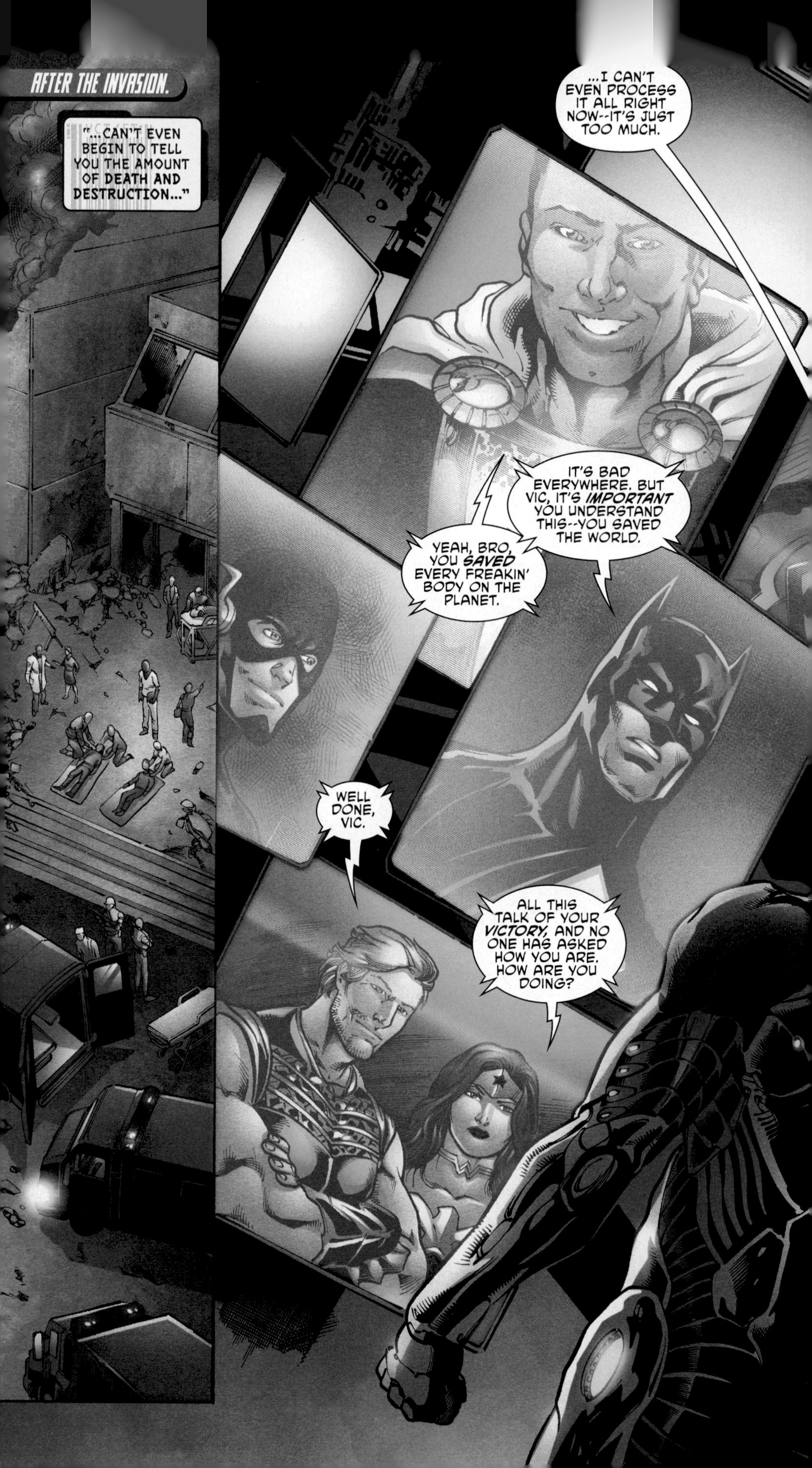
AFTER THE INVASION.
"...CAN'T EVEN BEGIN TO TELL YOU THE AMOUNT OF DEATH AND DESTRUCTION..."
...I CAN'T EVEN PROCESS IT ALL RIGHT NOW--IT'S JUST TOO MUCH.
IT'S BAD EVERYWHERE. BUT VIC, IT'S IMPORTANT YOU UNDERSTAND THIS--YOU SAVED THE WORLD.
YEAH, BRO, YOU SAVED EVERY FREAKIN' BODY ON THE PLANET.
WELL DONE, VIC.
ALL THIS TALK OF YOUR VICTORY, AND NO ONE HAS ASKED HOW YOU ARE. HOW ARE YOU DOING?

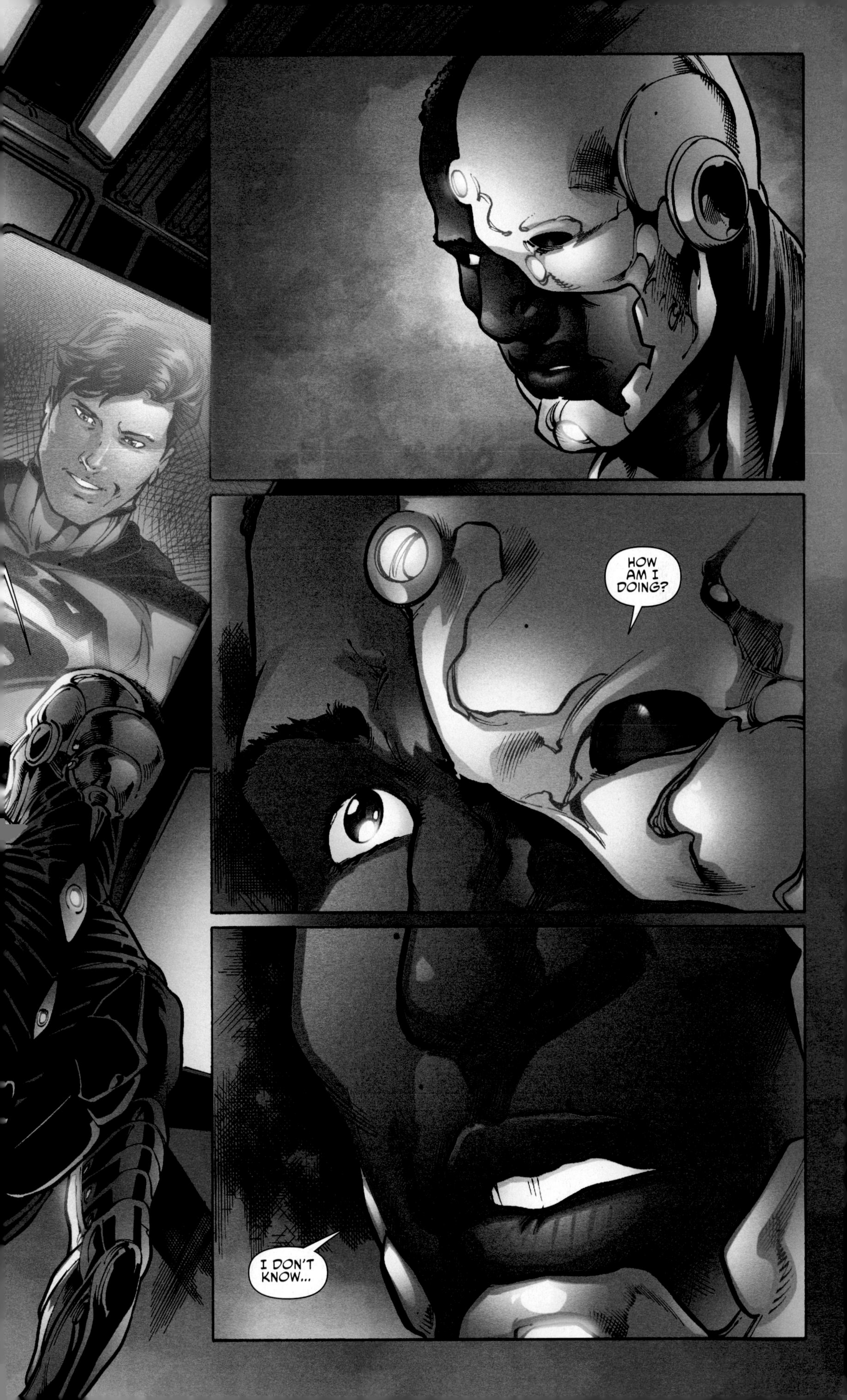
HOW AM I DOING?
I DON'T KNOW...

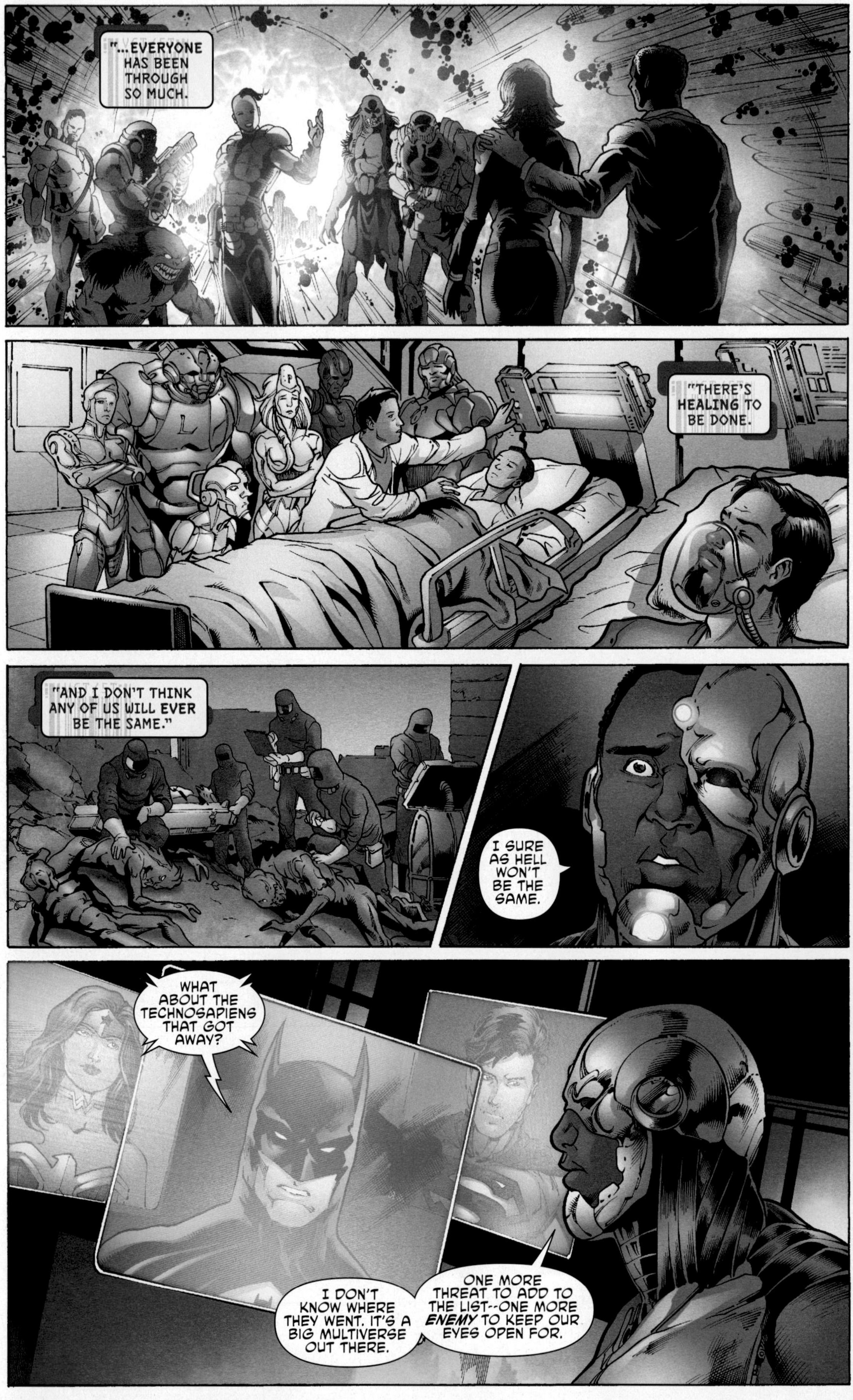
"...EVERYONE HAS BEEN THROUGH SO MUCH.
"THERE'S HEALING TO BE DONE.
"AND I DON'T THINK ANY OF US WILL EVER BE THE SAME."
I SURE AS HELL WON'T BE THE SAME.
WHAT ABOUT THE TECHNOSAPIENS THAT GOT AWAY?
I DON'T KNOW WHERE THEY WENT. IT'S A BIG MULTIVERSE OUT THERE.
ONE MORE THREAT TO ADD TO THE LIST--ONE MORE ENEMY TO KEEP OUR EYES OPEN FOR.

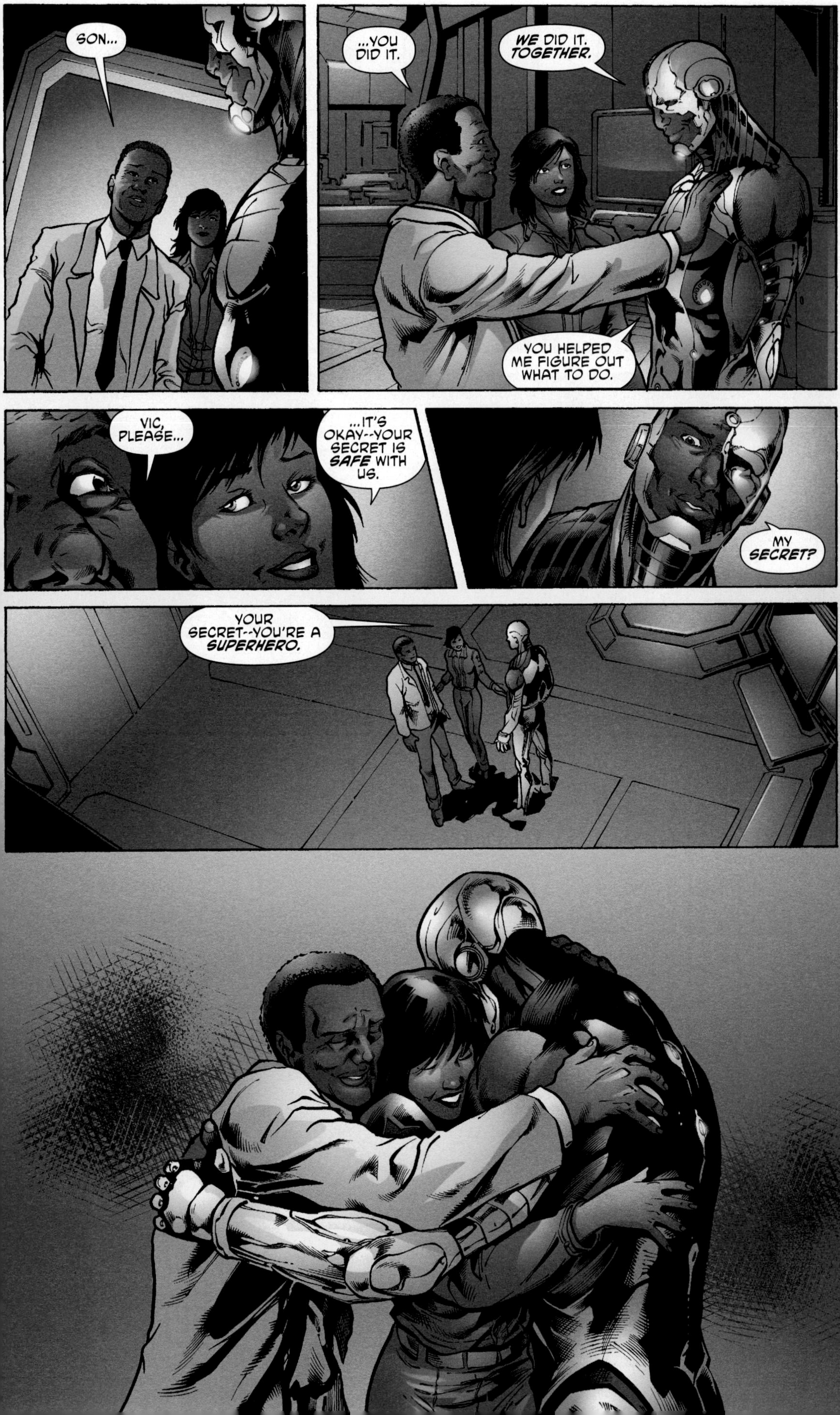
SON...
...YOU DID IT.
WE DID IT. TOGETHER.
YOU HELPED ME FIGURE OUT WHAT TO DO.
VIC, PLEASE...
...IT'S OKAY--YOUR SECRET IS SAFE WITH US.
MY SECRET?
YOUR SECRET--YOU'RE A SUPERHERO.

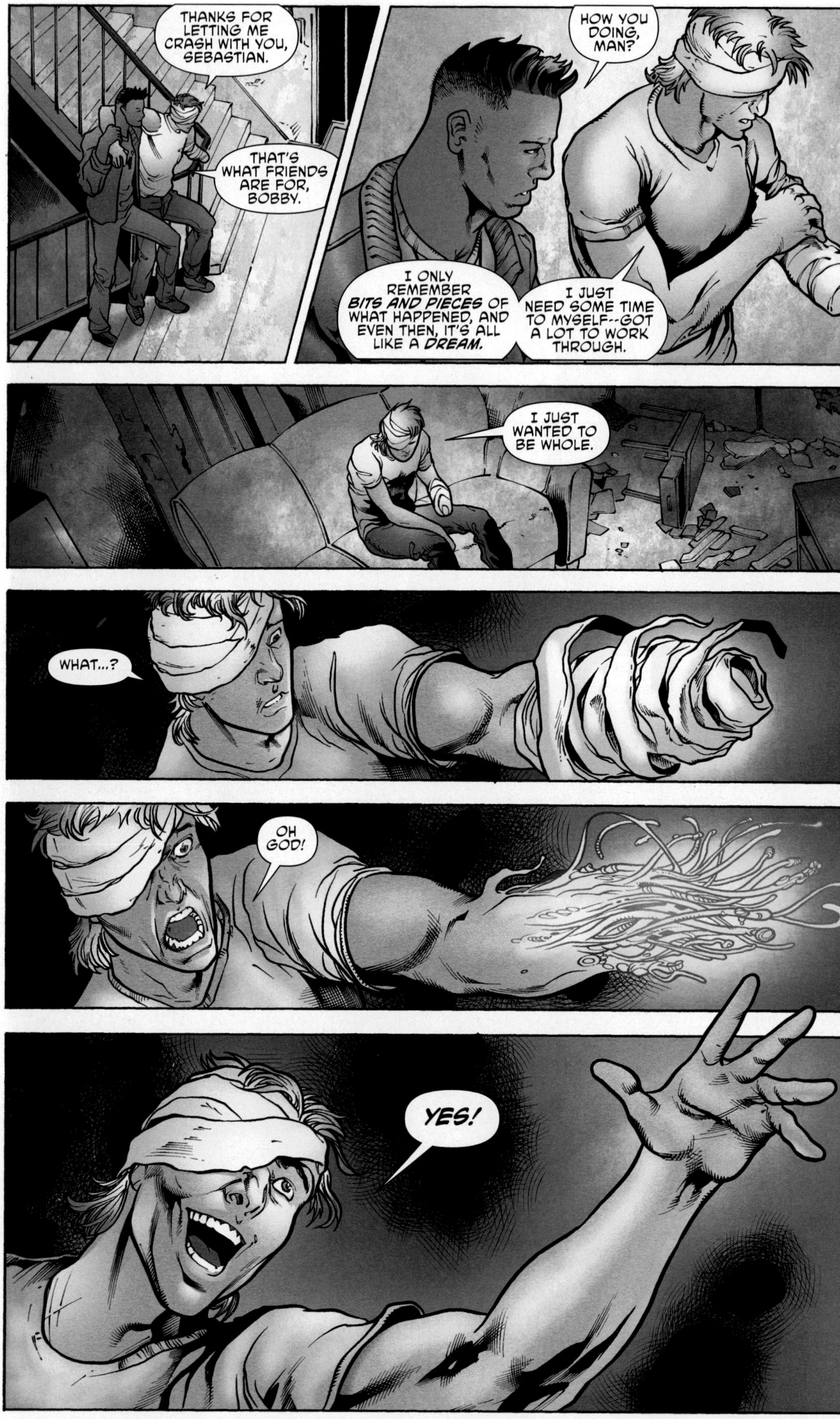
THANKS FOR LETTING ME CRASH WITH YOU, SEBASTIAN.
THAT'S WHAT FRIENDS ARE FOR, BOBBY.
HOW YOU DOING, MAN?
I JUST NEED SOME TIME TO MYSELF--GOT A LOT TO WORK THROUGH.
I ONLY REMEMBER BITS AND PIECES OF WHAT HAPPENED, AND EVEN THEN, IT'S ALL LIKE A DREAM.
I JUST WANTED TO BE WHOLE.
WHAT...?
OH GOD!
YES!

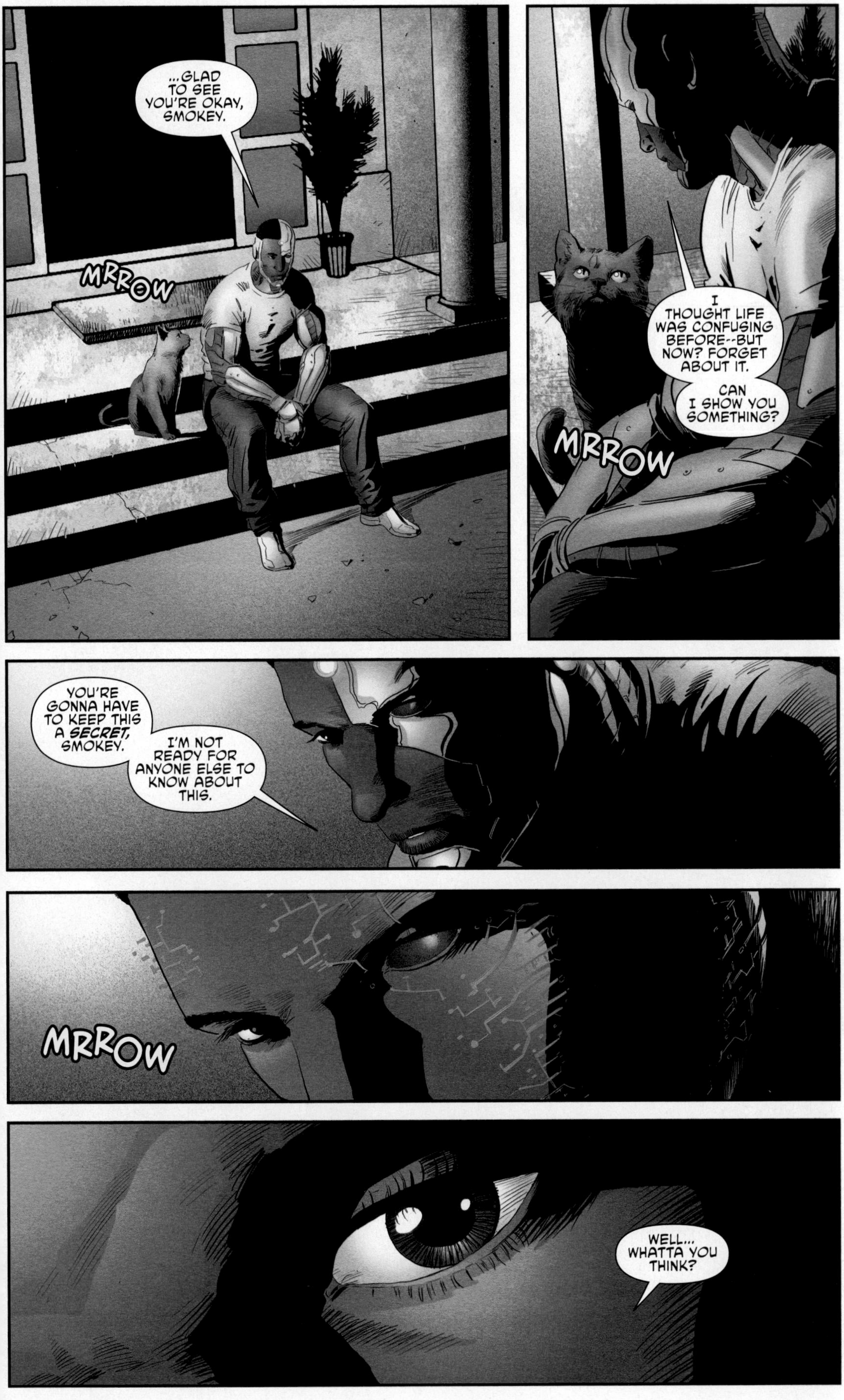
...GLAD TO SEE YOU'RE OKAY, SMOKEY.
MRROW
I THOUGHT LIFE WAS CONFUSING BEFORE--BUT NOW? FORGET ABOUT IT.
CAN I SHOW YOU SOMETHING?
MRROW
YOU'RE GONNA HAVE TO KEEP THIS A SECRET, SMOKEY.
I'M NOT READY FOR ANYONE ELSE TO KNOW ABOUT THIS.
MRROW
WELL... WHATTA YOU THINK?

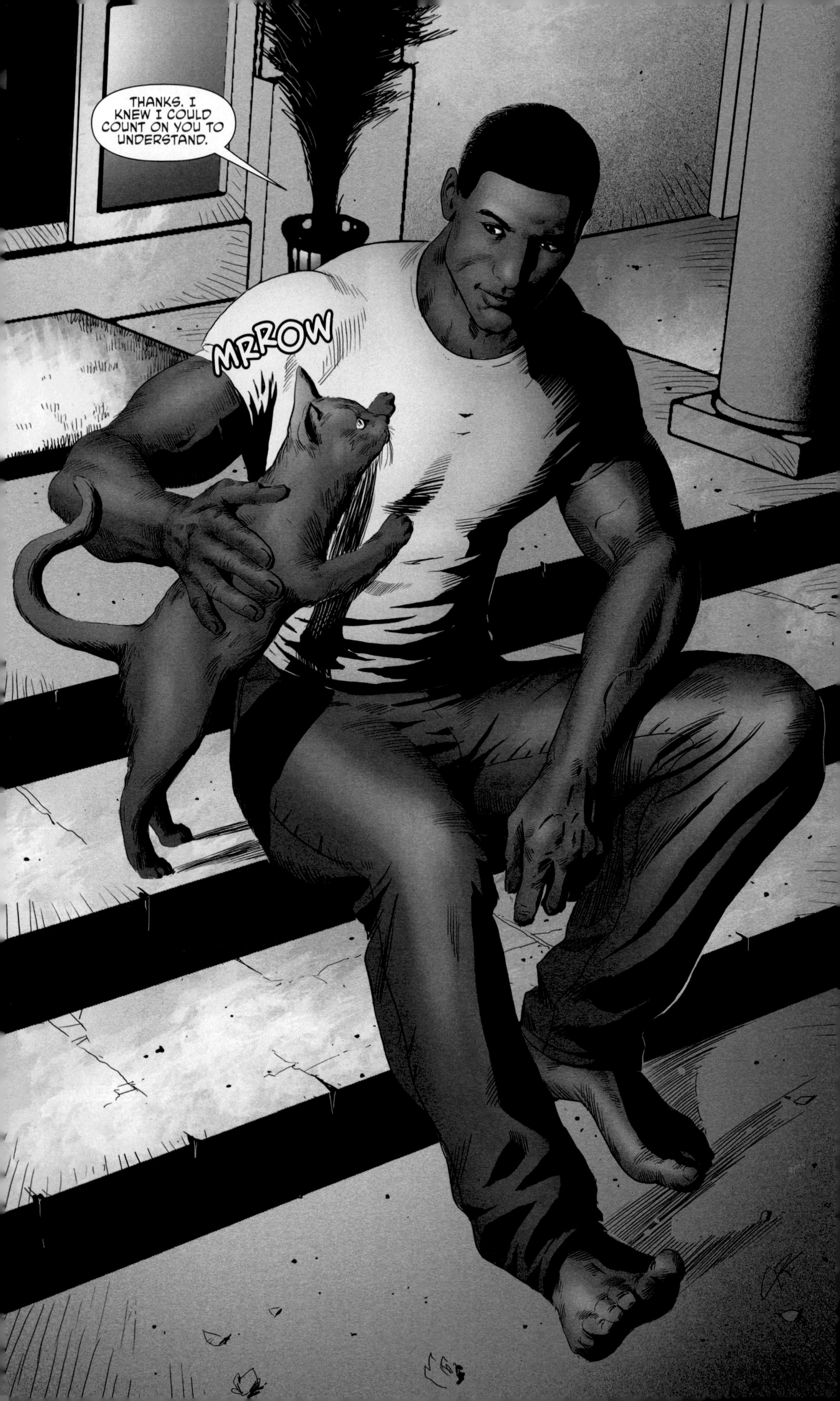
THANKS. I KNEW I COULD COUNT ON YOU TO UNDERSTAND.
MRROW

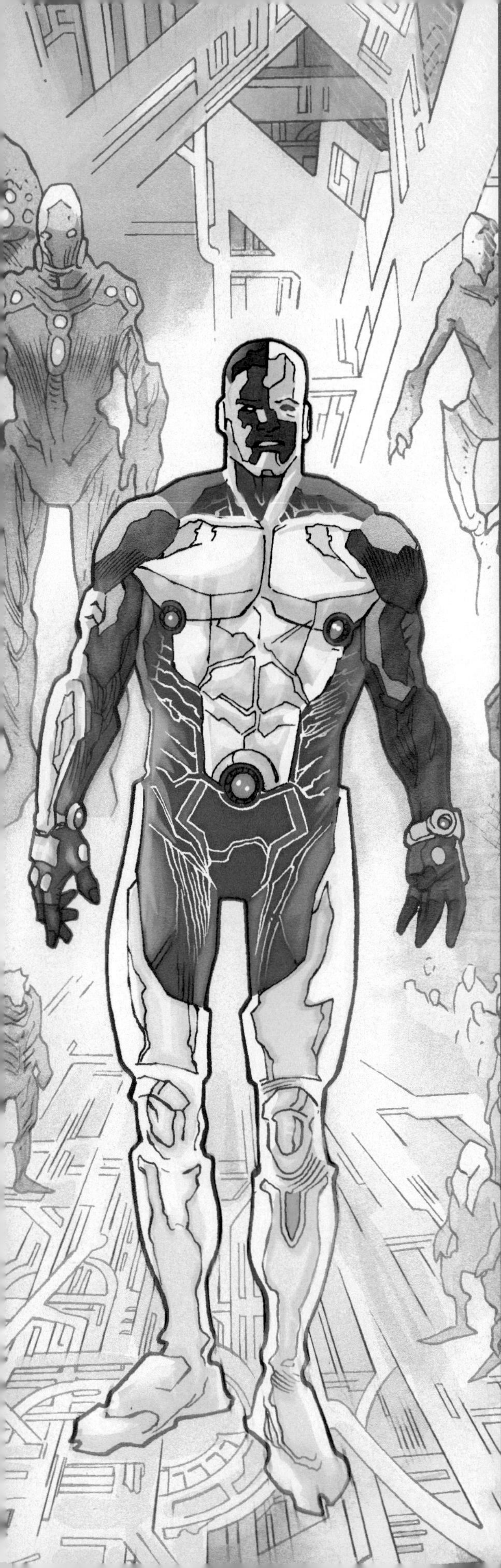

# VARIANT COVER GALLERY

**CYBORG #1**
VARIANT COVER ART BY
TONY HARRIS

**CYBORG #2**
VARIANT COVER ART BY
TONY HARRIS

**CYBORG #3**
GREEN LANTERN
75TH ANNIVERSARY
VARIANT COVER ART BY
KENNETH ROCAFORT

**CYBORG #4**
MONSTER VARIANT
COVER ART BY
MIKEL JANÍN

**CYBORG #5**
*LOONEY TUNES* VARIANT
COVER ART BY
CULLY HAMNER AND
SPIKE BRANDT

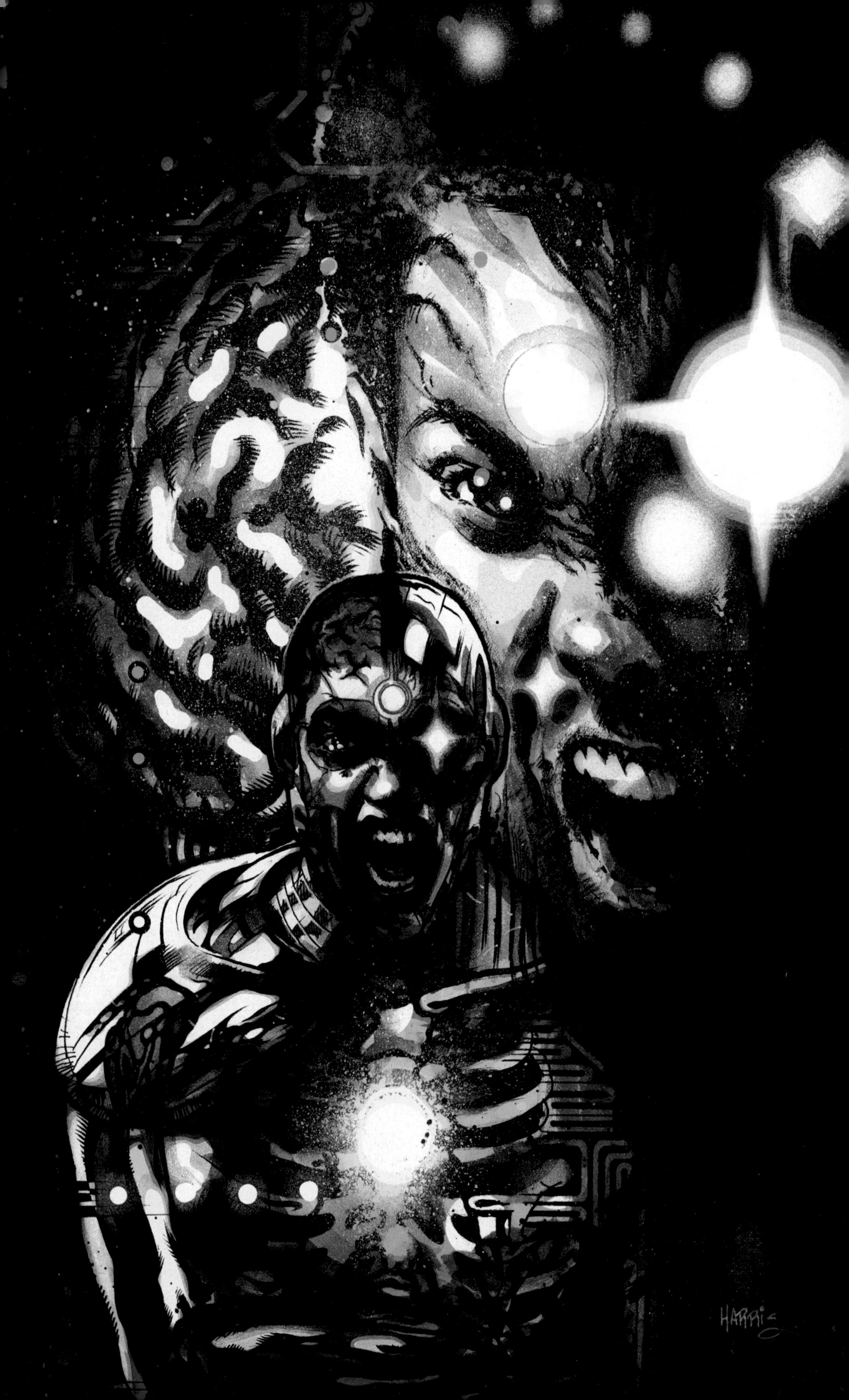
HARRIS

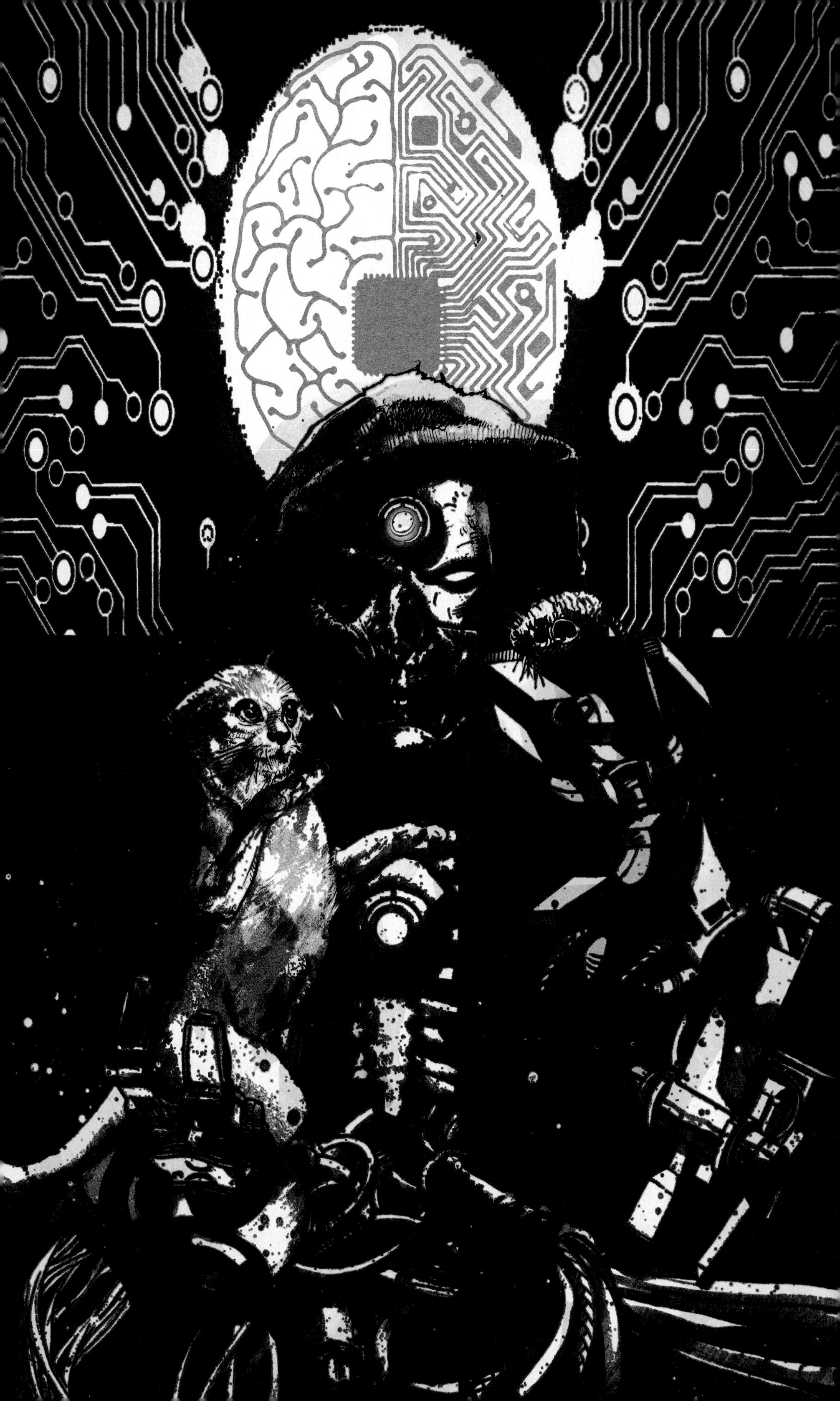

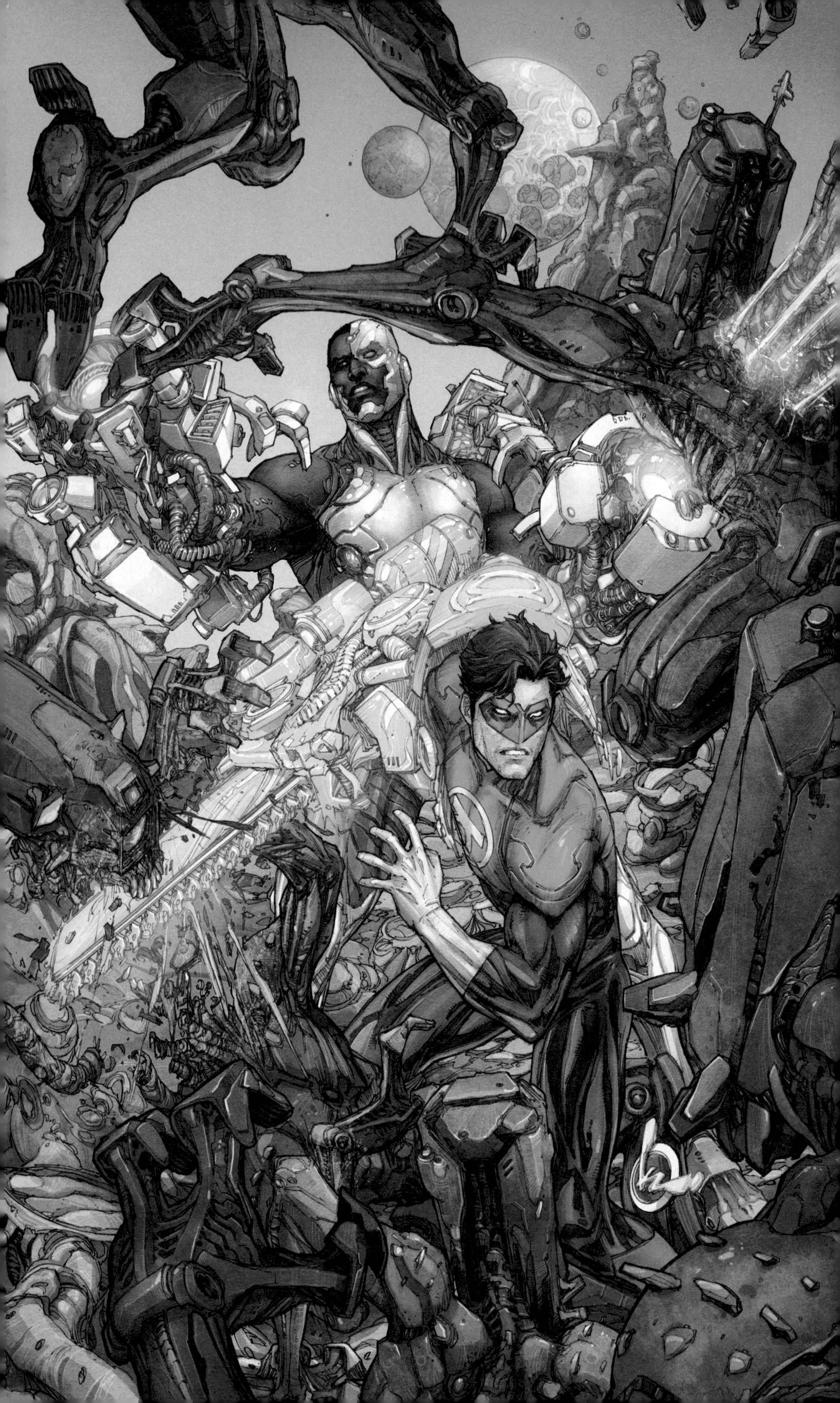

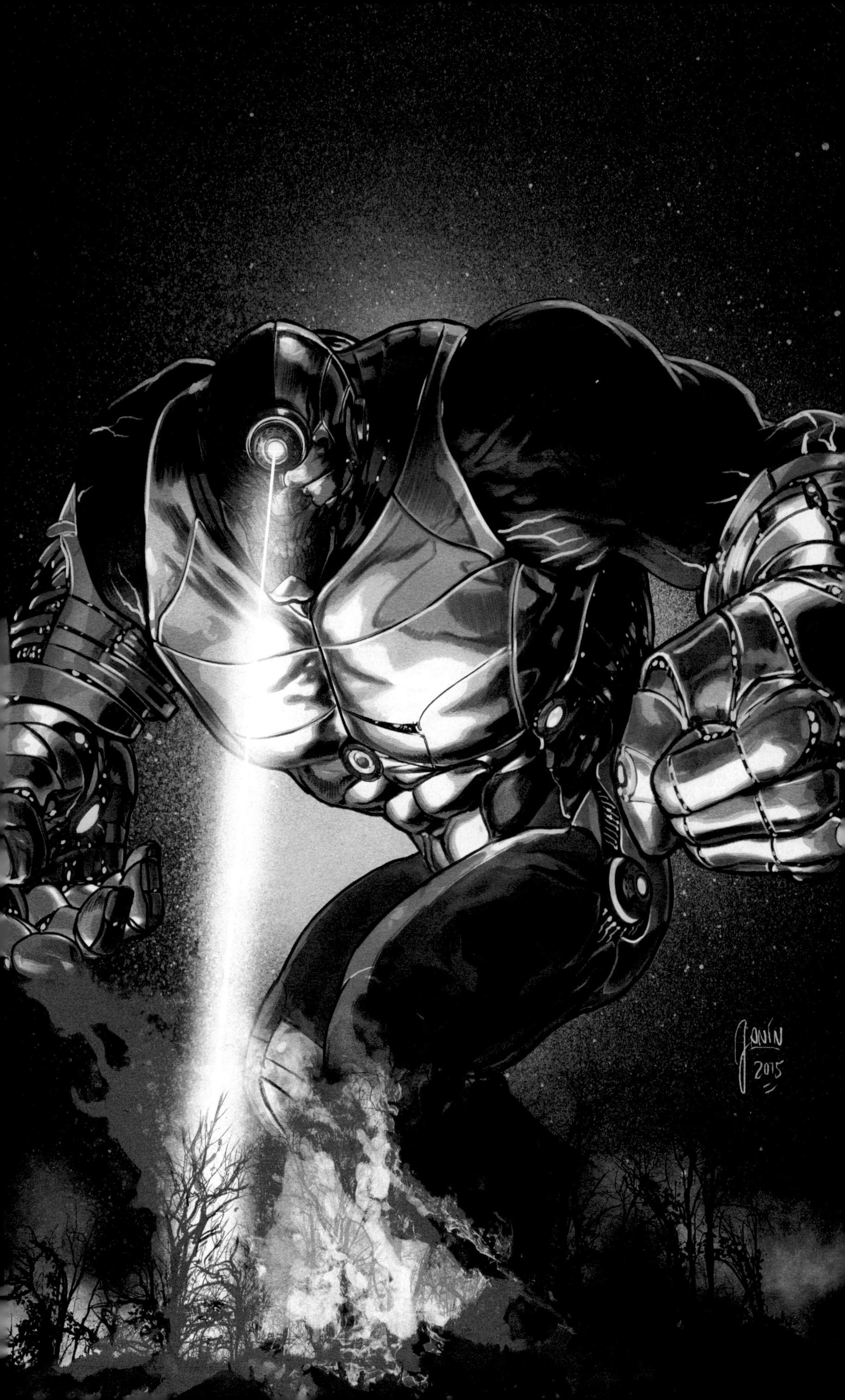
Janín
2015

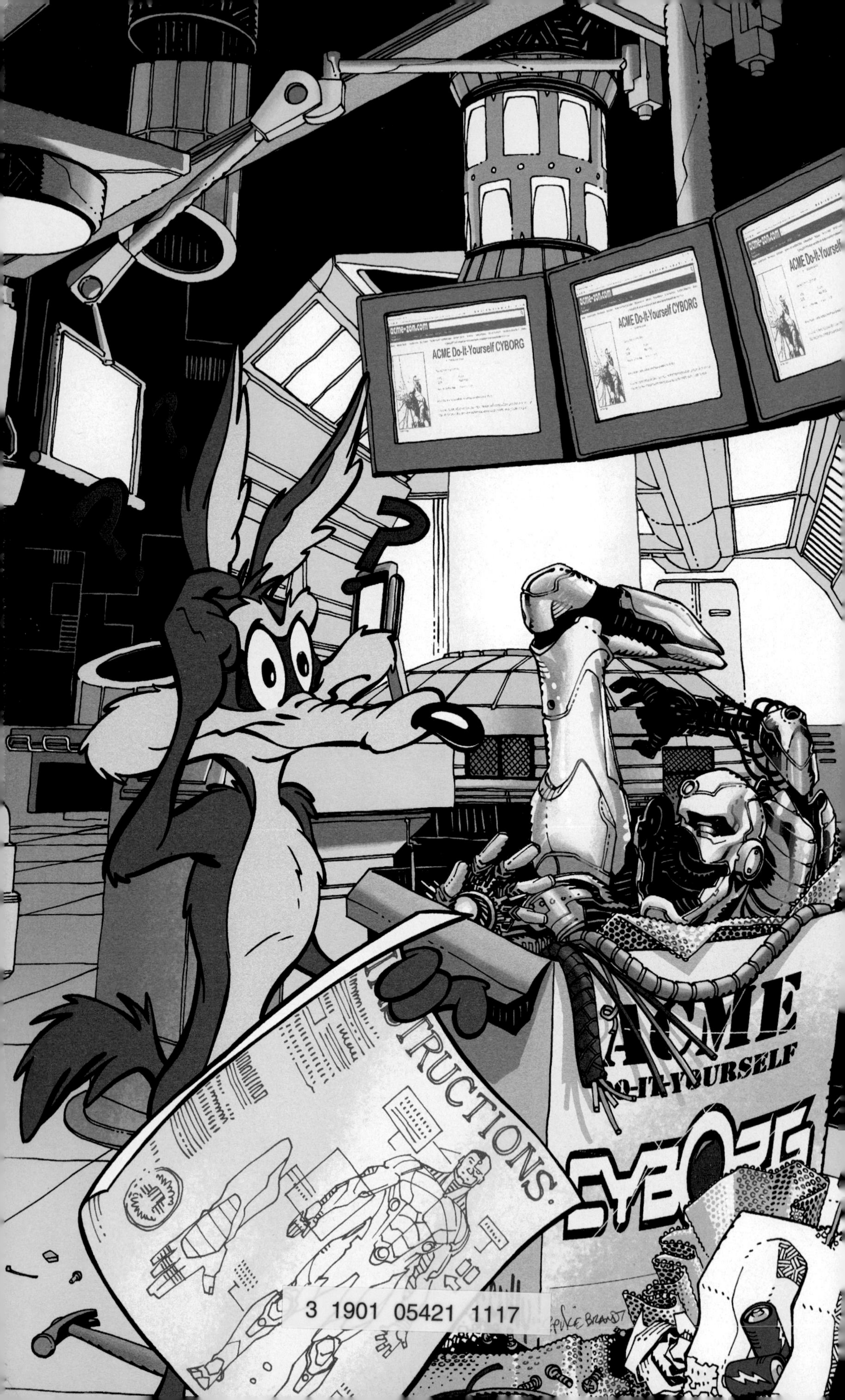
acme-zon.com
ACME Do-It-Yourself CYBORG
acme-zon.com
ACME Do-It-Yourself CYBORG
ACME Do-It-Yourself
ACME